The Rapture

***Also by Tim LaHaye
    and Jerry B. Jenkins
in Large Print:***

Left Behind®
Tribulation Force
Nicolae
Soul Harvest
Apollyon
Assassins
The Indwelling
The Mark
Desecration
The Remnant
Armageddon
Glorious Appearing
The Rising
The Regime

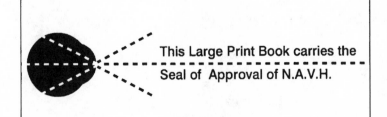

This Large Print Book carries the
Seal of Approval of N.A.V.H.

THE

In the Twinkling of an Eye

RAPTURE

Countdown to the Earth's Last Days

Tim LaHaye

Jerry B. Jenkins

Thorndike Press • Waterville, Maine

Published in 2006 by arrangement with
Tyndale House Publishers, Inc.

Thorndike Press® Large Print Basic.

The tree indicium is a trademark of Thorndike Press.

The text of this Large Print edition is unabridged.
Other aspects of the book may vary from the original edition.

Set in 16 pt. Plantin by Elena Picard.

Printed in the United States on permanent paper.

Library of Congress Cataloging-in-Publication Data

LaHaye, Tim F.
    The rapture : in the twinkling of an eye : countdown to the
earth's last days / by Tim LaHaye and Jerry B. Jenkins.
        p. cm.
    "Thorndike Press large print basic" — T.p. verso.
    ISBN 0-7862-8806-X (lg. print : hc : alk. paper)
    1. Steele, Rayford (Fictitious character) — Fiction. 2. Rapture
(Christian eschatology) — Fiction. 3. Large type books.
I. Jenkins, Jerry B. II. Title.
PS3562.A315R43 2006b
813'.54—dc22   2006009652

To Linda and Gerald Murphy,
my daughter and son-in-law,
who serve me in countless ways
T.L.

And to Roger Eide,
adviser, consultant,
but, above all, friend
J.B.J.

Thanks to David Allen
for expert technical consultation

As the Founder/CEO of NAVH, the only national health agency solely devoted to those who, although not totally blind, have an eye disease which could lead to serious visual impairment, I am pleased to recognize Thorndike Press★ as one of the leading publishers in the large print field.

Founded in 1954 in San Francisco to prepare large print textbooks for partially seeing children, NAVH became the pioneer and standard setting agency in the preparation of large type.

Today, those publishers who meet our standards carry the prestigious "Seal of Approval" indicating high quality large print. We are delighted that Thorndike Press is one of the publishers whose titles meet these standards. We are also pleased to recognize the significant contribution Thorndike Press is making in this important and growing field.

Lorraine H. Marchi, L.H.D.
Founder/CEO
NAVH

★ Thorndike Press encompasses the following imprints: Thorndike, Wheeler, Walker and Large Print Press.

The Principals

Abdullah ("Smith"/"Smitty") Ababneh, midtwenties, fighter pilot, Royal Jordanian Air Force, Amman

Nicolae Carpathia, 32, multilingual import/export business tycoon and member of the lower house of Parliament, Bucharest, Romania

Hattie Durham, 26, Pan-Continental Airlines flight attendant, Des Plaines, Illinois

Leon Fortunato, early fifties, Carpathia's personal and political adviser, Bucharest

Dr. Chaim Rosenzweig, late sixties, Nobel Prize–winning Israeli botanist and statesman, Haifa, Israel

Chloe Steele, 19, freshman, Stanford University, Palo Alto, California

Irene Steele, 39, wife and mother, believer in Christ for eight years, Mt. Prospect, Illinois

Rayford Steele, 41, Pan-Continental Airlines captain, Mt. Prospect

Rayford (Raymie) Steele, Jr., 11, believer in Christ for three years, Mt. Prospect

Jonathan Stonagal, eighties, billionaire American, banker and financier, Manhattan

Cameron ("Buck") Williams, 29, senior writer for *Global Weekly* magazine, New York City

Viv Ivins, sixties, lifelong friend of Carpathia, Bucharest

Prologue

From *The Regime*

Nicolae Carpathia had morphed into the consummate politician, diplomat, statesman, and international gadfly. He found reasons to travel, establishing alliances with heads of state who would not have thought to grant an audience to someone from the Romanian lower house, except that he was so persuasive. And he had become known as the most popular man in his home country, admired, respected, lauded by even his opponents.

He was a man of peace. A dove. Into disarmament. That tickled the ears of his colleagues in Europe and most of the world. He had not yet visited the United States, but he was certainly known everywhere else. Carpathia's brilliance, business acumen, and accomplishments seemed somehow known by all, without his having to trumpet himself. And the way he deflected praise made people pour it on all the more. The more he got, the more he needed, and often he nearly passed out from the thrill of it, only to come crashing down on his way from a public appearance.

Nicolae had learned the art of humility. Or at least of appearing humble.

His goal was to bypass the upper house and run for president of Romania when his second term expired. Pundits already called him the favorite. . . .

He wanted to get on with life. It was time to move, to expand, to take what he believed was rightfully his. He had bowed the knee, worshiped his lord and master in exchange for the kingdoms of the world. Was something more required of him? He was the smartest, most well-read, articulate, multilingual man he was aware of.

It was time for Nicolae Carpathia to emerge.

Within the space of a year or so, Rayford Steele realized that his life and career had reached both their zenith and their nadir at once. There was nowhere else for him to go within Pan-Con Airlines, unless it was management. And that held no appeal.

He was flying the flagships of the fleet, had his choice of routes, and virtually set his own schedule. Rayford had mediated the latest skirmish between Irene and Chloe, which resulted in Chloe's dropping out of church altogether. If anything, Irene had grown chillier than ever since then.

Rayford didn't know what her problem was with Chloe. They could not have asked for a more ideal daughter. She was a gem, a keeper, his friends would say, recipient of a full-ride academic scholarship from Stanford, and while he couldn't imagine her being that far away when it seemed she had been a toddler just a month ago, he was so proud of her he could hardly stand it.

He had the same high hopes for Raymie, but he worried about the kid. Was he becoming a mama's boy? There was nothing soft or sissified about him, except that he was so much into Irene's religion. That couldn't be good. What other boy that age — and especially older — was still enamored with church?

The only interesting thing on Rayford's horizon remained Hattie Durham. She had finally graduated to international flights and occasionally rode on his trips to England and other points east. Her goal was senior flight attendant and enough seniority that she could choose her routes. She had made it clear she would choose his flights, if that was all right with him.

Rayford had made it clear that this was his wish too.

That was ironic, because for as much of a thrill as it had given him to even say such a thing, it represented way more than had ever gone on between them. In point of fact, Rayford had never touched the woman.

He had been solicitous. He hoped his looks and gestures and tone of voice had made their points. But Hattie was the toucher in this relationship. She would lay a hand gently on his shoulder as she slid past him in the bulkhead. Would rest a hand on his back as she delivered coffee to the cockpit. She touched his hand while talking with him at the occasional dinner or while thanking him for frequent rides home.

Rayford had never been inside her place, and they rarely saw each other alone. But with his life going the way it was and his midlife crisis kicking up alarmingly, Rayford began allowing himself to think of the possibilities. He told himself that if something broke, if he was tapped to fly *Air Force One* or *Two*, or if he was publicly lauded by the CIA or the Defense Department for his clandestine but admittedly limited consulting, that might get him back on track.

He could quit fantasizing about the beautiful young flight attendant and somehow talk himself into robotically walking through his boring married life.

Buck Williams had been with *Global Weekly* nearly four years. He had already written more than thirty cover stories, including three Newsmaker of the Year pieces. He wanted to bag a fourth, so he went to the next staff meeting with his nomination in mind: Dr. Chaim Rosenzweig of Israel, the humble chemical engineer who preferred calling himself a botanist, but who had succeeded in concocting a formula that made the desert bloom like a greenhouse. The result was that the tiny nation of Israel had suddenly become one of the richest in the world.

In the end, the writing assignment went to Buck. He had, after all, done the story when Rosenzweig had won the Nobel Prize. During their interview in Haifa, Dr. Rosenzweig told Buck of the many suitors who had come calling, trying to curry his favor — and access to his discovery.

"Was *anyone* sincere?" Buck said. "Did anyone impress you?"

"Yes! From the most perplexing and surprising corner of the world — Romania. I do not know if he was sent or came on his own, but I suspect the latter because I believe he is the lowest-ranking official I entertained following the award. That is one of the reasons I wanted to see him. He asked for the audience himself. He did not go through typical political and protocol channels."

"And he was . . . ?"

"Nicolae Carpathia."

"Carpathia, like the — ?"

"Yes, like the Carpathian Mountains. A melodic name, you must admit. I found him most charming and humble. Not unlike myself!"

"I've not heard of him."

"You will! You will."

"Because he's . . ."

"Impressive — that is all I can say."

Later in the interview Rosenzweig said of Carpathia, "I believe his goal is global disarmament, which we Israelis have come to distrust. But of course he must first bring about disarmament in his own country. This man is about your age, by the way. Blond and blue-eyed, like the original Romanians who came from Rome, before the Mongols affected their race."

"What did you like so much about him?"

"Let me count," Rosenzweig said. "He knew my language as well as his own. And he speaks fluent English. Several others also, they tell me. Well educated but also widely self-taught. And I just like him as a person. Very bright. Very honest. Very open."

"What did he want from you?"

"That is what I liked the best. Because I found him so open and honest, I asked him outright that question. He insisted I call him Nicolae, so I said, 'Nicolae, what do you want from me?' Do you know what he said, young man? He said, 'Dr. Rosenzweig, I seek only your goodwill.' What could I say? I said, 'Nicolae, you have it.' I am a bit of a pacifist myself, you know. Not unrealistically. I did not tell him this. I merely told him he had my goodwill. Which is something you also have."

"I suspect that is not something you bestow easily."

"That is why I like you and why you have it. One day you must meet Carpathia. You would like each other. His goals and dreams may never be realized even in his own country, but he is a man of high ideals. If he should emerge, you will hear of him. As you are emerging in your own orbit, he will likely hear of you, or from you; am I right?"

"I hope you are."

Buck Williams had enjoyed a leisurely late evening meal with Chaim Rosenzweig a mile from the kibbutz and from the nearby military compound where Buck would stay before his dawn flight back to the States.

Rosenzweig's driver dropped Buck off at the military compound, where he headed through the command center toward his more-than-comfortable quarters. It was already after midnight, and he was fascinated by the alert attention the strategy room personnel gave the glowing computer screens. Earlier in the week he had met the brass and been given full access to the technicians who kept their eyes on the night skies. Many nodded or waved as Buck moved through, and a couple of the command personnel called him by name.

Before undressing for bed he stood by his window and gazed into a starry sky. He felt keyed up, not drowsy. He would have trouble sleeping; he knew it. It was at times like this when he wished he enjoyed wine the way a man like Rosenzweig did. That would have put him out.

Maybe some late reading would do the trick. Just as he was turning from the window to dig a book or magazine from his bag, the raucous blat of sirens shook the place. A fire? Some malfunction? Buck assumed the loudspeakers would advise occupants what to do, where to go. He pulled on his leather jacket and was then drawn back to the window by something new in the skies.

It appeared surface-to-air missiles had been launched. Was Israel under attack? Could it be? Sounds from the air overrode even the ear-rattling sirens. When the skies lit up like noon, Buck knew this was the real thing — a full-fledged air battle. But with whom? And why?

He bolted from his room and ran down the corridor toward the command center. "Stay in your quarters, civilian!" he heard more than once as he darted among ashen-faced men and women in various stages of dress. Many had emerged from their chambers pulling on uniforms and jamming on caps.

The situation room was chaotic already, and this crisis was less than a minute old. Command officers huddled around screens, chirping rapid-fire commands at techies. One man wearing impossibly large earphones shouted, "One of our fighters has identified Russian MiG fighter-bombers."

From another corner: "ICBMs!"

Buck reeled. Intercontinental ballistic missiles? Against little Israel? From the Russians?

Suddenly no one was sitting. Even the experts stood at their keyboards as if staring at something they didn't want to see. Every screen seemed lit and jammed with blips and points of light.

"It's like Pearl Harbor!"

"Like 9/11!"

"We'll be annihilated!"

"Hundreds of MiGs nearly overhead!"

"Hopelessly outnumbered!"

Then the explosions began. Sections of the building went dark. Some screens. Bombs sounded as if they had landed right outside the windows. So this was no grand-stand play designed to bring Israel to her knees. There was no message for the victims. Receiving no explanation for the war machines crossing her borders and descending upon her, Israel was forced to defend herself, knowing full well that the first volley would bring about her virtual disappearance from the face of the earth.

The sky was lit with orange-and-yellow balls of fire that would do little to slow a Russian offensive for which there could be no defense. It appeared to Buck that every command officer expected to be put out of his misery in seconds when the fusillade reached the ground and covered the nation.

Buck knew the end was near. There was no escape. Some personnel actually left their posts screaming, and their commanders did not try to stop them. Even senior officers dived under equipment and covered their ears.

As the night shone like day and the horrific, deafening explosions continued, the building shook and rattled and rumbled.

The first Israeli missiles had taken out Russian fighters and caused ICBMs to explode too high to cause more than fire damage on the ground. The Russian warplanes slammed to the ground, digging craters and sending burning debris flying. But radar showed the Russians had clearly sent nearly every plane they had, leaving hardly anything in reserve. Thousands of planes swooped down on the tiny country's most populated cities.

Buck's survival instinct was on full throttle. He crouched beneath a console, surprised by the urge to sob. This was not at all what he had expected war to sound like, to look like. He had imagined himself peeking at the action from a safe perch, recording the drama in his mind.

Cameron Williams knew beyond a doubt that he would die, and he wondered why he had never married. Whether there would be remnants of his body for his father or brother to identify. Was there a God? Would death be the end?

One

Buck Williams realized he would be no more dead outside under the erupting Haifa night skies than he would be inside the command center. This was not bravado; it was the unique, insatiable curiosity of the journalist. He would be the lone casualty at this post who would see and know what killed him. On rubbery legs, he made his way to a door. No one seemed to notice or care to caution him. It was as if they had all been sentenced to death.

He forced open the door against a furnace blast and shielded his eyes from the whiteness of the blaze. The sky was afire. Jets screamed over the din of the inferno, and exploding missiles sent more showers of flame into the air. He stood in stark terror, amazed as the great machines of war plummeted all over the city, crashing and bouncing and rolling and burning. But these all seemed to fall between buildings and in deserted streets and fields.

Buck's face blistered and his body poured sweat. What in the world was happening?

Nicolae Carpathia was a light sleeper, thus the quiet buzz programmed into a tiny device in his headboard woke him immediately at just after one-thirty in the morning.

He sat up, vigorously rubbed his eyes and face, and pressed the intercom button. "Gabriella?"

"Yes, sir. My apologies, but Mr. Fortunato is here and assures me you would want to be awakened."

So it had happened. It was done.

Less than a minute later, Nicolae had dragged a wet comb through his hair and pulled on a luxurious robe. He padded to the elevator, which opened into his parlor and brought him face-to-face with his most trusted adviser.

Carpathia fought to suppress a smile. "Leon, what is it?"

"Israel is being obliterated as we speak."

Nicolae clapped. "The Russians?" he said, as if guessing.

Fortunato nodded, smiling. "There's evidence Libya and Ethiopia are cooperating."

"Perfect. Dr. Rosenzweig knew exactly

what I wanted and would not budge. Wonder what he is thinking now. Or whether he will ever think again. Hoarding his formula was a waste. No one could maximize the benefits as I can."

Fortunato grimaced.

"What?" Nicolae said. He pointed to a divan. "Sit, my friend."

Leon settled heavily onto the couch. "Don't assume the Kremlin will bring you in on this, Nicolae. My sources tell me this offensive is as costly a single assault as they have ever attempted. The cadre I introduced you to will likely want to license you only a portion of the rights to market in certain areas."

Nicolae sat across from Leon on a large ottoman. "And you have some illusion that this would be enough for me? Surely you are sporting."

"I know how you feel, Nicolae; it simply may not be as easy as we'd like. Forgive me, chief, but why do you continue to grin like the Cheshire cat?"

A chuckle escaped Carpathia. "The deal has already been made, Leon."

"Sorry?"

"You did not hear me or did not understand?"

"The latter, sir."

"Between Jonathan Stonagal and me, we financed this operation and settled on terms before the first plane left the ground. Russia will have unlimited use of the formula for their entire expanse, as will Ethiopia and Libya, but the marketing of it throughout the rest of the world is under my purview, and they get an appropriate royalty. Seven percent."

Leon shook his head and leaned back, squinting at Nicolae. "You can't be serious."

"Of course I am. I would not make light of billions of dollars. Would you like the privilege of informing Mr. Stonagal? It is just before seven in New York, and the old man will be on his treadmill."

Leon sighed. "He's the one who informed me."

"But he did not tell you of the arrangement?"

Leon stood, jamming his hands into his pockets. "Neither of you did. My role has been clarified."

"Oh, make no mistake about that, Leon. You know more than anyone in my orbit, but you do not need to know all — neither shall you ever. You will know what you need to know and when I feel you should know it. Understood?"

"As I said, my role has been clarified."

Chunks of ice and hailstones as big as golf balls forced Buck to cover his head with his jacket as the earth shook and resounded, throwing him to the ground. Facedown in the freezing shards, he felt rain wash over him. Suddenly the only sound was the fire in the sky, and it began to fade as it drifted lower. After ten minutes of thunderous roaring, the fire dissipated, and scattered balls of flame flickered on the ground. The firelight disappeared as quickly as it had come. Stillness settled over the land.

As clouds of smoke wafted away on a gentle breeze, the night sky reappeared in its blue-blackness and stars shone peacefully as if nothing had gone awry.

Buck turned back to the building, his muddy leather jacket in his fist. The door-knob was still hot, and inside, military leaders wept and shuddered. The radio was alive with reports from Israeli pilots. They had not been able to get airborne in time to do anything but watch as the entire Russian air offensive seemed to destroy itself.

Miraculously, not one casualty was reported in all of Israel. Otherwise Buck might have believed some mysterious malfunction had caused missile and plane to destroy each other. But as he interviewed the shaken men and women who had monitored the thing on computer screens, they told another story.

A young female Israeli soldier, in heavily accented but precise English, told him, "It was a firestorm, along with rain and hail and an earthquake. That is what saved us from destruction."

It was the story of a lifetime, and Buck quickly appropriated a jeep and raced throughout the country, interviewing leaders, civilians, soldiers. Dotting the landscape for as far as he drove were hundreds and thousands of chunks of burning, twisted, molten steel that had smashed to the ground in Haifa, Jerusalem, Tel Aviv, Jericho, even Bethlehem — leveling ancient walls but not so much as scratching one living creature.

That was beyond Buck's comprehension; he simply could not make it compute.

As dawn broke several hours later, special task forces competed with buzzards and vultures for the flesh of the enemy dead, scrambling to bury them before their bones were picked clean and disease threatened the nation.

Buck was greatly relieved to find that Dr. Rosenzweig had escaped unscathed. "Had I not been here and seen it myself, I would not have believed it," he told the scientist. "It will take more than I have in me to make my readers buy it either."

Rosenzweig seemed strangely quiet.

"What is it, Doctor?" Buck said.

"Well, it is just that I feel strange broaching this subject, as an agnostic at best, but would you allow me to introduce you to some scholars who might have an interesting take on this?"

Rosenzweig introduced Buck to university professors who pointed out passages from the Bible that talked about God destroying Israel's enemies with a firestorm, an earthquake, hail, and rain. Buck was stunned to read Ezekiel 38 and 39 about a great enemy from the north invading Israel with the help of Persia, Libya, and Ethiopia. More stark was that the Scriptures foretold of weapons of war used as fire fuel and enemy soldiers eaten by birds or buried in a common grave.

Buck wasn't prepared to become religious, he told himself, but he certainly became a different person and a different journalist. Nothing would ever again be beyond his belief.

And if there was one person he wanted to talk to about all this, it was his Chicago colleague Lucinda Washington.

Two

Nicolae Carpathia sat behind the office desk at his estate in Bucharest, fully aware that steepling his fingers beneath his chin was a power cliché. Leon Fortunato squirmed in the chair across from him. Whether Leon had ever noticed that Carpathia's chair sat on a platform an inch and a half above the floor, Nicolae could not tell. The perch allowed Carpathia to subtly tower over any guest.

Nicolae was amused that Leon had been out of sorts ever since getting the drift that he was not as close to Carpathia as he had clearly come to believe. Nicolae's allowing his adviser to inform him of the Russian attack on Israel, then revealing that he himself had helped finance it, seemed to have crushed Fortunato's spirit. And, naturally, that was the point.

Fortunato was an asset, but there was always value in keeping everybody in one's orbit in their proper position. Leon could be useful but only if he knew and kept his place. The Roman was a strange combination of character traits. He could be obsequious yet also diplomatic. He was deferential but also sensitive to his station. Carpathia would have to start rebuilding the fragile ego while not softening the sting of the latest establishment of rank. Especially with the bizarre, otherworldly malfunction of the assault on Israel.

Oh, there were more millions where those lost on the operation had come from. But having come away from the fiasco without access to Chaim Rosenzweig's precious fertilizer formula, Carpathia had come to a hard realization. Seething, he deduced that his promised place at the top of the world would not be established on a foundation of wealth.

No, it would have to be built on diplomacy. Or what appeared to be diplomacy. In truth, his rise must be fueled by power.

"I have an assignment for you, my friend," Nicolae began.

Leon tilted his head back slightly and pressed his lips together, touching the knot of his tie, then pulling from his pocket a tiny leather note-card holder. "At your service, sir."

"You are troubled, Leon."

The heavier, older man sighed and shifted in his seat. "I simply prefer no surprises."

"Such as my part in the recent dustup in Israel."

"Yours and Mr. Stonagal's, yes, sir."

Carpathia covered his face with his hands and rubbed his eyes. "We need to clarify Mr. Stonagal's role as well, Leon."

"Clarify?"

"You must know that while he was in on this with me and he chose not to inform you, that was at my request. In reality, he serves me as you do."

"*He* serves you? Don't his financial resources outweigh even — ?"

"Mine, yes. But surely you must understand that he is, in essence, a supplier."

Fortunato appeared genuinely surprised. "Is that so? I thought the new golden rule was that he —"

"— who has the gold makes the rules, yes. That is hardly novel or original, and the fact is, neither is it true. My wealth potential is unlimited, and I expect to have not just access to but also ownership of Stonagal's fortune one day."

"Indeed?"

"If you do not believe that, Leon, perhaps you would rather be working for him."

Fortunato shook his head, and Carpathia saw sadness in his eyes. "Make no mistake, Nicolae. I have hitched my wagon to your star, and though you apparently don't appreciate that, I am willing to prove myself to you."

Carpathia studied the man. This couldn't be working more perfectly. "You realize that this room — in fact the entire estate — is surveillance-proof."

Leon appeared depressed. "Of course, sir. I oversaw that personally."

"And so what we say here stays here."

Leon nodded.

"Let us walk, shall we? And then plan to join me for dinner. What would you like?"

Nicolae rose and allowed Leon to help him don his jacket, then buzzed Viv Ivins and asked her to send their food order to the kitchen. When they arrived back, their meals would be served.

As they strolled the grounds of the rolling acreage that looked out over the vast Romanian capital, Nicolae was reminded of their first get-acquainted walk and how he had sensed king-making potential in the unprepossessing Italian with so many contacts.

At the highest point on the property, Nicolae suddenly stopped and turned to face Fortunato. Carpathia's two primary bodyguards held back about fifty yards, and four others lingered at their posts farther away on all sides.

"I want to be the next president of the republic —"

"I know. I am putting together a team of —"

"— but I have decided I do not want to wait for the next election."

"I don't understand."

"Of course you do, Leon. You once told me, on these very grounds, that you would do anything I asked, even to the ultimate degree."

Fortunato raised his eyebrows. "Surely you're not suggesting —"

"I am not suggesting anything. I am telling you that I want Vasile out and me in. Can you or can you not get that done?"

"I will do my best."

"Your best had better be success."

"You will have my whole heart, sir, but understand — I assumed you would campaign and be elected in the traditional way, and I fully expected you to win in a landslide."

Nicolae sat gingerly on an outcropping of rock and put his elbows on his knees, resting his chin in his hands. "That whole idea bores me, and it would take too long. The time is now."

"There is the matter of protocol, the law, the succession format."

"I am not interested in the obstacles, Leon. I am interested only in the outcome."

"Gheorghe Vasile is a proud man, Nicolae. He will not surrender easily."

"I do not care how easily he goes. I merely want this to be his idea, with his blessing, his urging of the government and the people to not only accept it but also ratify it."

"But how?"

Carpathia looked knowingly at Fortunato. "Do I have to do everything? You want me to plot this *and* effect it?"

"No, I — it's just that I —"

"You are so enamored of Stonagal; do you realize Jonathan holds the paper on Vasile's businesses?"

"Well, that's fortunate and could be strategic, but —"

"*Could* be? The man gets a kickback on billions of dollars worth of government contracts, and he gets them now. Every weapon of war, for instance, translates to a colossal boon to his secret bank accounts."

"But surely his business ventures are in trusts as long as he's in office."

"Oh, Leon! Do you really believe President Vasile would surrender access to his entire *avere* — his fortune — to live on the government stipend?"

"Well, I —"

"Of course he would not and he has not and does not," Nicolae said. "The man is guilty of not just political scandal but also crimes against his own people."

"If what you say is true, we could virtually blackmail him into stepping down. Ruin him. Make him destitute. Or threaten to."

Nicolae nodded slowly. "If necessary. But it must not actually come to that. I do not want to assume the power of a deposed ruler. For one thing, it would be more difficult to skirt the system. I am telling you that this must come from him, be his idea. I must reluctantly assume the role with his full endorsement as well as that of the government and the people."

"No small order, sir."

"You longed for a significant assignment. There it is."

Irene Steele had made the difficult decision and pulled the trigger. With her husband attending church with her less and less and her spiritually reprobate daughter off at Stanford, Irene had switched churches, taking son Raymie with her. How rich it was to sit under the teaching and preaching of the avuncular Vernon Billings at New Hope Village Church. And to see her dear friend Jackie every Sunday. And how Raymie loved everything about church.

That, she knew, bothered Rayford. He attended church no more than once every two months and slept in or golfed most Sunday mornings, then seemed to want to make up for it by urging Raymie to watch sports on television with him when he got home. The boy seemed to acquiesce reluctantly, and Rayford confided his misgivings to Irene.

"He doesn't have to be a jock," he said. "But does he have to turn every ball game into an opportunity to preach at me? If I wanted to know what he learned in Sunday school or church, I'd go."

Irene held her tongue, which wasn't easy. Not that long ago she would have immediately told him he *ought* to go. He had fallen wholly out of the habit, and the last time he had shown up on a Sunday morning was the previous Christmas, when Raymie had played a bathrobed shepherd in the children's drama. Rayford drove separately and slipped out as soon as Raymie's part was over.

Irene had been tempted to rail against him, to demand to know who he thought he was . . . to ask him what he was so afraid of.

But she was learning. Slowly, painfully, she was learning.

Jackie had urged her to go to the pastor for counseling about Rayford, and Reverend Billings had brought his own wife into the sessions — partly for appearances but also for her input. They had persuaded Irene that her best hope for Rayford was to stop nagging him. But Jackie's own story of how she loved her husband into the faith was most powerful to Irene. That, she told the Billingses, was one reason she had to counter their suggestion that she try to get Rayford to come for counseling too.

"He's just too far from this yet," she said. "It's as if we have an unspoken truce. I will not keep pushing him to attend church, and he will not disparage me for switching to New Hope."

Irene's new resolve was not easy. She had fallen into a habit of seemingly passive comments, and it didn't seem natural for her to put up with Rayford's lame excuses. Her last volley stuck in her brain and shamed her. He had said something about how he really wanted to go, but he was so tired and overworked that he really needed the break.

"As if sitting in a pew for a brief part of the morning is more taxing than eighteen holes of golf," she had said.

To his credit, he had simply fallen silent and left in a huff. She could be grateful for that.

When she arrived home from a convicting sermon, she and Raymie having picked up their traditional fast-food lunch on the way, Irene could hardly wait for Rayford to return from his golf outing. But when he got there, she nearly overwhelmed him.

No surprise to her, he was cautious and quiet, now wanting to just relax and watch TV. She wanted him to spend time with Raymie, of course, but she had to begin strong with this new effort to simply love and accept him. "How'd you shoot today?" she said, embracing him and clearly surprising him.

"Same old same old," he said. "Looked like a pro on a couple of holes. Made everybody else look better on the rest."

"Oh, I know you're better than that," she said. "I'll bet you shot the lowest score."

He looked embarrassed. "Actually, Jack won today, but I was second by only a stroke."

"See? If you had more time to play, you'd beat him regularly."

"That's what I was thinking."

When he went to raid the pantry for snacks, Irene said, "I'll get that for you, hon."

Again he looked suspicious. She went so far as to suggest he have a Coke, because she would rather he not drink in front of Raymie, and she had smelled alcohol on his breath.

He hesitated, as if he wanted to suggest a beer or something stronger, but he acceded and she set him up with chips and dip too.

"Four-wheeling today?" Raymie said as he ran through the house.

Normally Irene would have glared at Rayford, daring him to again deny the boy after having promised him so many times. But she just waited in the kitchen, out of sight, hoping, praying.

"Maybe next week, sport," Rayford said. "Come watch the game with me, eh?"

"Maybe next week," Raymie said, and Irene was impressed.

"Don't say I didn't ask," Rayford said.

"Then don't say you didn't promise."

Irene heard the front door slam and Rayford calling out, "Hey! Raymie!"

She bitterly wanted to scold Rayford and ask what he expected, but she merely came in and sat next to him, watching the game with him.

Later, while tucking Raymie in, she urged him to try to be understanding. "I know Dad's disappointed you many times, but we have to love him and accept him. And it wouldn't hurt you to do the right thing, even if he doesn't."

"Like watch the Bears with him? You know I'm more into basketball. I'll watch the Bulls with him in the spring."

After they had prayed together, Raymie said, "Mom, is Dad going to hell?"

She sighed. "Frankly, I can't tell where your dad is on all this. He claims to believe in God, and it's not for us to say."

"Well, I'm not letting him go to hell. What if his plane crashed or he got hit by a car or —"

"Oh, Raymie! Please don't talk like that."

"Well, it's either true or it's not, Mom. I mean, Pastor Billings talks about that all the time. We never know how much time we have on this earth."

"I know."

Maybe Raymie would be the catalyst to bring Rayford to Christ. Irene would have no trouble with that.

Lucinda Washington, *Global Weekly*'s Chicago bureau chief, had insisted that Cameron Williams visit her the next time he came through the city. It had not been that long since his story ran on the abortive Russian invasion of Israel. "You know you need to talk to me," she had e-mailed him.

She was right. And though she refused to call him by his nickname, he loved seeing and talking with her. She was like a second mother. Fiftyish and heavyset with a dark chocolate complexion, she was beloved by her employees, to whom she was ferociously loyal. They especially seemed to appreciate that when she was elevated from their ranks to be their superior, she had not moved to a corner office.

"What would I find there but more stuff to look at out of more windows? The authority, such as it is, doesn't come from the office. It comes from the heart."

"Cue the violins," Buck had said, and she just sat smiling and shaking her head.

"I read something in your piece, Cameron," she said.

"I figured you would."

"Between the lines," she added.

"Yeah, I know."

"God got your attention, didn't He?"

Buck sat facing her in her cluttered digs, slouching uncomfortably in a straight-backed chair, his feet crossed on a corner of her desk. He nodded.

"If you were my son I'd whup you upside the head, sitting like that, tearing up your spine."

"You don't still smack Lionel, do you?"

Buck said, peeking at the photo of the smooth-faced youngster.

"Can't catch him anymore, but he knows I can still take him."

Lionel was around twelve. Buck wanted to keep talking about the boy to keep Lucinda out of his head. As much as he admired her, she would not let up on him.

"And I can still take you, Mister Senior Writer all up into your young self. Tell me where you found that Scripture you used in your cover piece. They watch me like a hawk, so I can hardly ever get away with that. Next thing you know, they'll be letting you start proselytizing."

Buck told her that Chaim Rosenzweig, an avowed agnostic like himself, had put him in touch with religious scholars.

"You couldn't call me? I've been in the Word longer than those old coots, and I see stuff in the Old Testament they've missed."

"You'd have pointed me to the same passages?"

" 'Course I would! You think that wasn't the first thing that came to my mind when I heard of a massive attack gone bad? Prophesied, honey. Shouldn't have surprised anybody who knew a thing about the Bible. Which you don't."

"I do now."

"You don't know much, but I daresay what you do know has shaken you to your core."

"You got that right, Lucy."

She cocked her head and glared at him.

"Lucinda." She was anything but a Lucy; she had told him too many times to count.

"Cameron, why doesn't your Ivy-League head just admit you don't know as much as you thought you knew, humble yourself a mile or two, and come to church with me and mine? For one thing, it'd be a cultural thing you've never experienced before. Even if our enthusiasm and our music and all overwhelm you, if you keep your ears — and your mind — open, you might just learn something from people you didn't think had a thing to teach you."

"Now don't say that, Lucinda. I've told you and told you I've learned a lot from you."

She seemed to assess him. "God's gonna get you yet, boy. I mean, you were right there when it happened. And then you read ancient texts that look like they could have been written yesterday. You can't deny the miracle. You can't deny the hand of God. You can't even claim to still be an agnostic."

Buck shook his head. "You're right as always."

"You're just a step away from Jesus."

"Oh, I don't know about that. I can't deny the supernatural in what happened. It makes no sense otherwise. But if God protected Israel —"

"If?"

"Okay, so why did God protect Israel, a nation that denies Jesus as the Messiah?"

"Humph," Lucinda said. "So you *are* thinking. Well, let me ask you this: would you rather have a God who treats His children like they deserve to be treated? The Bible calls the Jews His chosen people time after time after time. He's not going to unchoose them. He's going to do what He promised, regardless of how they respond."

Three

Chloe Steele and her roommate strolled across the Stanford campus to their dorm from intramural volleyball, Chloe feeling scruffy in kneepads and a sweaty uniform.

"What?" Amy said in the twilight.

"What what?"

"You're looking away again. Crying?"

Chloe swore. "I wasn't going to do this!"

"It's hard," Amy said.

"He's not worth it!"

"You're right, Chlo'; he's not. But he was a big part of your life for a long time."

"Not even a whole semester. Just a few months, really."

"But you loved him. It's all right for you to grieve."

"I wish I *was* grieving. I wish Ricky were dead."

"Oh, don't say that!"

"The way he treated me? And now

married already? I mean it."

"I've been through this, you know," Amy said as they mounted the stairs.

"You have? No, I didn't know."

"First semester, senior year of high school."

"A year ago?"

Amy nodded.

"Tell me. The worst part of this is feeling so unique, so alone."

"You're kidding, Chloe. If we started a club we'd have to have the meetings in the stadium. Everybody's been dumped."

"That's it, isn't it? I was just flat dumped."

"His wife can have him, Chloe."

"You can say that again."

Amy threw back her head and laughed. "That's the best you can come up with? You want Ricky dead, and you spear him with 'You can say that again'? You of the silver tongue?"

Chloe had to smile. "I could invest the time he's not worthy of by coming up with creative insults."

"More creative than that? What, like his mother wears combat boots?"

They entered their room, and Chloe fell onto her bed. "This is just so maddening! I want to kick someone, punch something."

"Ricky."

"Yeah, but no. I can't ever let on how much he hurt me. I just have to do something with this anger."

Amy sat on the floor beside Chloe's bed. "What's your GPA?"

"You know."

"Off the charts, yeah. But it's still not as high as you're capable of."

"What're you, my dean?"

"No, I'm just sayin'."

"What?" Chloe said.

"Channel your angry energy into why you're here. You can do better than the dean's list. You could push toward a 4.0 the rest of the way and graduate summa cum laude."

"Oh, please!"

"You could! I know you. I see you work and read and study. You're not that far from straight As. Do it, Chloe. At least think about it."

Chloe rolled up onto her side. "You'll do it with me?"

"Ha! Not on your life! I'm here to also have fun, and anyway, I could work twice as hard as you — hey, I do — and accomplish only half. How unfair is that? But I'd support you. Give up your extracurricular stuff, maybe all but one thing — and don't make it volleyball; you're not good enough."

45

"You should talk!"

"But maybe you give up everything except debate and pour yourself into studying."

"No guys?"

"Are you kidding? What fun you'd be, seeing someone while sniffling over your old boyfriend. I mean, are you available already? Really?"

"No."

"Then write off guys for a while. You're never going to go long without one. I see the way they look at you."

"You do not!"

" 'Course I do! I pretend they're looking at me. Don't tell me you don't notice, Chloe. Don't even try that with me."

"I notice a little."

"Anyway, think about it. It'd be so cool to know someone who conquered this place."

"Academically? No one really does that."

"Then be the first."

Abdullah Ababneh — such a lover of Western culture, particularly the United States, that he had become known within the Royal Jordanian Air Force as Abdullah Smith, or Smitty — had hit the skids.

His wife, Yasmine, had become an infidel to Islam, a Christian. He had forbade it, they had fought, and she had left with the children. That had catapulted him into a descent into alcohol and adultery that exposed his own phony allegiance to Allah, and now he was living in a small barracks at the Amman air station.

Abdullah had long been a star pilot. Young and articulate and even dashing, he had been admired by his superiors and mates. But now he sensed their pity, their sideward glances. How he had fallen! It was all he could do to drag himself off his cot every morning and pretend to be praying. He carried out his duties like an automaton, never smiling, rarely conversing. His immediate superior officer told Abdullah he was worried about him, but Abdullah assured him he was just depressed, out of sorts.

"It will work itself out," he said. "I still believe the passage of time will help, provided Yasmine lets me see the children."

"You cannot win her back? She was so good for you."

Abdullah did not have the heart to tell the man that his wife had virtually died. She must be considered dead to him; that was certain. At times he believed that Allah would forgive him if he murdered her. In fact, perhaps that was Allah's will.

But Abdullah could not, for in spite of

himself and all that he knew, he still loved Yasmine with his whole being. He would sooner kill himself than lay a hand on her. Perhaps she would repent of her blasphemy and come back to Islam and to him.

Yet he knew better. Though he had ripped to pieces many of her letters, still he kept several. He did not understand everything in them, but one thing was clear: she was devout in her new faith. And she pleaded with him to consider it for himself. Yasmine Ababneh was not about to be dissuaded.

Things that had always endeared Irene to Rayford now irritated him. Her fastidiousness, for one thing. He knew he was being irrational. What else would account for such a good trait making him so crazy? Rayford was growing suspicious of Irene, of all things. This church switch had not made her more obnoxious, as he had feared. If anything, she was sweeter, easier to get along with. The sudden encouraging of his Sunday activities had to be some sort of ruse, but she acted genuinely interested, laid out his clothes, helped him get ready. All this while getting herself and Raymie ready for church.

Weekday mornings, especially Rayford's off days, were the same. He was an early riser even when he didn't have a flight, but he was rarely up before she was. The aroma of her special coffee blend, set on automatic timer to start heating up at six, roused him early. And though he tried, he only rarely succeeded in getting out of bed and into his workout clothes by the time her radio, tuned to the irrepressibly cheerful host of the local Christian station, came on at six-thirty.

Irene had taken to setting out Rayford's clothes, tuning the workout-room TV to ESPN, and being sure the bathroom was all his when he was ready to shower. By the time he descended the stairs, Irene had opened the drapes at the front and back of the house, and sunlight bathed the place. She had become a dream come true, and somehow he hated it.

It wasn't that she had become some perfect little Goody Two-Shoes. No, he could tell when he had frustrated her, angered her, made her want to attack. But somehow she restrained herself. She might stomp off, even slam a door, but when she had gathered herself, she was cheerful and helpful and even loving again. She was forgiving him without his asking, and it was driving him crazy.

Rayford had grown tired of the nagging and resultant bickering, mostly over church, his use of time, and his not spending enough time with Raymie. But now, this way, all those things were like the elephants in the room. He knew they were at the forefront of his wife's mind, and in some ways he'd rather have argued about them than pretend they didn't exist. On the other hand, if she was going to let these things slide, he could get used to that.

As Rayford pumped away on his stationary bike or rower or free weights, trying to concentrate on the sports news, he couldn't deny that he knew what was really causing his discomfort with Irene. She was pushing forty. In many ways he was proud of her. She worked out too, kept in shape, and he'd never had even a twinge of hesitation in introducing her as his wife. She had never been a classic beauty, a head turner, but she retained a youthful cuteness, and she could be described as vivacious. She had personality. People liked her.

So what was the problem?

Hattie Durham.

Rayford couldn't quit thinking about her. Young, tall, curvy, blonde, gorgeous. And while Rayford had never bought into the old saws about blondes being dumb — in fact, he knew many intelligent ones — it was true that Hattie was not the sharpest blade of grass on the lawn. It wasn't that she was dense; she had to be somewhat on the ball to already be so close to becoming a senior flight attendant, still shy of her twenty-seventh birthday. But she was a very young twenty-six, despite traveling the world. She was not well-read, not up on the news, and seemed to have no worldview other than her own interests.

But she was sure fun to look at. And be around. And it was clear she was enamored with Rayford, which is what made him so disciplined in his daily workouts. Was he actually hoping something might come of Hattie's flirtations? He knew better than to risk his marriage and family and reputation on a midlife fling.

If Irene were a shrew, liberal-minded people might understand some dalliance with a younger woman. No one he knew would question his taste, even if they questioned his judgment. Rayford believed Irene had been edging toward driving him away with her badgering and cajoling. That had made him look forward to flights with Hattie even more. There was a spring in his step when he knew she was on the schedule.

But now, suddenly, Irene was acting like they were courting again. She was putting her best foot forward for some reason.

51

Killing him with kindness? Trying to prove that her newfound religion had really changed her? This was worse than if she'd banged him on the head with her Bible every day.

Despite his mental turmoil, at least the cessation of fighting gave him some peace. Trouble was, Irene would have had the right to stay on his case about Raymie. Rayford had slid into simply slothful parenting. After having done fairly well scheduling time for the kids — especially when Chloe, his distaff image — was home, he was now failing with Raymie.

Four

Buck was as alarmed as anyone at the increase in war around the globe and a seemingly corresponding escalation of natural disasters. The months since the attempted Russian invasion of Israel had seen records set in the United States for tornadoes, earthquakes, hurricanes, and forest fires. President Gerald Fitzhugh had declared so many disaster areas that the novelty seemed to wear off. Charities began advertising aggressively, competing for funds, claiming some sites were worse off than others, when the truth was that any locale slammed by some force of nature had been left destitute.

And war. South America reeled under revolutions in several nations at once. The U.S. announced newer, tougher sanctions on Cuba for human-rights violations, and a new cold war settled over U.S.-Russian relations. Northern Ireland had erupted again.

The Arab-Israeli conflict reached new heights. North Korea threatened her entire hemisphere.

Every day brought more devastating news of conflict and disaster, and even Buck had to agree that there seemed to be almost a palpable hum in the air. He had drawn comfort from daily e-mails to and from Lucinda Washington. "Nobody in New York is interested in my take on this," she transmitted one morning, "but you know we're heading toward something, Cameron. Things can't just keep getting worse without something having to give."

How could he argue with that? Doomsdayers predicted the end of the world as he knew it, but what did that mean? The whole place blows up? A pandemic takes more than half the lives on the planet? World War III breaks out? What?

Buck actually found himself curious to know what his sister-in-law thought about what was going on. Sharon was the religious one in the family, nearly alienating her husband — Buck's brother, Jeff — and his dad in the process.

But the invitations to come home had ended with his mother's death. Buck did not feel wanted. And while he knew Sharon would happily engage in the very conversation that intrigued him, he knew better than to seek real story content from relatives.

Countless experts abounded on both sides of the issue of the future and where society was headed. Thing was, he was not being assigned stories on that subject. His beat was hard international news, geopolitical stuff. He would leave the other to the religion editor, personally intriguing as it might be.

Leon Fortunato was struck that Romanian president Gheorghe Vasile appeared to be an older copy of himself. They were of the same blocky height and build, though the president was much more jowly and his hair was gray. In his late sixties, Vasile was a humorless politico in private, gregarious and smiling in public. He had told the people he had one more term in his old body, and early polls showed him a huge favorite over several potential candidates.

But the polls did not reflect any public opinion over how he would fare against the much-younger Nicolae Carpathia. No one had ever reached the presidency directly from the lower house. However, everyone was, of course, familiar with the charismatic peacenik who had proved so eloquent and articulate, endearing himself to fellow party members and ingratiating himself with the opposition.

Vasile seemed bemused as he read Leon's card. "I am meeting with you, Mr. Fortunato, not because I have time or interest but because Mr. Carpathia begged my indulgence. And you serve him as chief of staff?"

"I serve him in many roles," Leon said, earnestness oozing from every pore. "But, yes, in his role as a member of the house, I am his chief of staff."

President Vasile had come out from around his enormous ebony desk that appeared as if it had grown where it stood and had rested there for centuries. He sat across from Fortunato at a small round table, the shape a recurring motif of the men themselves.

"I was unaware," Vasile said, "that members of the lower house had *echipi,* let alone chiefs of the same."

Fortunato smiled, trying to soften the bite of his words. "You well know that Dr. Carpathia is much more than a politician. Indeed his influence is wide and varied."

"*Dr.* Carpathia? Oh yes, the adjunct professorships. I am quite aware of the *flăcău*'s outside interests and influence."

"He is anything but a lad, Mr. President, despite his youth."

"So you say."

"Have you ever experienced Dr. Carpathia's opposition to one of your initiatives?" Fortunato said, writing on his small notepad all the while, clearly piquing Vasile's interest.

"Of course I have. What do you mean? He has spoken often and loudly in opposition to our defense initiatives, despite his connections with the military schools. His associations with them and then his insipid pandering to the public with his peace-mongering make garish his aim to unseat me someday."

"Someday?" Fortunato said dismissively, still writing. By now Vasile was leaning to see what he had written. But when Fortunato finished, he turned the paper upright and slid it across to the president.

Are you aware that Dr. Carpathia is a partner of Jonathan Stonagal's? He has been aware of and signed off on every transaction. Every transaction.

Fortunato fought to suppress a grin when Vasile blanched and cleared his throat. The older man checked his watch, stood, and buttoned his suit coat. "What is your schedule like, Mr. Fortunato? I would like to treat you to my favorite *băutură alcoolică*."

Fortunato, resolutely ignoring protocol by remaining seated though the president was standing, said, "I am not big on liquor, sir, but I will sample a taste if you insist. I assume, if it is your favorite, that you have a selection here."

Vasile glared at him. "I have a special place I like to go."

"Oh, I am fine right here," Leon said, which caused Vasile to grab his pen and scribble on the paper:

INSTALAŢIE ELECTRICĂ! PRIVATE!

Fortunato had known, of course, that the wiring in the presidential offices was bugged and that any serious discussion of this nature would have to take place elsewhere. "Very well," he said, rising and donning his overcoat.

Vasile told his secretary to cancel his appointments and have the *securitate* bring a car around and reserve a table at *Căruţaş*. He added that he wanted to be left alone with Fortunato, which Leon took to mean that the *securitate* would remain close but not close enough to listen in.

Interesting choice, The Waggoner. Leon, who had lied about his impartiality toward liquor, knew the place well. It was a hole in the wall less than two miles from the capitol, and the patrons had been trained to leave the president to his cups, should they see him there.

Leon loved the pomp and circumstance that surrounded a brief jaunt by car with the president. Citizens milled about on the street, hoping for such an occurrence and a glimpse of the man they had seen on state television for years. When they crowded the vehicle, the secret police held them back, and soon Vasile and Fortunato were on their way to the *cafenea*.

Knowing it would take a moment for the *securitate* to get the president from the vehicle to his favorite booth, Leon leaped out as soon as they stopped and rushed in, asking the manager if he was aware Vasile was coming.

"Of course. We are prepared."

"I will be joining him," Leon said, pressing a large bill in the man's palm. "What is the president's favorite drink?"

"A Russian vodka."

"Clear?"

"Yes."

"Make mine water, regardless of what I say. *Cuprinde?*"

"I understand."

Within minutes Fortunato and Vasile were jammed into tiny quarters and the public was kept away, though passersby stared.

When the vodka was brought to the table, along with two glasses, Fortunato panicked. "*Scuză,*" he whispered, waving for the manager. "A head of state should not be expected to pour his own drinks!"

"Nonsense," Gheorghe Vasile said.

But Fortunato insisted, and the manager, bowing and apologizing, took the bottle and glasses away, then returned with the glasses full. He winked at Fortunato, and Leon was grateful to discover that his was water.

"The impudence!" Leon whispered.

"Ach! They know me here. I often pour for myself."

"You should not. Never. You preside over this country. That is due some deference."

"But in here, in a bar, I'm just a man."

"May it never be so." Leon could tell he was making an impression on the man. He wondered if Vasile's chief of staff ever treated him this way. He did not know a leader whose ego did not crave such regard.

When Fortunato opened his mouth to

speak, Vasile held up a hand for silence as he downed one glass and held it up for another pour.

Leon waved for the manager, who handled the task. Leon had barely sipped his water.

"Excellent," Vasile said.

"Eh? You see? That is how you should be treated."

"I see." Vasile knocked back the second glass and set it down loudly.

"Another?" Leon said.

"Later," Vasile said. "Talk to me. What are you saying?"

Fortunato had long loved the directness of the powerful. They did not have the time for pleasantries and small talk, and that, naturally, was not what Leon was here for anyway.

"I am saying that your fortune, the one the public believes is appropriately tied up in trusts during the tenure of your presidency, is being managed by not only Jonathan Stonagal but also Nicolae Carpathia."

Vasile stared, glowering. "And what are the ramifications of this?"

"The ramifications? Need you ask? Surely you would not expect the Romanian people to believe your presidential salary alone finances your wife's annual stipend, your son's palatial estate that people think is funded by his lucrative stallion-breeding operation — but which you and I both know is a house of cards — your own storehouses of precious metals, American stocks and bonds, Asian securities, European land holdings. Were word to get out that you, sir, fund all this with income wholly criminally gained, why, it would all be in jeopardy."

Vasile squinted and leaned forward. "Carpathia is aware of all this?"

"How do you think I know?"

"And is he not also vulnerable, if he has such information and has not reported it?"

Fortunato sat back, still speaking softly. "No one can determine when this information came to him. But you well know that knowledge is power. He has both. He has no wish to humbly, reluctantly, sadly come forward and announce his abject disappointment in a worthy opponent he has long admired, despite political disagreements."

"But he would, would he not?"

"Of course he would." Fortunato was warm in the smoky, crowded place, and he wriggled out of his overcoat.

The president, flushed and sweaty, not only left his on but also left it buttoned to his neck. He folded his arms and lowered his chin, appearing sad. He stared at Leon and then at the table. "So, this is *stoarcere?*"

"It is indeed extortion, Mr. President."

Vasile rested his elbows on the table and pressed his palms against his generous cheeks. He sighed, inhaled as if to speak, then appeared to rethink himself. Finally, in a hoarse whisper, he said, "I suppose you are prepared to tell me what the man wants."

"Of course I am," Leon said.

Five

So this was why Irene had been buttering up Rayford. She had him in a good mood, wasn't on his case about anything. She gave him eye contact. She listened. She encouraged. In short, she was pleasant.

But then Irene sweetly lowered the boom. "May I talk with you about something without your being offended or getting upset?"

He smirked. "What'd I do now?"

"Oh no, nothing. It's just that I want to talk with you about something Pastor Billings is preaching about, but I don't want you to get the wrong idea."

"And what would the wrong idea be?"

"Well, for instance, your thinking that I'm trying to change you or get you to come to church or criticize you."

"And you're not trying to do any of that?"

"No. I mean, you know how I feel about

all that, so I'm not interested in starting anything. You're an adult and can make up your own mind, but Pastor Billings has been speaking on something so incredible that I would sincerely like your opinion about it."

Rayford was in a bind. She had pushed him into a corner, overwhelming him with pleasantness so that he was in a lose-lose situation. If he begged off this discussion, he would seem as unreasonable as she was. If he acceded, and he didn't seem to have a choice, he would have to endure yet another come-to-Jesus meeting.

"You know something?" he said, brightening.

"What?" Irene said flatly, clearly on guard against another lame excuse to delay the conversation.

"That stuff I promised Raymie is in, and I have to go pick it up."

"Can't that wait a day? Anyway, Rafe, stuff is not going to make up for your absence. He doesn't want stuff. He wants you."

"Three new toys all at once? And, may I say, big-boy toys? We're talking a four-wheeler, a snowmobile, and a bike for when the snow clears."

"You're trying to buy him."

Rayford snorted. "See how you are? See what you do?"

"I'm sorry, Rayford. Truly, I am. I shouldn't have said that."

"But you meant it. And you know better. I've just been so busy."

"Order that kind of stuff online and spend the time you used to shop for it just being with your son."

"You just don't know when to quit, do you?"

"How much?" Gheorghe Vasile said.

"How *much?*" Fortunato parroted. "Surely you don't think you can buy off a man like Nicolae Carpathia."

"What are you talking about?"

"Nicolae Carpathia does not want your money. He wants your job."

A laugh escaped Vasile. "Never. I'd die first."

Fortunato loved this more than life. With the authority vested in him by the most powerful man he had ever known, he leaned forward until his nose was six inches from Vasile's and told the president of the Republic of Romania, "That too can be arranged."

"I could have you executed for even hinting at such a thing."

"But you won't. If anything happens to me, the same thing would happen that would occur if you do not comply with Dr. Carpathia's wishes."

"Pray tell."

"I can tell you this, Mr. President: it will not be anything so pedestrian as taking the truth to the press, though the international media community would enjoy this. No, I believe the plan is to start with your son's operation. Maybe a barn burns, a few horses are lost. Harbingers of what could happen to your grandchildren."

Vasile flushed, obviously smoldering. He narrowed his eyes and pointed a sausagelike finger. "You leave them out of this. You wouldn't dare."

"Oh, this would be on you, sir. Not on me. Not on Carpathia. Not on Stonagal. The ramifications of your response are wholly up to you. You've had a good reign and you enjoy a fortune. Retire. Enjoy. Kick back."

"Romania is my life."

"The presidency will be your death. Give it up. You'll be a statesman. The people will continue to revere you, provided they are not made aware of your finances."

Vasile seemed to fade from red to gray. "So, what, I announce I will not run for reelection, and you think that paves the way for Carpathia?"

"Oh no, it's not quite that simple."

"Why did I not assume so?"

"You must resign within one week and engineer Carpathia's succession."

"Without an election? Impossible. There is the matter of protocol and many in place behind me —"

"That is why this must come from you."

"No one would buy it! No, Carpathia and I have not been bitter rivals, but everyone knows we disagree on something so fundamental as arms. Who would ever believe that I am stepping aside so a peacenik can assume the presidency?"

"I do not know, Mr. President. But that is your task. Your chore. Your price."

Yasmine Ababneh, the delicate and fair and soon-to-be-divorcee of Abdullah, left a message for him at the air base. She wanted a face-to-face, but she needed his pledge of civility. He called her immediately. "You have my solemn promise," he said.

Abdullah showered and shaved and dressed in his recently laundered uniform, topped with a clean turban. He was as nervous as a schoolboy on his first date. For all his bitterness and hatred — even considering murder — he wanted Yasmine back so badly that he was willing to concede almost anything. How he wished she would bring the children. His son and daughter would soften the meeting, make them all realize what they missed by not being a family.

But she arrived alone, as she had said she would. And Yasmine was so lovely Abdullah could barely breathe. He moved to embrace her, but she did not respond. "I love you," he said. "I miss you, and I'll forgive you if you will forgive me."

"For what are we forgiving each other, Abdullah?"

"You are forgiving me for being unkind. I am forgiving you for causing that by your religious infidelity."

"And your unkindness," she said, exhibiting a maddening sense of self, of purpose, of independence. "Are you confessing what that entailed, speaking of infidelity?"

"Yes, I have sinned. I was unfaithful to you. I took to drink. I became slothful. But Allah has forgiven me and I am on the path to spirituality now, praying at the prescribed times and remaining pure."

Yasmine's countenance seemed to soften, and Abdullah was encouraged. "Thank you for being honest and forthright with me, Abdullah. And if what you say is true, I am encouraged. Because though I believe you will stay entrapped should you remain loyal to Islam, seeing you try to live morally makes me feel better about allowing the children to see you occasionally."

"Occasionally? Why can we not reunite, Wife?"

"They are doing well. They miss you, naturally, but they miss the father they knew — the disciplined, decorated pilot. Not the man who has wasted his days."

"I told you! I am a new man. I am newly devout. We must restore our marriage. Why do you ignore my pleas?"

Yasmine sat back and crossed her legs, smoothing the flowing colorful *thob* that covered both her elbows and knees and yet favored her dark skin. "Because you have offered to forgive me of something for which I am not prepared to repent."

Abdullah stood quickly and paced. "You remain resolutely an infidel to god?"

"Not to my God," she said. "Abdullah, I could no more turn my back on the Christ than I could abandon my children."

"*Our* children! And you are abandoning *me!* You are turning your back on Islam and on Allah."

She leaned forward. "I do not mean to be unkind. And of course you are free to choose whom you will serve. But as for me and the children, we will serve the one true God and His Son, Jesus."

Abdullah covered his face and rubbed his eyes, shuddering. "And you do not fear the wrath of Allah."

"I fear nothing and no one, Abdullah. Not even you. If God be for me, who can be against me?"

Abdullah turned his back to her and stared out onto the empty tarmac, still shimmering in the late-afternoon heat. He lowered his voice and tried to sound reasonable, though he chose harsh, threatening words. "You know there is still enough Islamic influence in our government that I could likely regain custody." He heard her rise behind him, but he did not turn.

"Oh, Abdullah, listen to yourself. The world has passed you by. We live in an age of tolerance. Yes, we Christian believers remain in the minority here, and yes, I will be vilified by many. But there has not been official religious persecution here for more than a decade. And you do not want to force me to rehearse your own weaknesses in such a tribunal, even if one were to be staged."

Now he whirled to face her. "No! I don't! And the truth is I am hardly more devout today than I was a month ago. There is nothing for me in religion, mine or yours! I pray! I pray Allah will return my children to me, will soften your heart, change your mind, make you see your error. But he does not listen."

"Do me this favor," Yasmine said softly, and he was impressed that indeed she did not seem to fear approaching him. "While you are pondering all this, reread my letters. Consider my God. And in the meantime, maintain your personal discipline for your own sake, even when God seems far from you."

Abdullah was speechless. How could he argue with this woman? She made him so angry! He waved her off with the back of his hand.

"What?" she said. "You are dismissing me?"

He scowled at her and snapped off another wave, as if he could not stand the sight of her another second.

"You have nothing more to say to me?" she said, not seeming disappointed for herself but as if perhaps she was pleasantly surprised.

Abdullah turned away and marched toward the door to the corridor that led to his quarters.

"Very well," he heard her whisper. "I shall pray for you."

That made him slam the door, but he also had the feeling that he had seen her for the last time. And when he reached his cot, he collapsed in tears.

Predictably, Rayford's altruistic errand — rounding up expensive toys for Raymie — took much longer than necessary. With the crowds, the forms to fill out, the upselling by each salesperson, and the time it took to load the stuff onto a borrowed trailer, by the time he returned home Raymie had long been asleep.

But these had been no-occasion gifts, Rayford's language of love. Surely Raymie would know how much Rayford cared for him when he saw the bounty in the garage in the morning. Unfortunately, Rayford would be gone before dawn, picking up Hattie Durham on the way to O'Hare. But maybe he would be able to reach Raymie by phone later in the day, and he could set a date for them to play like real men with the boy's new gear.

"Are you asleep, Irene?" he said, peeking into the dark master bedroom.

"I was," she mumbled. "What's wrong? What took so long?"

"Oh, you know. Nothing's wrong. I'd just like someone to see what I bought."

She sighed loudly. "I've seen that stuff in the stores, Rafe."

"Fine, just forget it!"

But with his slamming around, Irene must have given up on rolling back into the syrupy river of sleep. "Oh, all right," she said. "Show me."

"No, it's okay."

"Seriously, Rayford, I want to see it. I know you're trying."

He tossed Irene her robe and led her down to the cold garage, flipping on the light.

"Wow," she said, and he could tell she wasn't faking it. "He's got to love those."

"You think?"

"Sure. But you know —"

"Yeah, I know. They're not going to make up for me not being around. Soon as I get back tomorrow night, we'll do something together."

"He'll be so glad."

"I hope."

"He will. And he would be even without all this. He just wants you."

"I know."

Rayford pulled away from the house before dawn, his BMW gliding into Hattie Durham's apartment-complex parking lot twenty minutes later. One thing he could say for her: she never made him wait. It was all he could do to keep his eyes on the road — she looked so good. The first couple of times he had picked her up he had leaped out and opened the door for her.

But she insisted he not do that. "It's quaint and you're chivalrous, Captain," she said. "But really, it's a new day, and you make me feel conspicuous."

"You sure you won't resent me, see me as boorish if I don't?"

"Don't be silly."

Hattie was typically perky for an early morning too. That's what made her so good with the passengers. Rayford knew she had the same complications and disappointments in her life that most people did, but she seldom brought them onto the plane with her.

And while she gazed at him when she spoke and frequently touched his arm, he stared straight ahead and did not return her touch. On their way from the O'Hare parking garage to the airport, he maintained an appropriate distance. And while they exhibited a professional air in front of the other personnel, something would happen on the flight that day that would affect their ride home.

Six

When Leon Fortunato reported back to his boss regarding the meeting with Romanian president Gheorghe Vasile, Carpathia seemed so giddy it was as if he had been there himself.

"So he left in a huff, did he?" Nicolae said.

Fortunato nodded. "Insisted on forty-eight hours."

"What did you tell him?"

"I agreed. Should I not have?"

"I thought you were a better negotiator, Leon. I would have responded with silence to see if he voluntarily reduced that. And if he did not, I would have countered with twenty-four. In fact, perhaps you should call and tell him you ran into a roadblock on this end and that twenty-four hours is the best you can do. I assume you traded private phone numbers."

"We did."

"Good. Do it."

Leon flinched. "Right here? Right now? In front of you?"

"What is the matter? Stage fright?"

"Well, I do better when I'm alone."

"Get over it. I am here and I want to be in on it."

"Should I put him on speakerphone?"

"No. He would be able to tell. I can listen in with my own earpiece. Go ahead. On one hand you are telling him that you are just my mouthpiece, but on the other you are exerting control. Okay?"

"As you wish."

Leon fished the tiny card with Vasile's pencil-scribbled private cell number from his pocket.

It was obvious the president knew who was calling. "Fortunato?"

"Yes, Mr. President. I'm afraid that —"

"Hold a moment so I can take this outside."

Carpathia raised his eyebrows and covered his mouth with his hand, obviously to keep from laughing.

A few seconds later Leon heard wind interfering with Vasile's transmission. "Now you listen here, sir. I'm not prepared to give my answer before forty-eight hours have passed, but I can tell you right now that I'm leaning toward exposing you and Carpathia and even Stonagal if need be. The people of Romania will not stand by and allow these strong-arm tactics. Now I am of a mind to —"

"Wait just one minute here, Gheorghe," Fortunato said, eliciting a wave and a huge smile from Nicolae, apparently for brashly calling the head of state by his first name. "You don't tell me how it's going to be; I tell you. I have run into a roadblock here on your request for forty-eight hours. Twenty-four is the limit, and —"

"Twenty-*four?* Why, I —"

"Twenty-four, and you are in no position to be exposing anybody. You are the one vulnerable, sir, and unless you want the international community to know of the duplicity within your —"

Click.

Leon slapped his phone shut as Nicolae applauded. "He hung up on you, Leon! He hung up on you! Nice work!"

"And so," Leon said, hiding his racing heart, "what do you do if he does not comply within the time frame?"

"Oh, he will. Trust me. He will. We have him, Leon. He is ours."

A few minutes later Carpathia's intercom chirped, and Viv Ivins said, "Mr. Stonagal for you, sir."

Nicolae pushed a button that put Jonathan on speakerphone. "How are you, my friend? I have Leon here with me, and we are wondering what time it is in New York."

"Same as it always is in relation to your neck of the woods. Now what in blazes do you think you're doing?"

"I beg your pardon?"

"You heard me. You think you can use a thug to threaten a government chief and not have it get back to me?"

"I was not under the impression that I reported to you, Jonathan."

"Well, you do when my name — not to mention my money — is invoked. And how dare you seek the presidency without my knowledge, let alone my blessing and that of the others?"

Fortunato had rarely seen Nicolae shaken. The younger man covered well. In measured tones he said, "Jonathan, you had better take a deep breath and think about whom you are talking to."

Stonagal swore. "I know whom I'm talking to, son. Now you listen to me. We have a meeting of the council coming up, and at that time —"

"When?"

"What?"

"When is your secret meeting with your

underground brotherhood? Are you deaf or do we not have a good connection?"

"Whom do *you* think you're talking to, Nicolae?"

"Someone I will not be speaking to for long if you do not answer me."

"Three weeks."

"I will be in office by then."

Stonagal was sputtering. "This is all premature, Nicolae. Now don't screw this up. We can set things in motion that guarantee you the presidency in the next election."

"Sorry, I am not waiting that long."

"But I . . . but you . . . we can't —"

"That is the problem, Jonathan. You cannot do anything. I will die from boredom before the next election. And why should I wait when we have what we need on this guy? You know we do."

"But why complicate things in such a dangerous way when we can grease the skids and —"

Carpathia stood. "Because I am not an employee, Jonathan! Anytime you want to pull your half of the money out and try to use it for more control over someone else, feel free."

"All right, calm down. Surely you must know that while I own only half a share in what we're doing with Vasile, there are seas of money necessary for global initiatives under my control elsewhere. It would behoove you not to run too far ahead of me. The other financiers need to be on board when you come to your rightful place of leadership."

"We all understood that that begins here in Romania."

"Of course, but —"

"But nothing! If I have to start here, I want to start now, this week."

"Vasile will never go for it."

"He has no choice."

Stonagal paused. "And how will you allow him to save face?"

"That is the least of my worries."

Irene kept checking her watch. For an hour after a late dinner, she had succeeded in keeping Raymie from the garage. Yes, she told him, the gifts were there, and, yes, his father had promised to take him out on one of them that very evening. But no, he could not see them until Rayford arrived home. And he was late. Late enough that she had tried his cell and, failing to reach him, called Pan-Con. The flight had landed on time.

She waited thirty more minutes, then called Rayford's cell again.

"Hi, hon," he said, and she heard restaurant noises.

"Rayford, tell me you didn't forget."

"Of course I didn't. What time is it? Oh no! On my way."

"Where are you?"

"An hour away."

"An hour! Raymie won't have time to do anything tonight."

"You didn't show him the stuff, did you? At least I get to see the look on his face."

"You might find that mixed. He doesn't just want to see the stuff, Rafe. He wants to enjoy it with you. Now where are you?"

"Oh, well, we had a snafu on the flight. We were shorted some dinners so the staff didn't get to eat. I thought I should take them out before we headed home."

"How thoughtful of you."

"Wasn't it?"

"Yes, you're extremely thoughtful, Rayford."

"Why are you being sarcastic, Irene?"

"I can't imagine. So, you're out to dinner with your whole crew."

"Yeah! Well, some of them just headed straight home. But whoever wanted to come along came along."

"Just hurry, will you?"

★ ★ ★

Rayford rang off and signaled for the waiter.

"Gotta go?" Hattie said.

"Yeah."

"And am I your whole crew?"

He sighed. "Yep."

"At least I'm *those* who decided to come along."

"Right."

"That was a little white lie, wasn't it?" she said, grinning.

Rayford nodded. But it hadn't been a white lie at all. It had been a big, black, ugly thing, and he would just have to remind himself that Irene's knowing the truth would be more hurtful than not.

The drive home was one of the longest of his life, because he still had to drop Hattie off, and his rationalizations were not helping him feel better. At the very least he could have called Irene. And he could have asked to talk with Raymie. But nothing had happened with Hattie. And he had told mostly the truth, hadn't he? They *had* been shorted some meals, and both he and Hattie had been hungry. Sure, they could have stopped for fast food, and, yes, he had forgotten his promise. At least temporarily.

But Raymie was a good kid. He'd understand. And he would be forgiving.

Seven

Leon was proud of himself, believing his plan was foolproof. Even if his scheme to intimidate the president of Romania fell apart at some juncture, he was certain nothing could lead back to him or to Nicolae Carpathia.

Fortunato began in a seedy area on the east side of Bucharest, where blue-collar workers and their families were crammed into housing units too small for even half of them. Bars teemed with customers, and hooligans of all ages milled about on street corners. Leon cruised through the district to the unit where his contact lived. As he parked on the crowded street and emerged from his vehicle, Leon recognized the man's girlfriend marching down the steps, clearly agitated.

"Do me a favor and shoot him," she said. "Would you?"

"Sure thing, Ecaterina," Leon said.

Family, friends, acquaintances, and lovers were always complicators in these matters.

He found Stefan Marin slouched on a sagging couch, nursing a beer.

"What's her problem?" Leon said.

"Money. What else?"

"Could you use three grand?"

"In U.S. dollars? Could I!"

"That's almost forty thousand in the old *lei*."

"Trust me, I know."

"Easy job, but it has to be done right."

"I'll do anything for three thousand, long as it's not perverted."

Fortunato smiled. "That never stopped you before. But no, this is conventional, straightforward. Just find the man called Teodor, who drives the Vasile grandchildren to school and serves as their security. Offer him eight thousand dollars for merely saying that someone has asked him for the kids' daily itinerary. That's all he has to do and all you have to do."

"Sounds *bănuitor*."

"There's nothing to be suspicious of, but fine, I'll find someone else."

"No, no. I need the money."

"Of course you do. Now rehearse it for me."

"I got it. But how do we know he follows

through? And if he does, how does he get his money?"

"He has to make the call in front of you. He tells his supervisor what you tell him to say; you give him the cash. Simple as that."

"He doesn't have to tell me anything? give up anything about the kids?"

"No. He can tell his superior that someone he didn't know approached him and offered him money and that he told them to get lost, that he's loyal and just thought the boss should know. And this has to be done tonight."

"How do you know I won't skip with the money?"

"You disappear with the eight thou, you'll be dead before you see Ecaterina again. Or she'll be."

"Don't worry. You can trust me."

"Of course I can. I know where you live. I know where she lives. I even know where your mother lives."

"My mother?"

"You don't have a mother? Everybody's got a mother."

"I've never mentioned my mother."

"Is that so? Then how do I know Paraschiva Marin lives 3.1 miles from here and works six days a week in the lace factory?"

Stefan seemed to freeze. "There is no reason to involve her in any of this. She does not know what I do. And she does not need to."

"You continue to do your job for me; I forget what I know about your mother. A churchgoer. Devout."

"A saint."

"May God keep her safe. May *you* keep her safe, Stefan."

By the time Raymie arrived home from school the next day, Rayford had the new four-wheeler and the new snowmobile loaded onto a trailer and was ready to head out to the forest preserve to try them out. It was not lost on Rayford that the boy's enthusiasm seemed to be directed at the machines, not at his father. And he well knew that this did not really counter Irene's contention that Raymie wanted Rayford, not toys. Rayford had alienated his son by all the broken promises and lack of attention, so he knew this was Raymie's way of being polite and avoiding the issue.

Unfortunately for Rayford, that would not last. Because the outing soured shortly after they unloaded the equipment. The snow was too deep for the four-wheeler, and Raymie was too young and too small to handle the snowmobile. He had to sit behind Rayford and hang on while Dad had all the fun, racing about.

And it was fun. The thrill of flying had nearly left Rayford after years in the cockpit, carefully maneuvering heavy craft from city to city. He was still at the top of his game, and there was just enough of an edge from the load of responsibility and accountability he felt for the passengers. But the chance to open the snowmobile wide and lean into turns, making Raymie squeal, reminded Rayford of the person he had once been.

On the way home, Raymie wanted to talk. And that was something Rayford had hoped to avoid. The boy was nothing if not direct.

"Dad," he said, "do you believe in Jesus?"

"Well, yeah, sure. I mean, I guess so."

"You either do or you don't. You know you have to believe in Jesus to go to heaven."

"Do you?"

"Of course. Doesn't everybody know that? Mom said you grew up going to church and that you used to go all the time with her."

"I know. Yeah, I did. But there are lots of people who go to church who don't agree that you have to believe in Jesus to go to heaven."

"But they're wrong, aren't they? I mean, Jesus is the one who said it. He said that nobody can come to God but through Him."

"Now, Raymie, I'm glad you're going to church, and I'm sure it's going to be good for you in the end. But you know the last thing I want is for something that's meant for your good to wind up making you intolerant. You know what that means?"

"Tell me."

"As you get older you'll realize that there are a lot of well-meaning people who think they have God all figured out and really believe that their way is the only way to God. Frankly, that doesn't make sense to me. I think there are a lot of different paths to God, and one is just as good as another. I don't think God would punish somebody who never heard of Jesus and was doing the best he could in the religion of his choice. Or no religion. As long as he's trying to be a good person."

"Wow."

"Wow what?"

"You sound just like the people Pastor Billings talks about. People who think they have it all figured out, but they don't really believe in Jesus."

"I told you. I believe in Jesus."

"But you don't believe what He said."

"Now, Raymie, Jesus was alive two thousand years ago, so it's hard to know what He really said. He was a wonderful man, a religious man, a good teacher. The fact that He's still famous and still remembered means He must have been on the ball."

Raymie laughed. "On the ball! I've never heard anybody say that about Jesus before. You want to know what I believe?"

"I think I know, but sure, let's hear it."

"I think Jesus was either crazy or a liar or telling the truth."

"Oh, it doesn't have to be that cut-and-dried, Son."

"Sure it does. Pastor Billings has talked about this. You said Jesus was a great teacher, but He said He was the Son of God and the only way to His Father. If that's not true, He was either lying or thought He was something He wasn't, right?"

Rayford pretended to be more interested in the traffic. "Well, like I say, Raymie, we can't be totally sure He was quoted exactly, can we?"

"If we can't," Raymie said, "how do we know what to believe?"

"That's my point, Son. Don't be so quick to assume that everything you read and hear, even in church, is the whole truth."

"So you don't believe Jesus is coming back either, right?"

"Coming back?"

"Mom was going to talk to you about what Pastor Billings has been preaching about. Jesus coming back."

So that's what she was trying to get to. "Uh, no, we haven't gotten a chance to discuss that yet. I've been real busy."

"Tell me about it. We were supposed to do this weeks ago."

"I know, and I'm sorry. Now that we've got this stuff, we can get out together more."

"Now that we've got this stuff? How does that give you more time?"

"Hey, are you hungry?"

"Soon. Right now I'm just kinda worried about you."

"You don't need to worry about me. I said I was sorry, and I promise to carve out the time for us. Okay?"

"That's not what I'm worried about. Okay, it is a little, because sometimes it seems like you just promise me to keep me from bugging you, but then it never happens, and —"

"Never happens!? What are we doing right now?"

"I know. But what I'm worried about is that when Jesus does come back, you won't be ready."

"Ready for what?"

"To go to heaven with Him. You should

really come to church Sunday. Pastor Billings is finishing his series on this, and it's really great. Even I can understand it."

Good for you. "So Jesus comes back and everybody goes to heaven with Him?"

"Not everybody, Dad. That's just it. You have to believe in Him."

"I do. I'll be okay."

"You don't really."

"Okay, can we just disagree about this and still love each other, Raymie? I don't want to spoil our time together with arguing."

"I do love you, Dad. That's why I'm worried."

"Well, don't worry about me. If good people are floating up to Jesus someday, I'll be right with you."

"But it isn't good people who go. It's forgiven people."

He sounds just like his mother! "All right, end of discussion, okay? As you get older you'll realize there are all kinds of ways to look at this stuff, and each person is free to come to whatever conclusions he wants."

Raymie fell silent, and while Rayford hoped he hadn't hurt the boy's feelings, he was relieved to take a break from all the religious mumbo jumbo.

At home Raymie helped get the vehicles off the trailer, but as Rayford finished putting them up in the garage, he overheard the boy talking with Irene, who had asked how things went.

"Dad's going to hell," Raymie said. "He doesn't think he is. He thinks he isn't. But he doesn't believe in Jesus. Not really."

"He's at the top of my prayer list," Irene said. "Yours too?"

" 'Course."

Eight

Though Leon Fortunato was licking his wounds over having to prove himself to his boss anew daily, he couldn't deny that Carpathia treated him well in many respects, not the least of which was the exquisite apartment he enjoyed. Nicolae had given him his choice between lavish quarters within Carpathia's own estate or the entire top floor of a palatial apartment building in downtown Bucharest. Leon had chosen the latter.

He lounged next to a dancing fire and before the TV, watching today's staged presidential event that depicted the gregarious Gheorghe Vasile being serenaded and waved at with flowers by schoolchildren in yet another parade in his honor. That made it all the more surreal when Leon's cell phone chirped and the president himself was on the other end.

Leon had to admit it was disconcerting

that the angrier Vasile grew, the more calmly and directly he spoke. "I am not a happy man, Mr. Fortunato. You must understand that, despite your efforts and the wishes of Nicolae Carpathia, I remain president of this republic and have access to more power than you can imagine."

If he only knew the power to which Carpathia and I have access! "And you are threatening me why?" Leon said.

"Because someone came nosing around my grandchildren, and I will not have that."

"Nosing around?"

"Do not play ignorant with me, sir. You predicted the same if I did not comply with your boss's ridiculous deadline."

"Which fast approaches."

"And if I tell you what you can do with your implications and threats?"

"I believe you know the answer to that, Gheorghe. You may find in office your number-two man — perhaps whom you prefer over Dr. Carpathia — but you will be vilified and ruined in the process. Your scandalous dealings will be made known all over the world. Whatever legacy you think you have nurtured will be seen for the sham that it is, much like the fiction I am watching on TV even as we speak. And for the record, I know nothing of any 'nosing around' your grandchildren, as you put it."

"Is that so?"

"What reason would I have for lying about that? If it was true, it seems I would be eager to take credit for it, would I not?"

"You're telling me you know nothing about someone contacting my grandchildren's driver and bodyguard and offering him four thousand U.S. dollars for information regarding their itinerary?"

"I beg your pardon?"

"You heard me. The equivalent of fifty thousand of our old *lei.*"

Four thousand U.S. dollars? Is Vasile testing me, or did Stefan try to pull something after all? Maybe Teodor pocketed half of it and gave the other half to his superior to prove his innocence?

"I repeat, Mr. President: I know absolutely nothing of that. But let me tell you this: If I do not have your decision — the only one we will accept — by midnight tonight, I merely inform my superior and a series of events is set in motion that will make you wish you had committed suicide."

And as Gheorghe Vasile sputtered and protested and tried to bluster, Leon slapped his cell phone shut, reopened it, and dialed.

"Matei?" he said. "A job for you." He gave

the man descriptions and addresses for Stefan Marin's mother and girlfriend. "The old woman must disappear, never to be seen again. And the young woman must be incapacitated to the point that Stefan has to take care of her for several months."

"Got it."

"And one more thing: if you do not hear from me by midnight, here is the location of a structure that must be torched, the livestock not allowed to escape, and security immobilized. Understood?"

"Understood."

During a tense meal, with Rayford clearly trying to keep the subject off what Raymie and Irene wanted to talk about, Irene urged her son to accede to his dad's wishes and spend even more time with him watching sports on TV.

"But no more church talk tonight," Rayford said. "Fair enough?"

"Rayford!" Irene said.

"Well, I got both barrels today, and I don't think it's right that you're filling his head with all this at his age."

"Okay! All right! Stop. Raymie, let me talk with your father about this. You stick to talking sports for a while."

Raymie shrugged, and Irene glared at

Rayford until he looked away.

Once Rayford and Raymie were camped out in front of the television, Irene suddenly felt alone. And lonely. She missed her daughter. They had not spoken much since Chloe went off to Stanford. Irene was determined not to let the barrier between them rise any higher. She called Chloe's room and reached her roommate, who told her that Chloe was at debate club but that she would give her the message.

"Thanks, Amy," Irene said. "And tell her it's nothing urgent. I just miss her and love her and want to hear her voice."

"Oh, that's so sweet!"

"Well, we'll see how sweet Chloe thinks it is if she calls me back."

"If she doesn't," Amy said, laughing, "I'll mimic her voice and call you myself."

Matei Prodan was Fortunato's most trusted operative. He was expensive, but he was ideal. Quiet. Ruthless. Above all, thorough. Somehow he never left evidence, and when he took a job, it was soon done and forgotten.

Matei and a younger associate — Lazar — took care of Stefan's mother first. As Lazar mounted the steps to her one-room apartment, Matei phoned her from his cell phone in the car. "Mrs. Marin?"

"Yes, who is it?"

"I'm calling from Fundeni Hospital, where your son has been admitted. Your son is Stefan Marin, correct?"

"Stefan? Yes! What has happened?"

"An accident, ma'am. I am sorry to tell you that you must come immediately."

"He is dying? I have no way to get there!"

"We have sent an attendant to drive you. Can you be ready momentarily?"

"Of course!"

"He should be nearly at your door."

"But I'm undressed for the evening after a day at work! I'll need to change!"

"Do it quickly," Matei said. "And you will need nothing more than identification."

Moments later Lazar opened the back door of Matei's car for the bent woman, and she entered, weeping. "I am so grateful for your kindness," she said. "What can you tell me? Will he live?"

"Would you like to speak with him?" Matei said, handing her his phone. "It is ringing."

"Stefan! What happened? I am on my way! Hold on for my sake. . . . What? But I was told . . . these gentlemen are bringing me to the hospital! . . . What? Help me, Stefan! They told me —"

The woman thrashed about, trying to open the back door, but it had been locked from the driver's door. She pulled herself forward. "What is this? What are you doing? My son says he is fine!"

Matei nodded to Lazar, who turned and said softly, "Perhaps it is a case of mistaken identity."

From the phone came shouts of warning from Stefan, and with that Lazar drove an elbow so savagely into the face of the woman that Matei heard bones shatter as she flopped onto the seat and then onto the floor. The shouting continued from the phone until Lazar fished it from the floor and slapped it shut.

Matei followed the Danube out of the city and pulled off to a secluded grove. "Is she still alive?"

Lazar nodded, and Matei motioned with his head toward the back while reaching into the glove box to trip the trunk latch. The young man got out and returned with two forty-pound blocks of concrete with handles made of bent rebar.

Stefan's mother breathed laboriously through blood-caked nostrils as Lazar moved to the other side of the car and forced her feet through the openings in the ersatz handles. When Matei helped heft her from the car, he wondered if she weighed much more than the concrete.

The men carried her to a steep embankment and rolled her over the side, waiting a few seconds for the splash. By the time her body deteriorated and freed itself from the boots of death, there would be too little of her left for anyone to recognize. And who knew where she might wash up onto the bank of the rapid river?

Matei and Lazar cleaned themselves off and reentered the car. Matei pulled a small slip of paper from his pocket and held it up to the dim dash light. "Our next stop."

"You tell me where my mother is and you tell me right now," Stefan shouted, gushing profanities.

Fortunato lowered the volume on his TV and pulled the hem of his robe over his bare feet. "Your mother?" he said, pressing the phone tight against his ear.

"Don't do this!" Stefan said. "Where is she?"

"Hmm," Leon said. "If I knew something like that, I wonder how much I should charge for such information."

"I'll give you the four thousand with interest!" Stefan said.

"So it was you and not Teodor who

worked the con. Maybe I should hire a responsible young man like him to replace you."

"Mr. Fortunato, please! Come after me; just don't let anyone do anything to my mother."

"Well, that's fair," Leon said. "Tell you what — next time you see her, tell her that I promised to look after her from now on. You're going to be busy."

"Busy? I'm going to be busy? What am I going to be doing? I'll do anything to get square with you again."

"Oh, I know you will, Stefan. And in the meantime, it would help my business if you warned people against trying to pull anything on me."

"I promise, sir! I promise! Now, please! Don't let anything happen to my mother!"

"I'm sorry, Stefan. We'll have to continue this another time. I have to take this call."

"Wait! No!"

Leon disconnected from Stefan and answered Matei.

"You've already heard from Stefan? You're not worried he will tip off the girl?"

"Trust me," Leon said. "He's thinking of nothing and no one but his sainted mother right now."

"He can think all he wants about her,"

Matei said. "It's done."

"As planned?"

"No hitches, no evidence, no witnesses."

Nine

Raymie's bedtime arrived by halftime of the ball game, and Rayford knew it would soon be time to face the music. On the way up to Raymie's room, Rayford said, "Hey, I forgot. I brought you something."

"Something else?" Raymie said.

"Yeah, come on."

The boy followed him to the garage, where Rayford pulled from the backseat of his BMW a padded envelope with a framed picture of himself in uniform in the terminal, his cap under his arm, a 747 showing outside the window. Rayford had signed it, "To Raymie with love, Dad." Under that he had written, "Rayford Steele, Captain, Pan-Continental Airlines, O'Hare."

"Cool!" Raymie said. "I'll put it in my room."

But on their way back inside, Raymie said,

"Hey, Dad, look. Flat tire on the four-wheeler already."

Rayford swore, then apologized.

"Dad, can I ask you something?"

Uh-oh.

"Will you come to church with us this Sunday?"

"I don't know. Maybe."

"Why not?"

"I said maybe."

"That's what you said last week."

"Well, this Sunday I'm going to have to fix this tire."

"C'mon, Dad!"

"Do you want me to fix this four-wheeler for you or not? I don't have all the time in the world."

"Next Sunday then?"

Rayford sighed. "For sure."

As they mounted the steps toward Raymie's room, Irene called out from the kitchen, "His Bulls pajamas are laid out. Don't let him wear his socks to bed."

A few minutes later Rayford was back in the living room, and he could tell Irene was on her way. He instinctively picked up a newspaper as a diversion.

"You mind if I turn the sound off until the third quarter?" she said. "Or do you want to see last week's highlights?"

"It's all right," he said, the newspaper in his lap.

"Rayford," she said, "I don't want to fight, but please don't undermine what has become so important to Raymie."

"All right," he said. "I'll try to behave."

"Don't make light of it," Irene said. "Please."

"Fair enough. I guess a little religion won't hurt him, but you know my concerns."

"It's not like he's going to become a missionary or a pastor," she said. "Although that wouldn't be all bad. He's just a young boy very interested in the things of God, as I am."

"He's only interested because you are."

"And what's wrong with that? Aren't we supposed to be examples to him?"

"Not of fundamentalists."

Irene made a face. "It's not fair to use inflammatory language, Rafe. Fundamentalists have come to be known as people who kill those they disagree with. When was the last time you heard of a Christian doing that?"

"Granted. But do you know what someone asked me the last time I went to that new church with you? They asked what God was doing in my life."

"And what did you say?"

"I said He was blessing my socks off. You'd have thought I'd made their day. Now what's all this both you and Raymie are trying to tell me about the preacher and some hobbyhorse he's on lately?"

"It's not a hobbyhorse," Irene said. "It's one of the major thrusts of this church. They believe in Bible prophecy, which says that Jesus is coming back someday, and we don't know when. That's why I wish you'd come with us this Sunday, because Pastor Billings is finishing up his series on the topic and he's really going to put it all together. It's amazing."

"So it *is* a hobbyhorse."

Irene shook her head and looked away, as if interested in the muted highlights on TV.

Rayford used the occasion to peek at the sports section of the paper. He fully expected her to scold him for not listening, but she was not talking. Rayford found something intriguing in the paper and was soon reading for real.

"I'm reading everything I can get my hands on about the rapture of the church," Irene said.

"Hmm?"

"Nothing."

"That's what Raymie was trying to tell

me. Jesus is coming back and all that."

Suddenly she was engaged again. "Can you imagine, Rafe? Jesus coming back to get us before we die?"

"Yeah, boy," he said, peeking over the top of his newspaper, "that would kill me."

She was not amused. "If I didn't know what would happen to me," she said, "I wouldn't be so glib about it."

"I *do* know what would happen to me," he said. "I'd be dead, gone, *finis*. But you, of course, you would fly right up to heaven."

He hadn't meant to offend her. He was just having fun. When she turned away he rose and pursued her. He spun her around and tried to kiss her, but she was cold. "Come on, Irene," he said. "Tell me thousands wouldn't just keel over if they saw Jesus coming back for all the good people."

She pulled away in tears. "I've told you and told you. Saved people aren't good people, they're —"

"Just forgiven, yeah, I know," he said, feeling rejected and vulnerable in his own living room. He returned to his chair and his paper. "If it makes you feel any better, I'm happy for you that you can be so cocksure."

"I only believe what the Bible says," Irene said.

Rayford shrugged. He wanted to say,

"Good for you," but he didn't want to make a bad situation worse. In a way he envied her confidence, but in truth he wrote it off to her being a more emotional, more feelings-oriented person. He didn't want to articulate it, but the fact was, he was more intelligent. He believed in rules, systems, laws, patterns, things you could see and feel and hear and touch.

If God was part of all that, okay. A higher power, a loving being, a force behind the laws of nature, fine. Let's sing about it, pray about it, feel good about our ability to be kind to others, and go about our business. Rayford's greatest fear was that this religious fixation would not fade like Irene's Amway days, her Tupperware phase, and her aerobics spell. He could just see her ringing doorbells and asking if she could read people a verse or two. Surely she knew better than to dream of his tagging along.

Irene had become a full-fledged religious fanatic, and somehow that freed Rayford to daydream without guilt about Hattie Durham.

Buck Williams had never seen Jim Borland like this. The longtime religion editor of *Global Weekly* had been a Princeton religious studies major a couple of decades before, and while they did not see eye to eye on everything, Buck considered Jim one of the savvy veterans on the staff.

But here was Borland, moping about the New York office, appearing in shock. Buck was dying to ask him what was wrong, but Borland surprised him by knocking softly on his door. "You got a minute?"

"Sure, Jimmy. What's up?"

"You know where I am on this God stuff, right?"

"God stuff?" Buck said.

"The whole religious thing. I mean, I'm the religion guy but not that religious, okay? I come from the school of thought that believes a little bit of god is in everybody — whoever or whatever you consider god. Probably a strength for someone in my job."

"As long as you know about and understand a lot of religions, sure."

Borland reluctantly sat when Buck pointed to a chair. "Well, you know I was in Eastern Europe on some religious confab stories. Somebody invited me to what they call an evangelistic crusade. No interest. None. I have always wondered what these evangelists were thinking when they decided to call these mass rallies crusades, when they're the first ones to howl when we remind them of the shame of the Crusades in the name of their God."

"Right. So you don't go."

"No, I go."

"You do?"

"Yeah, and here's why. The so-called crusade is being held in Albania, okay? And the evangelist is not an American TV–type guy. I mean, I guess he's an American citizen now, but it's this Gonzalo Islando from Argentina. Heard of him?"

"Don't think so."

"Came to this country when he was young, patterned himself after Moody, Sunday, Graham — those types. Preaching salvation to the masses, you know."

"Okay."

"So I'm intrigued, because this is real cross-cultural stuff. This guy may be a naturalized American citizen by now, but he's an Argentine and he's preaching in Albania. Might be interesting. I'm thinking maybe I'll catch him in some cultural gaffe, some ignorant move. So I check it out, and guess what? I end up going back two more nights in a row."

"That impressive, eh?"

"Well, no. He wasn't that big a deal. I'll give him this — he knew the culture, was self-effacing, handled the press well, was self-deprecating, had a sense of humor, really seemed to love and care about the people of Albania — who knows why? As a preacher he was good, I guess. These guys are pretty simple, you know. Nothing deep. Nothing earth-shattering. You hear one hellfire-and-brimstone-except-that-Jesus-died-for-your-sins sermon, you've heard 'em all. I decided he was no charlatan; he really believes this stuff. You can't earn your way to heaven, trust in the blood of Christ — all that."

"So you became a believer."

Borland snorted. "Hardly. I became convinced of Islando's sincerity; that's all. What got to me was the response. I've been to these things before, Williams, and I've always found them a little strange and amusing. There's lots of emotion, a bunch of people following each other like sheep, people coming forward and getting saved — you know the drill."

"Sure."

"But this is different. Islando holds this deal at a stadium that holds around fifty thousand, and it's packed. There's cheesy music, then people witnessing or giving testimony or whatever they call it when they tell everybody else how bad they used to be and how good they are now because of Jesus. Then Islando preaches this simple message — pretty much the same every night. Being good isn't good enough. You can't earn it. Trust Jesus."

"Same old same old."

"Except that people start getting out of their seats and coming forward long before he invites them to. And it's not just a bunch of counselors getting into position. I've seen that happen. It serves as a sort of priming of the pump. You realize the first thousand people down there are part of the deal, carrying their Bibles and their literature and wearing their badges."

"But . . . ?"

"But not this time. Well, some of them, sure, but there were people weeping, crying out. It was like they couldn't wait to get down there and pray and repent and get saved. There were way more converts than counselors at first, and it was a mess. I thought it was interesting. I was racking my brain to remember what it was that made Islando's message so compelling to so many, and I couldn't come up with it. Like I said, I went back the next night and the next, and thinking back on it, I can hardly tell you the difference between one service and the next. Except the response. That first night was the most I'd ever even heard of, let alone seen. But the next night topped that, and the next was even bigger. Buck, that was last week. Those meetings are still going on and getting bigger every night. It's like that whole nation is going Christian."

"True definition of revival."

"I guess. Just blew me away."

"And so?"

"So that's not all. I'm on my way back to France, and I hear this Texas-based guy — fella by the name of Sandy Tibbitts out of San Antonio, younger than Islando but at this thing more than forty years himself — is doing the same thing in the Ukraine. Well, I'm a long way from Ukraine, but this I have to see. I can tell by the look on your face you've never heard of Tibbitts; neither had I. I find out he's some kind of a Southerner and a Baptist, so I'm guessing big hair and slick suit and a wide grin, plus a lot of media, right?

"None of that. Discover this guy spends most of his time overseas, doing the same kind of thing Islando does, only a little less slick, a little less organized, more simple and direct. Not polished, just a loud, powerful preacher who somehow connects with people on some elemental level. And the same thing is happening. These people are running down the aisles to get Jesus."

"So is it worth a story?"

"That's just it, Buck. I don't know what to do with it. These types of guys have been around forever, but as an observer of the religious world, I've got to tell you, I've never seen anything like this. These guys aren't healers, aren't miracle workers — those types naturally draw big crowds and lots of response. But here are these two flat-out salvation preachers seeing some sort of response even they have never seen before. I talked to them both, and they both used the same word for it: *harvest*."

"Sounds like a horror movie," Buck said. "*The Harvest of the Dead.*"

"Um-hmm." It was clear Borland's mind was somewhere else.

"This is really bothering you, Jimmy. Why?"

"I don't know. I guess because I'm finding out that it's happening all over the place. All over the world. Anybody involved in this game — even if they're sincere and not just playing at it for who knows what motive — is seeing the same kind of thing. It's becoming a story as big as all the natural disasters. But what can I write about it? The whole world is coming to Christ? I'd be laughed out of the profession."

"Truth never hurts. But maybe all the disasters are causing this renewed interest in God."

"I've thought of that," Borland said. "Sure, people are scared, and they want to somehow keep nature from falling in on them, but wouldn't the conventional response be to blame God or to question Him? These people seem to be genuinely embracing Him, and this is from all over. You know, Buck, the U.S. is not immune."

"To what?"

"Same phenomenon, and it's happening in churches all over. Attendance is up. Conversions are up. No one knows what to make of it."

"Well, there's your angle, your story. But frankly, you seem handcuffed by it."

Borland stood and looked out at the Manhattan skyline. "That's the best assessment I've heard about its impact on me," he said. "I flat don't know what to make of it. Are we experiencing another revival, this one global? It's been a century since the last one. Something's up, Buck. Something's happening, and I have no idea what it is."

"Tell me something, Jim. You ever envy these people, wish you had a little of what they've found in all this?"

"Seriously? No. I don't believe the message, don't get it, consider people weak who go that route. But I can't deny that whatever appeal this ever had has somehow escalated.

People are getting religion like never before, and it'll be interesting to see what it means to society as a whole."

Ten

"We can be kind," Matei told a pale and whimpering Ecaterina as she cowered in the backseat. "This is not your fault. This is Stefan's fault. You have to suffer, and he will be forced to care for you."

"I'm sitting in someone's blood," she said, her voice quavery. "What are you going to do to me?"

"My associate here is going to give you an injection to dull the pain. Then we are going to break your tibias. Without the anesthetic, you would pass out."

"No, no!" she wailed. "You don't have to do that! Isn't there anything I can do?"

"You can sit still for the injection. This has to be done. You don't have to understand it. *We* don't have to understand it. We're trying to make it as easy as possible. But I warn you, nothing can make this pain-free. The less you move about, however, the

118

better. We will leave you where Stefan can find you, and it would be wise of you to tell him immediately that you should be moved only by professionals and treated as soon as possible."

"Oh, please!"

"Hush."

"What did he do? Why aren't you hurting *him?*"

"Trust me, he is already suffering. Now the best thing you can do is submit to the injection. This is going to happen either way."

"Do you have to break both legs?"

"Afraid so. You must be totally dependent on Stefan for a while."

"I'm going to kill him," she said. "Whatever he did, I had nothing to do with it."

Whether Lazar acted too quickly following the administering of the anesthetic or Ecaterina simply had too low a pain threshold, she passed out from the pain of the first break.

"Do I need to do the other?" Lazar said.

"It will be easier," Matei said. "We'll just have to be careful moving her. And Stefan better hope we reach him so he can get to her before she's fully into shock."

The park bench where they placed her, wrapped in a scratchy woolen blanket and quivering uncontrollably, was six blocks from Stefan's place.

When they reached him by phone, he cursed them, sobbing.

"Are you up for a while, sir?" Fortunato said on the phone at about midnight.

"I plan to retire by 1 a.m.," Carpathia said. "Come now."

A few minutes later Leon sat across from him in his parlor. "Before I left the car," Fortunato said, "I assigned the arson."

"I am stunned, troubled, I must admit, by Vasile's not cracking yet."

"He will by dawn."

"Likely."

Leon told Nicolae of the other complications and how he had dealt with them.

"You actually had an innocent old woman tossed into the Danube?" Nicolae said, narrowing his eyes at Fortunato.

Leon nodded, heart racing.

"Stand please."

"Sorry, sir?"

"Stand, I said, Leon!"

Fortunato stood, tensing.

Carpathia approached and looked up into his face. They were nearly nose to nose. "And you had an innocent young woman's shins shattered?"

Leon nodded slightly, preparing his defense.

Carpathia spread his arms wide and beckoned Fortunato close. He wrapped his arms around the big man and squeezed tight. "I love you, Leon! Do you know that? I love you."

And Fortunato basked in the affection.

His phone chirped. "I should take this," he managed, his face pressed into Carpathia's shoulder.

"Certainly."

It was Stefan, hysterical. "You didn't have to do this, you —" and he raged profanely. "Do you know what I had to do?"

"About what, Stefan?"

"You know about what, you filthy excuse for a man! I had to shoot her!"

"That's distasteful. Shoot whom?"

"You know who! She was dying anyway! There was no time to call anyone. She regained consciousness and nearly passed out again when she saw her legs. You destroyed her, Leon! Her shin bones were showing! She was bleeding to death!"

"I'm sorry, Stefan, but I do not know to whom you are referring."

"You lying scum! I had to kill my own girl-friend!"

"Well, you shouldn't have done that. However she hurt herself was surely treatable by competent medical professionals."

"Tell me where my mother is, Leon! I mean it! I'll kill you if anything's happened to her."

"You'll kill me? Perhaps you can accomplish that when you return my four thousand, hmm? But don't let too much time pass. Unlucky things keep happening to those around you."

"I'll kill you!"

"Excuse me, will you, Stefan? I need to place another call."

"Don't hang up on me! I'll —"

Click.

"Matei," Leon said a moment later, seated again under the beam of Carpathia's smile. "We'd best put the young man out of his misery. He's no good to me anymore."

"Done."

By dawn Bucharest police were searching for the murderers of Ecaterina and Stefan and beginning to process a missing person's report on one Paraschiva Marin, who had not shown up for work.

There was also the matter of a suspicious fire on the grounds of the breeding ranch of the son of the president of the republic, which had taken the lives of sixteen purebred Arabian stallions valued at millions of euros.

"Mom, it's Chloe. What's up?"

"Nothing. I just wanted to hear your voice. How are you, sweetie? I miss you."

"Doing well. How's everyone there?"

"Good. Good." Irene hated that Chloe had not returned any of her sentiments. Couldn't she say it was good to hear from her mother, that she missed her too, that she wanted to hear her voice? Irene guessed that was too much to ask.

"And how are you doing since your disappointment?" Irene said.

"My disappointment?"

"Your breakup with Ricky."

"Oh, that! Over it."

"Are you sure?"

" 'Course. You know he's married already."

"You're not serious."

"Yep."

"That has to hurt. A little anyway. No?"

"Nah! She can have him."

"Well, that's a pretty mature response."

"Oh, you know me, Mom. Ms. Mature."

Irene asked her about studies and friends and extracurricular activities, getting banal, noncommittal responses until she wanted to scream, to demand whether Chloe ever even thought about her, cared about her at all. Irene loved this child to the depths of her soul, but it was as if Chloe were made of stone.

Irene finally rang off with a series of wishes and expressions of love and cheerfulness, to which Chloe merely responded with courtesy. Hanging up, Irene sat on the edge of the bed and wept.

She thought she heard Rayford on the stairs and quickly wiped her eyes. But he did not come in, so she opened her Bible and reviewed her prayer list:

Rafe, for his salvation and that I be a loving wife to him.
Chloe, that she come to Christ and live in purity.
Ray Jr., that he never stray from his strong, childlike faith.

Early the next morning Carpathia called Leon. "What do we hear from Vasile? Surely you would have told me if he had called?"

"Of course. Nothing."

"What now?"

"I would advise you to involve Jonathan," Leon said.

"You heard my last conversation with

him, Leon. I will not crawl to him asking for his help."

"I will."

"You will?"

"Sure. I'll tell him what has happened up to now, tell him that even if he disagrees and finds it distasteful, now is the time to accept the lesser of two evils and do what he has to do to get Vasile out of the way."

Carpathia paced. "You scare his family and kill his son's horses, and he responds in silence? What is he up to, Leon?"

"Frankly, it wouldn't surprise me if he thinks he is going over your head."

"Over my head! Who is over my head?"

"Stonagal."

"Jonathan is not over my —"

"*You* know that, Nicolae. And *I* know that. But Jonathan does not know that yet. That's why I should call him."

Eleven

Irene looked forward to Sunday as she hadn't in a long time. Sure, since she had switched to New Hope she had enjoyed church more than ever. But this was different, special. Even Raymie was eager to hear the last sermon in Pastor Billings's series on the end of time, and much of it was above the boy's head.

"Let's both plan on taking notes," Irene told him. "Then we can talk about it later."

"We can tell Dad all about it," Raymie said.

She hesitated, nodding slowly. "We'll need to be cautious about that. Judicious. You know what that means?"

"I think so. Careful?"

"Using good judgment, sound thinking, choosing our timing carefully. Something is going on in your dad's life, Raymie. I don't know what it is, but he's not himself."

"Why?"

"I don't know. His drifting from church is just a symptom. Sometimes when adults get to be your dad's and my age, they take stock of their lives and aren't happy."

"But Dad's successful! He's done everything he ever wanted to do. Didn't he always want to be an airline captain?"

"Yes, but that's the problem. Sometimes you point your whole life at a goal you think will make you happy, and when you reach it, it doesn't satisfy you. That's quite a lesson, isn't it? You see how you want to set goals that really satisfy?"

Raymie fell silent, clearly thinking. Irene was impressed that he would admit when he didn't understand something, and he was never quick to respond until he did.

"You mean like if I dreamed of becoming a professional basketball player and making millions of dollars and being famous, I might not like it once I made it?"

"You know what the Bible says about living for ourselves and being rich. . . ."

"Yeah. Something about setting your sights on eternal stuff."

"Fame and fortune aren't going to mean a thing in heaven, are they?"

"I guess not. You know, Mom, I've been starting to worry more about Dad than ever."

"Worry how?"

"You know, like when he's flying. I never used to worry, because he always told me how safe airplanes are. He said that every time I hear or read about a plane crash, I should remember how many hundreds of thousands of flights were made without anything going wrong. Before I never worried about it at all. But now, not knowing if he'd go to heaven if he died, I keep hoping and praying he doesn't crash."

"I worry too," she said.

"You do?"

"Of course."

"Wouldn't it be cool if we didn't have to die to go to heaven? Like what Pastor Billings has been talking about. Do you think Jesus could come back before I get old?"

"You never know," Irene said. "We're supposed to live as if it could be today. Nothing more has to happen before He returns."

"Then why doesn't He come?"

"Who can know the mind of God?" she said. "But He loves the world so much, maybe He's just waiting for one more person to turn to Him."

"Maybe He's waiting for Dad."

"Maybe He is."

Leon stood on the veranda at Carpathia's estate, watching his boss meander across the property, his face toward the sky. Suddenly he stopped and raised his arms. Then he dropped to his knees.

The head of Nicolae's security team glanced at Leon and began to advance toward his client. Fortunato waved him off and made a gesture with his cell phone. The security man called Leon.

"Let him be," Fortunato said. "If he needs you, he'll let you know."

"But what if I hang back and then find out I should have — ?"

"I'll take full responsibility," Leon said.

"No disrespect, sir, but I don't answer to you. I need to cover my —"

"I said I would take full responsibility. If necessary, you may tell Dr. Carpathia that I forbade you to approach him."

"Very good, sir. Thank you."

Nicolae — trim, fit, working out daily — had felt a sudden rush of fatigue. He was trying to communicate with his spirit guide when he was driven to his knees.

"Worship me," came the voice he would never forget from his first encounter with the being, "and I will communicate solely with you."

"I am your servant," Nicolae said, his voice weak and shaky.

"All will go with you if you can discipline yourself to never forget that, subject."

"You have my word."

"Your path is being cleared."

"My path? My path to where?"

"Your path to the fulfillment of my promise."

"The world and its kingdoms?"

No response.

Nicolae was tempted to repeat his question, but he knew from experience that the spirit had no patience and no interest in repeating the obvious. "I am ready," he said.

"Do not run ahead of me."

"Have I?"

"Do not."

"If I have, it is only because —"

"If you had, I would have told you. Events currently set in motion will result in your initial ascension. Be prepared but do not be premature."

"How more should I prepare? Spirit? How? Spirit? Do not depart from me! I wish only to do your bidding and accept what you have promised. Spirit? Spirit?"

Leon took an aircraft-to-ground call from Jonathan Stonagal. "I will be in Bucharest within two hours. You tell Carpathia that I —"

"Excuse me, Jonathan, but please do not forget that we are employees of Dr. Carpathia. You may feel free to tell him things, but I do not. I do his bidding."

"*We* work for Carpathia, Leon? *We?* Perhaps you're his lackey, but I most certainly am not. Now you be sure and tell him that Gheorghe Vasile has gotten the message and wants a truce. He needs more time, and —"

"Let me make myself perfectly clear as to where my loyalties lie, Jonathan. I am not your errand boy, nor your mouthpiece. I repeat, I do not tell Nicolae anything. If you have a message for him, come and tell him in person or call him yourself."

"Listen, Fortunato, you're going to find out who has the power here, and you're not going to like what you find. Do you think when Carpathia crashes and burns I'll be even half interested in your services?"

"Then I'm gambling my professional life on a different horse, sir."

"You sure are. Now I want a meeting with Carpathia at the airport when I arrive. And you had better call off your dogs in the meantime."

"My dogs?"

"The people you have terrorizing Gheorghe and his people."

"Did you want me to request an audience

for you with Dr. Carpathia?"

"No! I want you and him at the airport when I arrive."

"May I ask you a question, Mr. Stonagal?"

"Stop being so formal. What?"

"Is it fair to say that you are the instigator of this meeting?"

"Of course! Why? What's your point?"

"It would be true then that you wish to see Nicolae, not him you?"

Silence.

"Are you there, Jonathan?"

"Would you quit being obtuse and tell me what you're trying to say?"

"I thought you'd never ask. It seems to me that if you are the one asking for the meeting, protocol requires you to come Nicolae's direction, not him yours."

"I've flown halfway around the world! Now you tell him to meet me —"

"Oh no, you don't understand, sir. I won't be telling him anything. He doesn't want to talk to you. You want to talk to him. If you would like me to pass along your request to his assistant, I'll be happy to do that. She'll get back to you with a time that might be convenient for you to drop in on him here."

"What? Are you serious? The first thing I'll do is have him fire you, you —"

"You may expect a call from Ms. Viv Ivins then, Jonathan. Good day."

"Listen, Fortunato —"

"I said good day."

Buck Williams's intercom buzzed. "Yeah, Marge," he said. Marge Potter was really his boss, Steve Plank's, secretary, but due to a recent budget cut, she took some of his calls too.

"Dirk Burton for you from London. I just love his accent."

"You know he's Welsh."

"I knew it was something like that."

Dirk had been a classmate of Buck's and working in the London Stock Exchange since graduation.

"Lefty, my friend, how are you?"

"Cameron, you really must come over here." The usual levity was gone from Dirk's voice.

"What now? The Illuminati? The Bilderbergers? The Trilateral Commission? Who's meeting now to affect the heads of state all over the world?"

Not even a snicker. "You finished, Cameron?"

"Yeah, sorry, Dirk. What's up?"

"You know I was right about Jonathan Stonagal being one of the biggest movers and shakers in the secret world of international finance."

"Gotta give you that one."

"And the head of the London Exchange, you know who . . ."

"Joshua Todd-Cothran, right."

"Well, something's brewing."

"Pray tell."

"You don't sound serious, Cameron."

"I am, Dirk. Really. You know I think you're nutty but only a little. Tell me what you've got."

"That's just it. I don't know what I've got. All I know is that Stonagal is on the move, apparently on his way to Eastern Europe, and he's going to stop here to meet with Todd-Cothran on his way back."

"Not unusual for a couple of big-money guys."

"Maybe. But when they get together, things happen."

"Okay, I'm listening."

"I can't say any more right now. There's not much to tell. But once I find out anything about their meeting, can I call and leave a message at the secure center?"

"Sure."

"Dad," Raymie said, "I've got a thing at school this week. An evening program."

"Oh! Sorry, bud. Do well, but I've got a London flight this week."

"Wish I could go."

"Me too," Rayford said, imagining how that would cramp his style should he ever follow through with any of his designs on Hattie Durham. "You'd love England."

"I'll be at the program," Irene said.

"See?" Rayford said. "There you go."

She was staring at Rayford.

"What?" he said. "I can't do anything about my schedule."

She nodded toward Raymie and whispered, "At least ask him."

"Ask him what?" Rayford mouthed.

"About the program."

"Yeah! Raymie, what's your part in the program?"

"I play a tree."

Rayford guffawed. "A tree! What do you have to do, bark?"

"Very funny, Dad. I've got lines. I'm a talking tree."

"Well, I really wish I could be there."

Twelve

"After I phone this in, Nicolae, I need to tell you how far I have gone with Jonathan," Leon said.

"Then hurry. I can hardly wait. And I have much to tell you as well."

Leon checked the phone book for the number of the private school Gheorghe Vasile's grandchildren attended.

As he dialed, Carpathia said, "You are certain your cell phone is untraceable?"

"Of course," Leon said. "It is the latest in scrambled security code technology." He held up a hand as a woman answered, announcing the name of the school. "I want you to listen carefully," Leon said, "because I will say this only once. You may want to take a note."

"Excuse me? Who is this?"

"One time," Leon said. "A bomb has been planted in the school by members of the Romanian People's Party. You have —"

"This is not funny! I'm going to hang up."

"— exactly nine minutes to evacuate the building. I would urge you to remove the —"

"I don't know who you think you are, but —"

"— students and personnel at least a quarter mile from the site. Eight minutes and forty-five seconds and counting. Goodbye."

Fortunato put his phone away and sat across from Nicolae. He was shaking but not from fear. Rather from excitement.

"Leon," Carpathia said, and Fortunato detected genuine admiration in his tone, "you are priceless."

"Thank you, sir. I only wish I didn't have to prove it to you every day."

"I am getting the picture."

"You may not, however, be so pleased at how far I have pushed Jonathan." Leon told him of their conversation.

The younger man cackled and howled. "I love it!" he said. "Perfect! And correct! He wants to see me; I do not want to see him. Excellent. Of course, the fact of the matter is that I *do* now want to see him. Vasile will crack by the end of the day, and if he does not, it will be time to strike not just his livestock but also his loved ones."

"I'm prepared. Now that we've taken the first step down this road, there'll be no turning back."

"I could not have said that better myself, Leon."

Carpathia told Leon of his contact with the spirit world.

"That's wonderful, Nicolae. It's been a long time, hasn't it?"

"But worth the wait. Your Romanian People's Party was a stroke of genius, by the way. I will come out strongly against them as soon as I am given the chance. They will, of course, deny any connection with the harassment of Vasile."

"Of course."

"Let us see how long it takes your scheme to reach the news," Carpathia said, releasing a screen from within the wall and tuning it to a news channel. Within moments camera-mounted helicopters showed frantic teachers running children out of the school, and the type on the screen read, *Romanian People's Party bomb threat . . . Securitate link scare with Vasile family horse fire . . .*

As the men sat chortling, Fortunato grew suddenly serious. "But really," he said, "should you not try to reach Jonathan? Surely you're not ready to be independent of him just yet."

"Soon."

"But still."

"No. He will call. And by the time he does, Vasile will have caved."

"Look!" Fortunato said, pointing to the television.

Running text along the bottom of the screen announced: *President of the Romanian Republic Gheorghe Vasile announces a press conference for two this afternoon. Resignation rumors flying.*

As soon as technicians had swept the school and reported no explosive, every station moved to minute-by-minute coverage of the speculation over Vasile's press conference.

The man in line to succeed him immediately put to rest speculation about his own future. "I do not know President Vasile's intentions," he said. "But what he has endured in the last few hours would try any man. I have been told nothing, except not to expect to succeed him. I do not know what this means. If he were to step aside, and I pray that he does not, I would be entitled by law to be elevated to his chair, and I would pursue every legal recourse to ensure that.

"However, Gheorghe Vasile has long been a statesman and leader who has given his heart and soul to our motherland, and I hope he resists to the end any attempt by the cowardly minority party to force him from power."

That elicited immediate denials on the parts of the leaders and the rank and file of the Romanian People's Party, who pointed out that they would never stoop to such tactics, that such acts had never been their hallmark, and that thinking people would realize the lunacy of their even wanting to take credit for such.

A couple of hours before Vasile's press conference, Viv Ivins entered the office where Leon and Nicolae sat staring at the TV. "Mr. Stonagal on the line for you, sir," she said.

Nicolae pushed the speaker button, dismissed Ms. Ivins, and winked at Leon. "Jonathan! How good to hear from you! How are things in New York?"

"You know perfectly well I'm not in New York! We're about to land here, and I want to see you."

"I am in my office all afternoon. I will look forward to seeing you."

"Come and meet me at the airport!"

"You are breaking up, Jonathan. I will see you here this afternoon then?"

"At the airport!"

"I think I have lost you, Jonathan. If you

can hear me, know that I am honored by your visit and look forward to seeing you here."

"Meet me at the airport, Nicolae! I know you can hear me!"

"I seem to have lost him, Leon. I hope he got my message. It will be good to see him, will it not?"

"It will!" Leon exulted, covering his mouth.

A few minutes later Leon's phone rang, and he answered to Vasile himself.

"Will you stop at nothing, Mr. Fortunato?"

Nicolae waved at Leon and pantomimed taping his mouth shut. *"He is likely recording,"* he mouthed.

"Who's calling, please?" Leon said.

"You know well who this is."

"Your voice sounds familiar. You sound like the president of Romania. Is this President Vasile?"

"You know it is."

"What an honor to hear from you, sir. To what do I owe the privilege?"

"I think you know that too."

"Well, just let me say, I've been watching the news, and I can't imagine what you must be going through. Is there anything I or any member of Nicolae Carpathia's team can do for you? Anything at all?"

Nicolae was holding his stomach and looked nearly apoplectic with glee, making it difficult for Leon to maintain his composure. He could hear Vasile's frustrated breathing.

"I was so sorry — we all were here, Dr. Carpathia included — to hear of the loss at your son's horse farm. But tell me, are the grandchildren all right? That was horrifying for the whole country, let alone Grandfather, eh? I'll bet that'll be a precious reunion."

"Let me talk to Carpathia."

"I'm sorry, sir?"

"You heard me, Fortunato. Put him on."

"I'm afraid he's unavailable at the moment, Mr. President."

"It is rather urgent. Are you not right there with him?"

"Oh no, sir, you've reached me in my own apartment downtown. You know this is my cell number. You might call his assistant, Ms. —"

"Give me that number!"

Carpathia pretended to clap and laugh aloud.

Fortunato passed along the number, and within seconds, the office phone rang, Viv buzzed Nicolae, and he picked up, indicating that Leon should listen in on the other phone.

"Yes, sir, Mr. President. A surprise but an honor to hear from you on what must be a very difficult day for you."

"You have no idea."

"Of course I do not."

"Do we have to go through this charade, Carpathia?"

"I beg your pardon?"

"Oh, I get it. We *do.* Very well." And here Vasile's voice fell into a singsong of script, like a child forced to render an apology he doesn't own. "Dr. Carpathia, I am about to announce my resignation from the office of president of the Republic of Romania."

"Oh no! Sir, surely you are not letting terrorists intimidate you. Even as a man of peace, I would gladly serve on a committee authorized to retaliate against such —"

"Please, Carpathia. Let me get through this. I'll make clear to the public and to my colleagues in the houses of government that the crises of last night and this morning have not spurred this action and that in fact I do not believe our worthy adversaries, the People's Party, would ever have anything to do with something like this.

"It is simply that the time has come. I am tired. I am persuaded we need new blood. I

143

do not wish to wait until the next election. I am going to go to the people and to my colleagues and urge them to accept you as my choice to first fulfill what's left of my term and then to be free to run for reelection in the normal course."

"Oh, Mr. President, I am honored, deeply flattered, moved that you would think of me in this way — especially given our less-than-amicable history. But I simply could not accept. The legal ramifications, the havoc you would wreak on our constitution, the inability of the people to officially ratify something like this . . ."

"You're going to take it, right? I mean, this is all so much *prosti,* is it not? You don't need to do this for my benefit."

"Balderdash? Not at all, sir. It is just too much for a young, inexperienced man to take in."

"Oh yeah, right. So I'll make my announcement, and you'll be ready for the media onslaught?"

"I will be ready."

"I just hope you're prepared for the hue and cry, not to mention the lawsuits."

"I have a plan for that too, Gheorghe."

"Somehow I thought you might. Will you be available to appear with me at my press conference at two?"

"No, sir, I do not believe that would be a good idea. Let us allow this to all play out in a normal fashion, which I realize — due to its unique nature — is highly unlikely. You may say that you have approached me with this idea, but it is your wish that the will of the people prevail."

"The will of the people."

"Correct, Mr. President."

"You are beyond words, Carpathia."

"Well, thank you, sir."

Not half an hour after Nicolae got off the phone with Vasile, Stonagal and his entourage stormed into the house.

"You have an impeccable sense of timing, Jonathan," Carpathia said. "Let us — you and Leon and I — meet privately, and I will bring you up-to-date on all that is going on."

"I have crucial team members who should be in on this, Nicolae. It's important that they hear for themselves —"

"They will hear what you and I want them to hear, Jonathan. And I do not have a lot of time now, because shortly after two this place will be overrun by the international press, wanting to know whether I will accept President Vasile's invitation to succeed him."

"You're convinced he's going to make that invitation? Last time I talked to him he promised me anything if I would intercede and buy him at least another week."

"The deed will be done today, Jonathan. In fact, it is already done. The rest is just playacting."

"Well then, you had better bring me up to speed."

"After you," Nicolae said, sweeping an arm toward the elevator that led to his office.

Thirteen

By the time they finished their meeting, Leon could tell that Jonathan Stonagal was aghast. On top of everything else, he had been assigned to somehow wrangle Carpathia, in his current role as a member of the lower house of Parliament in the Romanian government, an invitation to speak to the General Assembly of the United Nations.

Fortunato sat amazed at his boss in action, laying out for Stonagal how it was going to be, how he needed introductions to heads of state all over the world during the next forty-eight hours, and how he also wanted in on the secret meetings of the world's leading financiers. "This has gone on long enough," Carpathia told him, "your seeing me as your man for the future and pretending that you and your secret-society cohorts are the kingmakers. I have engineered this myself, with no small contribution from my man Fortunato here. So regardless of the financial backing and political skulduggery you may have effected on my behalf, I will soon be a head of state and shall expect to be treated that way."

It was clear Jonathan's wheels were turning. Fortunato decided the octogenarian had likely never been treated this way and didn't appear eager to start enduring it now. To his credit, while his jaw was set and his temples throbbed, he held his tongue.

"You have an assignment, Mr. Stonagal," Carpathia said. "You may use one of our phones, but I suggest you get on it."

"An invitation to speak at the U.N."

Nicolae nodded. "Do we need to rehash everything I have said?"

"I just want to be sure I have it."

"Oh, you have it. Your hearing aids are working; are they not?"

"I do not need to be insulted, Nicolae."

"And I do not need to be stalled, sir. I need to be able to say, by two o'clock here, that I have the invitation in hand. And then I am prepared for a bit of a world tour with you."

"I have pressing business in the States."

"It will have to wait. Now call whomever you have to call at the U.N."

"It's five o'clock in the morning in New York!"

"Is it? You will be rousing someone early then; will you not?"

President Gheorghe Vasile's resignation hit Romania like a tidal wave. And his suggestion that he be replaced by Nicolae Carpathia rocked all of Europe, especially when the young politician appeared at first to decline.

Within an hour after Vasile's press conference, Carpathia was coaxed out onto his lawn and in front of the microphones and cameras of all the major news organizations in the world. He appeared thoroughly stunned.

"First I want to wish President Vasile well in whatever he chooses to do. Let me add my voice to the many within our government on all sides of the political landscape in urging him to reconsider. Should these efforts fail — and of course only President Vasile can make this decision — I would urge him to follow our constitution and protocol by allowing his number-two man to succeed him. If I were to seek the office, I prefer to do it at election time next year.

"I have recently been extended an honor superseded only by President Vasile's confidence in me, and that is to address a meeting of the General Assembly of the

United Nations. Those who know me — and I realize they were relatively few until this fifteen minutes of fame was thrust upon me — know that I have long been an aficionado of that august body. I have studied the history of the U.N. and have gratefully accepted their invitation. I look forward to sharing with them — and with the world — my stand on peace among all nations. This is something from which I will never waver.

"Already many within the government have asked me to accept the presidency, including several who would otherwise stand in the line of succession. To be honest, this alone nearly persuades me. Let me say this: I would only even entertain this possibility if I was guaranteed that the people of Romania would have the freedom, as soon as possible, to ratify the same. It would be, in effect, a yes-or-no vote on one candidate. If the will of the people is that I should not be in office, I would retreat from it immediately.

"The presidency is not something I am seeking, at least at this time. But if it is the will of my president, my colleagues, and — primarily — the people, knowing full well my determination to push for peace in all matters, then I will reluctantly consider this and study the possibilities with my closest advisers. Should I decide to accept, I pledge to undertake the role with total commitment and enthusiasm."

It was becoming more and more difficult for Irene to maintain her resolve. She did not want to become unattractive to Rayford. She always regretted overreacting, and Jackie — though younger — had wisely counseled her that badgering her husband would more likely drive him away than draw him in.

Sunday morning she could hear that Raymie was already up and getting ready. Amazing. On school days she often had to be sure he was out of bed. But never on Sunday. How Irene wished she'd had that love for God and for church and everything associated with it when she had been his age.

"Rayford?" she said quietly, and he mumbled a response, his head still buried in his pillow. "You know Raymie would really love for you to go with us today, what with your London trip coming up and all."

No response.

"So I'll just tell him no?"

He grunted again, then rolled onto his side, pulling the blankets over his face. "I've got to fix that four-wheeler tire," he managed. "But I'll be here for lunch with you guys, and the Bulls are on after that."

It was all Irene could do to keep from suggesting that he fix the ATV tire during halftime of the game and just once force himself to do something he didn't want to do for the sake of his son. But no. She wasn't going to do that. She was not going to get Rayford back to church, especially to New Hope, by nagging him.

Pastor Billings had often said that sometimes it took real defeat in people's lives to bring them to God. "Sometimes they have to come to the end of themselves."

As Irene got ready for church, she wondered what might make that happen in Rayford's life. He was more distant, testier than ever. Clearly he was not happy, and she didn't know what to do to fix that. She sensed it was caused by the distance between him and God, but she also knew that no one could bridge that gap but Rayford himself.

Raymie's Sunday school class met during the first morning service, so to be sure she could sit with him during the sermon, Irene volunteered to assist Jackie in teaching her primary girls class. She and Raymie would meet in their favorite pew after that.

The little girls were so precious, and Jackie was a natural with them. They seemed bright and happy and curious, and because they were so young, they drank in the Bible stories and lessons. Irene was struck that the class seemed bigger this week and mentioned that to Jackie.

"Yes," her friend said. "At least three new girls. And Dooley said the men's pancake breakfast yesterday was packed. There was a story in the *Herald* about church attendance being on the rise. Did you see it?"

Irene shook her head. Interesting though. More and more people interested in church and her husband less so. What could she do but pray for him? It wasn't like her to take such a passive approach, but enough people had warned her against pushing him that she had to take their word for it that it would do more harm than good.

When Irene reached the fifth pew, aisle end, organ side, Raymie was already there. How long, she wondered, would he unashamedly sit with his mother in church? She guessed not another whole year. How old had she been when she decided that being seen with her parents was the worst embarrassment she could imagine? With his being her baby, that was going to be hard to take. It seemed only last week he had been

153

born, and already she knew puberty was coming on. Irene could only hope and pray that even if Raymie endured the usual healthy stages of starting to separate from his parents, he would not lose his tender heart toward God.

"What'd you learn about today?" she whispered.

"The rich young ruler," he said. "Do you think Jesus really meant for him to get rid of everything he had, or was He just testing the guy?"

"I don't know," Irene said. "But either way the rich man failed, didn't he? He got to keep all his stuff, but he had to be miserable. He didn't really want the Kingdom of God. He wanted to serve himself."

"Kind of like Dad."

Irene flinched. She hadn't thought of that, maybe because she had never seen Rayford as particularly wealthy, and he certainly wasn't a ruler. "How so?"

Raymie shrugged. "It just seems like everything is about him. I mean, he's not nasty about it or anything. It's just that what he wants comes first, and then if he's got time for anybody else, then maybe he'll . . . I don't know."

"Your dad can be a very kind and gentle man, Raymie."

"I know. I remember. Maybe he just liked Chloe best. Now that she's away, he's different."

Now there was something Irene had never put together. "First of all, Raymie, I've never once heard your dad compare you with Chloe or say he liked either of you best. I believe he loves you both deeply and to the same degree. It might interest you to know that Chloe assumed your dad liked you best because you were a boy."

"Really?"

Irene nodded. But the idea of Rayford's biggest change coming with the departure of Chloe . . . now that was something to consider. When Chloe had been around, the emphasis had been on her. And she and Rayford had been partners in this anti-church, anti-God thing. Now Rayford had to be more creative, and he had no compatriot. But was it also possible that what was beginning to look like middle-age angst was just a man deeply missing his daughter? Irene could certainly be sensitive to that. She herself ached for Chloe, especially because there had risen between them some sort of rift that seemed to change their relationship — she hoped not forever.

After all the usual preliminaries — call to worship, prayer, singing, special music, offering, and announcements — it was finally time for Pastor Billings's sermon.

Irene had come to appreciate the humility that exuded from her new pastor. She had attended many churches in her life, and most had pastors barely able to conceal their egos. Here Vernon Billings had built a small but growing congregation that had to have two morning services — not because they were so huge but rather because their sanctuary was so small — and he was respected by the congregation. Yet he seemed to put the spotlight on everyone else who worked in the church. He never failed to acknowledge those who helped out.

Most of all, though, he always began by praying that he would say what God wanted him to say and that the people would hear what God wanted them to hear. While preaching, his focus was always on Jesus, and he clearly revered the Bible.

"Those of you who have been in your seats for a few moments may want to glance around before I begin," he said. "This may be the largest crowd ever accommodated by this building."

Irene swiveled to see every pew filled, even in the tiny balcony. Could anyone explain this renewed interest in the things of God? And was there some cosmic explanation for why it did not extend to Rayford Steele?

After Pastor Billings opened with his usual prayer, he ran through a fast recap of what he had already covered in the series, emphasizing that "no man knows the day or the hour of the return of the Lord, not even Jesus Himself. He told His disciples that only the Father knew when the end would come, so anyone who says he knows when this will occur is engaging in the highest and most shameless form of folly.

"One thing we know, and that is that there is nothing left on the prophetic calendar that must occur before Jesus comes from heaven with a shout and the trumpet blast and gathers true believers from all over the globe. Scripture teaches us to live in light of His imminent return and to conduct ourselves as if it could be today. And yet God in His mercy might wait one more day, which in His economy of time — the Bible says — is a thousand years. My faith would not be shaken if He tarried past my death. But it behooves us to know what it means to live as if He could return today.

"He will not return to the earth this time, but rather He will appear in the clouds. And the dead in Christ shall rise first, and then we who remain shall be snatched away in the twinkling of an eye, and so shall we ever be with the Lord.

"Oh, make no mistake — He will return and set foot on this earth again someday, but that is not the Rapture. That will be the Glorious Appearing, seven years after Antichrist signs a fake covenant with God's chosen people. Some teach that this seven years begins with the Rapture, but I believe it begins with the signing of that covenant, which could take place anywhere from a few days after the Rapture to a couple of years later.

"Regardless, true believers who are raptured will enjoy seven years in the house of God with Christ, who has spent two thousand years preparing that place for us. We have covered many times who will go, but it is always good to rehearse it. Good people? No. The Bible says, 'There is none righteous, no, not one.' Religious people? No. God is no respecter of persons. The kind, the generous, the serving? Well, hopefully, those who qualify will exhibit these qualities. But Scripture is also clear that it is not by works of righteousness we have done but by God's mercy that He saves us. It is 'the gift of God, not of works, lest anyone should boast.'

"Acts of service, works of righteousness — surely these are good and positive and necessary things for the believer. But they will not save him. They will not get her into heaven. They will not prepare one should the Rapture occur today. Those are things that should be done in response to the free gift of salvation that has been offered . . . and to whom? To those who believe. To those who trust in the sacrificial work of Christ on the cross for the forgiveness of their sins.

"You have heard me say before that some of the people who go may not be as nice as some of the people who are left. Just because all men and women are sinners — either saved by grace or still lost in their sins — does not mean there are not nice and pleasant people around.

"I'm often asked, 'Isn't this discriminatory? Aren't you being exclusivistic? Who are you to say that sincere, devout people of other religions will be lost, left behind?' I realize that we live in a pluralistic society and that people of all faiths and persuasions deserve respect and have the right to make their own decisions. I want to be as tolerant as anyone, and you will never hear that Vernon Billings or New Hope Village Church or — I pray — any true follower of Christ would condemn another person simply because they choose to disagree with us. We are to love even our enemies, let alone colleagues and friends and acquaintances and relatives who simply disagree with us.

"But it is also our responsibility as ambassadors of Christ to tell the truth as we know and believe it, that Jesus Himself claims to be 'the way, the truth, and the life' and that it was He Himself who said He was the only way to God. We may not like that. That may not have been the plan had we been God. We don't have to understand it. God's ways are not our ways. So, we don't share this news to offend or divide. We share it simply to inform and to urge people to make up their own minds about what they will do with this alarming statement.

"Our job, our obligation, is to spread the word, to plead with people to investigate the claims of Christ so they might be ready when that great day comes. What they do with the message is up to them. And how we respond to their decision reflects on our Lord Himself. You will not hear of true Christians hating, condescending, terrorizing, bombing, killing, or flying planes into the buildings of those who exercise their freedom to disagree. Christ tells us to love and pray for them."

Irene sensed an unusual stillness in the sanctuary. Often when the place was full there seemed to be a hum or a buzz of activity, and one had to work at concentrating. But today, despite the biggest crowd ever, no one seemed to even move. Pastor Billings had once said that when prophecy is preached and taught, the body is challenged to holy living. He was hardly one who advocated turning one's back on the ills of society merely because you hoped to one day be miraculously rescued from it. Rather, he said, we should be all the more concerned with poverty, hunger, widows, orphans, and those in need.

"But now," he said, "and I know you were wondering if I would ever get to it, I would like to conclude my series with what we might expect on that great day."

Pastor Billings announced three separate Bible texts, and while these were projected on a screen behind him, Irene also thrilled to the sound of onionskin pages being riffled all over the auditorium. She and Raymie were among those who found all three passages and kept a finger or marker in each one.

The first was John 14:1–6, where Jesus was talking to His disciples:

"Let not your heart be troubled; you believe in God, believe also in Me. In My Father's house are many mansions; if it were not so, I would have told you. I go to prepare a place for you. And if I go and prepare a place for you, I will come again and receive you to Myself; that where I am, there you may be also. And where I go you know, and the way you know."

Thomas said to Him, "Lord, we do not know where You are going, and how can we know the way?"

Jesus said to him, "I am the way, the truth, and the life. No one comes to the Father except through Me."

Next Pastor Billings directed them to 1 Thessalonians 4:13–18, where the apostle Paul had written to the church in Thessalonica:

But I do not want you to be ignorant, brethren, concerning those who have fallen asleep, lest you sorrow as others who have no hope. For if we believe that Jesus died and rose again, even so God will bring with Him those who sleep in Jesus.

For this we say to you by the word of the Lord, that we who are alive and remain until the coming of the Lord will by no means precede those who are asleep. For the Lord Himself will descend from heaven with a shout, with the voice of an archangel, and with the trumpet of God. And the dead in Christ will rise first. Then we who are alive and remain shall be caught up together with them in the clouds to meet the Lord in the air. And thus we shall always be with the Lord. Therefore comfort one another with these words.

"I don't want to assume that everyone here knows what Paul meant when he wrote of those who have 'fallen asleep,' " Pastor Billings said. "Those are the dead. So we are not to mourn those who die in Christ, for we believe that they too will be snatched away to be with Him on that great day — even before we are, should we be alive at the time."

Finally he asked people to turn to 1 Corinthians 15:50–58:

Now this I say, brethren, that flesh and blood cannot inherit the kingdom of God . . .

"In other words, we cannot live with God the way we are. Something has to change, and this is not something we ourselves can accomplish."

. . . nor does corruption inherit incorruption. Behold, I tell you a mystery: We shall not all sleep, but we shall all be changed — in a moment, in the twinkling of an eye, at the last trumpet. For the trumpet will sound, and the dead will be raised incorruptible . . .

"Our bodies will be changed and glorified to be like Jesus' body."

. . . and we shall be changed. For this corruptible must put on incorruption, and this mortal must put on immortality.

"In other words, our sinful, fallen, mortal bodies must be changed by God into incorruptible, immortal bodies."

So when this corruptible has put on incorruption, and this mortal has put on immortality, then shall be brought to pass the saying that is written: "Death is swallowed up in victory."
"O Death, where is your sting?
O Hades, where is your victory?"
The sting of death is sin, and the

strength of sin is the law. But thanks be to God, who gives us the victory through our Lord Jesus Christ.

Therefore, my beloved brethren, be steadfast, immovable, always abounding in the work of the Lord, knowing that your labor is not in vain in the Lord.

"Paul is saying here that while our works will not save us, the hope of the resurrection makes them all worth it. Nothing done in Jesus' name is wasted.

"So do you see the progression here, people? The dead in Christ shall rise first. Can you imagine? Bodies in graves and crematoria, lost at sea, buried by natural disasters, entombed in sunken ships, obliterated by bombs, consumed in fires, aborted . . . all rising before those who remain alive in Christ.

"And then I foresee a great reunion of believers — perhaps a billion or two from all around the globe — in the clouds. Then we shall rise to meet Jesus. And then He will take us to His Father's house. I don't know about you, but I can't wait. I wish I could describe this to you, but Paul, writing to the Corinthians, echoed the writing of Isaiah when he said, 'Eye has not seen, nor ear heard, nor have entered into the heart of man the things which God has prepared for those who love Him.'

"The only passage in the Bible that describes God's house is Revelation 21, where it is seen descending out of the heavens to the earth at the end of the Millennium — Jesus' thousand-year reign of peace on earth following His glorious appearing at the end of the Tribulation.

> Now I saw a new heaven and a new earth, for the first heaven and the first earth had passed away. Also there was no more sea. Then I, John, saw the holy city, New Jerusalem, coming down out of heaven from God, prepared as a bride adorned for her husband. And I heard a loud voice from heaven saying, "Behold, the tabernacle of God is with men, and He will dwell with them, and they shall be His people. God Himself will be with them and be their God. And God will wipe away every tear from their eyes; there shall be no more death, nor sorrow, nor crying. There shall be no more pain, for the former things have passed away."
> . . . And he carried me away in the Spirit to a great and high mountain, and showed me the great city, the holy Jerusalem, descending out of heaven from

God, having the glory of God. Her light was like a most precious stone, like a jasper stone, clear as crystal. Also she had a great and high wall with twelve gates, and twelve angels at the gates, and names written on them, which are the names of the twelve tribes of the children of Israel: three gates on the east, three gates on the north, three gates on the south, and three gates on the west.

Now the wall of the city had twelve foundations, and on them were the names of the twelve apostles of the Lamb. And he who talked with me had a gold reed to measure the city, its gates, and its wall. The city is laid out as a square; its length is as great as its breadth. And he measured the city with the reed: twelve thousand furlongs. Its length, breadth, and height are equal. Then he measured its wall: one hundred and forty-four cubits, according to the measure of a man, that is, of an angel. The construction of its wall was of jasper; and the city was pure gold, like clear glass. The foundations of the wall of the city were adorned with all kinds of precious stones: the first foundation was jasper, the second sapphire, the third chalcedony, the fourth emerald, the fifth sardonyx, the sixth sardius, the seventh chrysolite, the eighth beryl, the ninth topaz, the tenth chrysoprase, the eleventh jacinth, and the twelfth amethyst. The twelve gates were twelve pearls: each individual gate was of one pearl. And the street of the city was pure gold, like transparent glass.

But I saw no temple in it, for the Lord God Almighty and the Lamb are its temple. The city had no need of the sun or of the moon to shine in it, for the glory of God illuminated it. The Lamb is its light. And the nations of those who are saved shall walk in its light, and the kings of the earth bring their glory and honor into it. Its gates shall not be shut at all by day (there shall be no night there). And they shall bring the glory and the honor of the nations into it. But there shall by no means enter it anything that defiles, or causes an abomination or a lie, but only those who are written in the Lamb's Book of Life.

Irene was scribbling as fast as she could, and Raymie was too. It was nearly overwhelming, all this detail. Never before had she so looked forward to the return of Christ.

But Pastor Billings was not finished. He also told of the judgment seat of Christ, where the deeds of believers would be tested and rewarded — or not. "Just as our works cannot save us, neither can they cause us to lose our salvation. But it is clear from Scripture that they will determine the level and extent of our heavenly reward. So for those who say they have believed in Jesus just for fire insurance, just to stay out of hell, they would be wise to consider that everything they have ever done will be revealed in that judgment."

Pastor Billings concluded with a resounding treatise on the symbolic marriage ceremony in heaven of Jesus the Lamb to His bride, the church. "The wedding supper, the celebration, will be reserved for the Millennium seven years later," the pastor said. "But imagine the ceremony itself.

"Then as the Tribulation draws to a close on earth, the raptured will be marshaled to accompany Jesus on His glorious appearing for the Battle of Armageddon and the setting up of His thousand-year reign. The terrible Great White Throne Judgment, in which the sheep and goats will be determined and judged, will also take place during the Millennium.

"And you know, my presumption is that we will not experience time there as we do here. If a thousand years is as a day to the Lord and a day a thousand years, imagine how brief seven earthly years must seem from the other side of the portals in glory. It might seem to us but a moment, and then we shall be united with those who were left behind and came to Christ. Oh, what a day. What a day."

When Pastor Billings finished, Irene was struck by what happened and what didn't happen. Normally there would be a closing prayer, during which the music worship team would return to the platform for a last number as people filed out.

But now Pastor Billings merely stepped away from the pulpit, descended the three steps from the platform, and stood at floor level before the first pew. He stretched his arms wide and said quietly, "If you would be ready, come."

And from every corner of the sanctuary they came. Ones and twos, then groups of a dozen and more, weeping, rushing, kneeling at the front, eager to receive Christ, to be ready for the Rapture regardless of when it occurred.

Irene could not help herself. She found herself turning to see if by some miracle, like in a sappy movie, Rayford had somehow been nudged to show up. Perhaps he had sat in the balcony or stood in the back, and now he was coming forward.

But no. All Irene saw when she scanned the surging crowds was the enigmatic assistant pastor, the slightly pudgy, curly-haired, bespectacled Bruce Barnes, whom everyone so loved. He seemed to be watching what Irene was watching, and their eyes met briefly. He seemed detached, but she assumed he would soon join the crowds at the front to help counsel and pray and lead people to Christ.

Fourteen

Buck Williams checked his secure voice-mail box and found a message from Dirk Burton in London:

"Cameron, you always tell me this message center is confidential, and I hope you're right. I'm not even going to identify myself, but you know who it is. Let me tell you something major and encourage you to come here as quickly as possible. The big man — your compatriot, the one I call the supreme power broker internationally — met here the other day with the one I call our muckety-muck. You know who I mean. There was a third party at the meeting. All I know is that he's from Europe, probably Eastern Europe. I don't know what their plans are for him, but apparently they're something on a huge scale.

"My sources say your man has met with each of his key people and this same European in different locations. He introduced him to people in China, the Vatican, Israel, France, Germany, here, and the States. Something is cooking, and I don't even want to suggest what it is other than in person. Visit me as soon as you can. In case that's not possible, let me just encourage this: watch the news for the installation of a new leader in Europe. If you say, as I did, that no elections are scheduled and no changes of power are imminent, you'll get my drift. Come soon, friend."

Dirk might be an alarmist, Buck thought, *but he's also an astute, smart thinker.* Buck stepped out to Marge Potter's desk. "You've got me going to Chicago next week, right?"

"To see Mrs. Washington, yes."

"Can you get me to London directly from there and then back to New York?"

"I'm sure. I'll let you know what I find."

Playing hard to get made Nicolae Carpathia irresistible to the people of Romania. Almost immediately they seemed to rise up en masse and call for his installation. At every turn he added conditions. Everyone in the official line of succession had to agree. The number-two man had to withdraw his legal objections. Both houses of Parliament must vote favorably. Of course, this was said after the will of the people had become clear. Hourly polls showed support for Carpathia rising astronomically, so no politico in any party dared risk his own future by opposing the wishes of his constituents.

Finally, when it appeared Carpathia had set the requirements for his acceptance impossibly high, all were met. He announced that if the public referendum could be engineered as soon as possible — and if he was permitted to rename a wing of the capitol building in honor of the outgoing president — he would surrender to the desire of the people of the nation he loved so much.

"I just want to know," Leon said. "Is that too much to ask?"

"Of course not," Nicolae said. "Be specific and I will do the same."

"I would like a strategic role on your leadership team. An office in the capitol. I want to be known as your most trusted adviser."

"Thank you for sharing that, Leon. The fact is, I have given this a great deal of thought. It might surprise you — and it might not — to know that I just yesterday had the same conversation with Viv Ivins."

"She sees herself in the same role?"

"She knows better than that. But she wants to stay close, to be on staff, to be in the inner circle, to also have an office in the capitol."

"You can hardly blame us. We are loyal and would like to see that reciprocated."

"Of course. But I am going to tell you what I told her. I have need of both of you in New York."

"New York!"

"You will be my advance team. You see, Leon, I have been working on my address to the U.N. since long before Jonathan secured the invitation for me. My speech there, if I may say so, will be a tour de force. If you think my acceptance of the presidency was impressive, trust me — it will pale in comparison to what will happen at the U.N. And I can see it now. On the biggest media stage in the world, Romania will suddenly become too small a venue for me. Everyone will recognize that. I will be thrust onto the international scene so fast that I may then need to send you back here to run the country while I take my place globally."

Leon didn't know what to say. He felt proud. He had seen this potential in Carpathia, and he believed he had played a major role in helping him achieve it. But he wanted to stay close, not be banished to some outpost to serve as an advance man or be left to mundane matters of state while Nicolae conquered new horizons.

"What's in it for me if I succeed in setting up for you a welcome in New York worthy of your station? If you, as you hope and plan, take the city — and the world — by storm, then what?"

"That, Leon, is the best part. If you are worried that you will be relegated to such a role long term, do not fret. You and Viv may be waiting in the wings for a season, but the time will come — when I truly come into power — that you will be right there with me, front and center."

Rayford had expressly forbidden Hattie Durham to call him at home. It wasn't that Irene was suspicious. It was that Rayford did not need even the possibility of that eventuality in his life just now. The truth was that he had become obsessed with Hattie, which made Irene, for all her efforts to resurrect their marriage, seem old, cold, plain, and shrill.

Rayford knew better. Yes, there were times when she reverted to the Irene of old — the one who used anger or sarcasm to try to make a point. But in his heart of hearts he knew that was his fault too. He had drifted to where the only discipline in his life showed behind the controls of the jumbo jets he piloted. He always looked right and was prepared for that work. But his marriage, he knew, was failing. He did what he wanted to when he wanted to, looking out for number one, his own wife and son largely ignored.

And his mind, it seemed, was constantly on the young woman he so enjoyed being with in the car, in the air, at more and more private dinners, and on the phone. But only his cell phone.

The irony was that he had still never touched Hattie. At least not on purpose. She did enough touching for the both of them, and somehow that kept her in the forefront of his mind all the time. It reminded him of crushes he'd had in high school. The difference now was that he knew Hattie Durham was attainable. She was not some impossible, far-off dream of an ideal girl. In high school he had set his sights on the same girls every other guy worshiped and only the rare guys ever got.

But here was one of the most alluring women he had ever seen, fifteen years younger than he, and she wanted him. He could tell. He didn't have to be a Rhodes scholar to figure that out.

"I'm on the London run," she announced on his cell phone that Sunday morning, and he felt his face flush, even in private.

"Great, Hattie. I'm looking forward to that."

"Me too," she said. "More than you know. More than I can say. But maybe not more than I can show."

There was something about going that far from home that seemed to justify in Rayford's mind some more overt dalliance with Hattie than he had ever allowed himself. It was juvenile. Complicating. Wrong too. He knew better. Might it cost him his marriage? his son? Chloe would understand. She had the same issues with Irene that he did. Lots of people went through difficult breakups. He would survive it. And so would Raymie. Kids were resilient, right? Wasn't that what everyone said?

Oh, what was he thinking? Hattie was just a diversion, a mind game. He had been inappropriate, sure, with his eyes, his words, his white lies to Irene, the private times he'd spent with Hattie. But he hadn't even touched her, and here he was thinking through the ramifications of a divorce.

If Hattie did tear him from his family,

what then? Could he ever expect her to be faithful to him? It was one thing to be over forty and have a twenty-seven-year-old wife, but what about when he was fifty? And sixty? She was clearly the kind of woman that was going to age slowly and be a knockout for years. How long would she remain interested in him? Especially when he quit playing hard to get? Now he might just be a challenge for her. Surely she couldn't have had much experience being interested in men she couldn't win. Would he all of a sudden become less attractive to her if he yielded to her advances and turned his back on his wife and family?

This was crazy, he told himself. Ludicrous. He was going to have to put it out of his mind. At least until he again picked her up for work, watched her get into the car, felt her hand on his arm, looked into those huge, inviting eyes.

Rayford had it bad.

In fact, he was feeling guilty, his mind occupied with the other woman who had not yet really become the "other woman," while his wife and son were at church without him. He would need to steel himself against their insipid and always-renewed enthusiasm as soon as he heard Irene's car pull up.

Guilt had caused Rayford to hurriedly set the table with paper plates and plasticware, in anticipation of the drive-through chicken bucket Irene brought home every Sunday. This time Rayford would resist already being parked in front of the TV. Often he had insisted on taking his lunch there, knowing full well that Irene wanted just a brief sit-down at the table together. He could manage that — at least today.

Next weekend he would go one better. He had promised Raymie he would go to church. How he had let the kid finagle that out of him, he couldn't even recall. But he was way past the point where he could renege even one more time. Going once couldn't hurt, he decided.

Unless it made him feel even guiltier about his obsession with Hattie Durham. The fact was, he wasn't ready to give that up yet . . . or her.

Anticipation, Buck Williams had come to realize, was his favorite part of the job. Buck simply liked the planning of his days as much — if not more — than the days themselves. Nothing fulfilled him more than taking a Sunday afternoon, idly watching sports on television and scoping out his next week on his computer, then downloading his schedule to his personal digital assistant.

As each task — rated by order of importance — was checked off, he felt better and better about himself. Someone had referred to him as an overachiever, but he didn't see it that way. He believed the difference between him and a thousand other guys — stalled or stuck in jobs they didn't like — had less to do with luck than it did with doing a thousand little things right.

He knew he lived a charmed life. He traveled extensively; met interesting, important people; drew great assignments; and was paid well. More than well. He lived way beyond a level that would have easily satisfied him. His tastes were simple, yet his apartment in Manhattan was unattainable for anyone below his station.

Buck left little to chance. Everything was planned and plotted. And as he made his lists and double-checked them to be sure he had what he needed, he imagined each experience. If it was a tense reunion, as was scheduled with Lucinda Washington in Chicago this week, he knew it was time to take her up on her promise to expose him to her culture in a great restaurant on the South Side of Chicago.

And then, thanks to Marge Potter's finding a direct Pan-Continental flight out of Chicago, it would be on to London to see Dirk. His quirky friend had been the source of some great and some not-so-great leads over the years, but this one was sure worth pursuing. Second to reuniting with Dirk, though, was the prospect of all those hours in first class over the Atlantic. Sometimes Buck believed he was getting old because of how much he looked forward to the simple things in life — the really simple things. Like being able to plug in his laptop, ignore a chatty seatmate, skip the movie, and catch up on myriad tasks uninterrupted as a 747 tore through the skies.

The highlights of my life are solitude and work in a comfortable leather seat? Old, old, old.

But Buck was barely thirty.

Irene and Raymie had come home from church psyched up before, but this was ridiculous. Irene, apparently encouraged by Rayford's table-setting gesture, did not intervene when Raymie started in about how incredible the sermon had been.

"You've got to get the tape, Dad. Really. You'd love it."

"Maybe I will."

"Promise."

"Okay, I promise."

"That's two promises now, Dad."

"How well I know."

"You do?"

"Sure."

"Next Sunday?"

"Yep. Promise."

Raymie spent the rest of the meal, not to mention the Bulls game, regaling Rayford with point after point from Pastor Billings's sermon. Amazingly, Rayford actually found it interesting and wondered if perhaps he should have gone. But he wasn't about to admit that. Who knew what a torrent of information that would unleash?

Why couldn't he just have a normal life, a normal family, a normal wife, a normal son? Nobody he knew had a kid this interested in church. Maybe they went, but what happened in church stayed in church. It wasn't something you discussed ad nauseam at meals and while watching ball games on TV.

Fifteen

Leon Fortunato had never been a ladies' man. And while he respected, even somewhat admired, the elderly (to him) Viv Ivins, he was not excited about enduring an international flight with her. He had been impressed by her efficiency and especially her loyalty to Nicolae. But as so often happens with teammates on a powerful person's staff, jealousies arose.

They had never had words, but Leon found himself passive-aggressively ignoring her suggestions and comments, unless they clearly reflected Nicolae's wishes. In truth, he had little to fear, because he had learned a few things about Carpathia. First, he was a chauvinist of the old school. Second, though Nicolae called Ms. Ivins "Aunt Viv" — Leon was aware of their interesting background and connection — Nicolae did not treat her with familial respect.

Viv was close to him, obviously — part of his inner circle. And Nicolae relied on her a great deal. But Leon had never heard him say anything affectionate or even affirming to her. Neither did Leon feel slighted because Viv had known Carpathia longer. Viv's role had certainly shifted from spiritual adviser and parental figure to day-to-day logistical assistant and manager of the private household. She had become more of a background person, a servant.

Leon wondered if she resented that and anyone who got between her and her boss. He detected a certain coolness in her, perhaps even suspicion of his motives. But Leon did not feel the need to defend himself. His proximity to Carpathia — despite this temporary and necessary separation — brought with it great capital, which he intended to invest wisely.

He was pleasantly surprised, then, during the trip to New York, to find Viv Ivins remarkably warm and effusive and even solicitous. She proved polite, self-effacing, helpful, and curious about him and his background. Leon sensed no ulterior motive in this, though he was careful to not be too forthcoming. Nicolae was the only person who really needed to know Leon's history, and he was fully aware of it.

"My expectation," Viv said after they had enjoyed their first in-flight meal, "is that you will handle the more public arrangements and I the private. I am open to suggestion and correction, of course, but in other words, I will make certain Nicolae's accommodations are acceptable, including all the amenities and so forth. Correct me if I am wrong, but I assumed you would handle diplomatic arrangements, the press, and the like."

Leon nodded. "All I know, ma'am, is that budget is to be no object, that we are all to stay and set up headquarters at the Plaza, and that President Carpathia expects to be accorded the privileges commensurate with his office."

To Leon's delight, he and Viv worked separately and efficiently, and within a day of their arrival, nearly everything had been set in motion for a successful visit by the new president and guest U.N. speaker. The Carpathia retinue took over an entire wing of an upstairs floor, augmenting Romanian *securitate* with New York policemen and both U.N. and U.S. security personnel.

Leon and Viv enjoyed beautiful rooms on either end of the corridor, and a set of rooms turned into an office separated Viv's quarters from Nicolae's. Every technological marvel known to man was installed in the office suite within twenty-four hours, and Leon busied himself arranging meetings for Nicolae with a list of dignitaries that covered three computer printout sheets.

Leon's most strategic private meeting was with U.N. Secretary-General Mwangati Ngumo. The large, very dark Botswanan, known for a beatific smile, exhibited no warmth. While he vigorously shook Fortunato's hand, he did not utter any variation of the normal nice-to-meet-you sentiments. He seemed busy and preoccupied, and within minutes of Leon's being seated — across from Ngumo, who stayed behind his desk, despite two separate, more informal meeting tables — they were interrupted by a reminder that the secretary-general had fewer than twenty minutes.

"That should be enough," Leon said.

"I certainly hope so," Ngumo said.

"This is just a get-acquainted session."

"I trust we can accomplish more than that and eliminate the need for redundancy."

"I'll certainly try. First, of course, I bring you greetings from the honorable Dr. Nicolae Jetty Carpathia, president of the Republic of Romania."

"Thank you. What an unusual middle name. One of its meanings is 'black,' as you may know. But I have seen photographs of President Carpathia, and he is anything but dark. Do you know the origin of that name?"

"I do not."

Ngumo waved him on.

"President Carpathia thanks you for your kind invitation, and —"

"Can we, in the interest of time, dispense with these rote sentiments? I accept his greetings; I send mine back; he's been invited; he's thankful; he's welcome — all right?"

"Well, uh, sure. Is there a problem, Mr. Secretary-General? Something I should be aware of?"

"You are his chief of staff and you are not aware of how this invitation came to him?"

"I suppose I'm not, if there was anything untoward about it."

"Untoward? Only that it was coerced from outside standard diplomatic channels. It was suggested not by a friend or associate of this body but rather by an international financier with whom, I am without doubt, you are acquainted."

"Jonathan Stonagal, sure. And that is a problem?"

"It doesn't have to be. But neither should I be expected to celebrate it. The invitation has been treated by the international press at its face value: the U.N. seeking to familiarize itself with a new leader. Fine. Misleading. Untrue. But fine. We will adjust."

Leon crossed his legs, shifting his weight and making the chair squeak. "I can assure you that President Carpathia had nothing to do with angling for an invitation, sir."

"You'll forgive me if I find that difficult to believe. We have file cabinets full of such requests. But even if that is true, that is all the worse. It makes some sense, a head of state wishing to address us. The interests of a billionaire, on the other hand . . ."

"Then why did you acquiesce?"

Ngumo shook his head. "You're asking a question to which you know the answer."

"Because you, like anyone else, have to be concerned about a bottom line."

Ngumo cocked his head at Leon, as if to say, *So we do understand each other.*

"Well, let me tell you my goal for this event, Mr. Secretary. In spite of how it came about, I hope you will be glad you extended the invitation and that President Carpathia will prove a worthy occupant of the lectern."

"We shall see."

Leon told the man of Nicolae's fascination with the U.N. and his savantlike memory of its history. "Trust me, sir, he will

189

be able to tell you the day of your inauguration, how many five-year terms you have served, and how many you are expected to serve."

Buck Williams was off the plane and headed for his rental car at O'Hare when Steve Plank called.

"We're clear that you're making nice with Lucinda, right?"

"That's why I'm here, chief. And to see if I can scoop her and her people on another story."

"Not funny."

"Seriously, Steve, I can't believe she complained about this . . . especially to you. We're buddies, she and I. We always got along great, I thought."

When Buck reached the Chicago bureau, he bribed the receptionist to let him sneak to Lucinda Washington's office unannounced. She had stepped out, so he leaped into her chair and turned his back toward the door. That put him face-to-face with her gaudy religious knickknacks. He was studying a fake gold-leafed one when he heard her enter.

She hesitated, obviously wondering if she herself had turned her chair around, and when she swung it back to sit down, she jumped and squealed to find it full of Cameron.

"You gonna shoot me?" he said. "Can I still work here?"

"Only if you get on your knees and beg my forgiveness," she said.

He slid onto the floor, but she reached and yanked him up. "Quit that now," she said. Buck settled into a side chair, and Lucinda planted herself where she belonged.

"I'm sorry," he said.

"You are not. You don't even know what I'm mad about."

" 'Course I do. Bears Hall of Famer finally gets the money together to buy a football franchise, and I sniff it out, track him down, and run with the story."

"I admire you, Cameron. I always have, as irritating as you can be. But the very least you should have done was let me know."

"And let you assign somebody who should have been on top of this anyway?"

"Sports isn't even your gig, Cameron. After writing that Newsmaker of the Year thing and covering the defeat of Russia by Israel — or I should say by God Himself — how can you even get interested in penny-ante stuff like this? You Ivy League types aren't supposed to like anything but lacrosse and rugby, are you?"

"This was bigger than a sports story, Lucy, and —"

"Hey!"

"Sorry, *Lucinda.* And wasn't that just a bit of stereotyping? Lacrosse and rugby?"

They shared a laugh.

"I'm not even saying you should have told me you were in town," she said. "All I'm saying is, at least let me know before the piece runs in the *Weekly.* My people and I were embarrassed enough to get beat like that, especially by the legendary Cameron Williams, but for it to be a . . . well . . . total surprise —"

"That's why you squealed on me?"

Lucinda laughed. "That's why I told Plank it would take a face-to-face to get you back in my good graces."

"And what made you think I'd care about that?"

"Because you love me. You can't help yourself. But, Cameron, if I catch you in my town again on my beat without my knowledge, I'm gonna whip your tail."

"Well, I'll tell you what, Lucinda. Let me give you a lead I don't have time to follow up on. I happen to know that the NFL franchise purchase is not going to go through after all. The money was shaky and the league's gonna reject the offer. Your local legend is going to be embarrassed."

Lucinda was scribbling furiously. "You're not serious," she said, reaching for her phone.

"No, I'm not, but it was sure fun to see you swing into action."

"You creep," she said. "Anybody else I'd be throwing out of here on his can."

"But you love me. You can't help yourself."

"That wasn't even Christian."

"Don't start with that again," he said.

"Come on, Cameron. You know you got your mind right when you saw what God did for Israel."

"Granted, but don't start calling me a Christian. Deist is as much as I'll cop to."

"Hey, how long you in town for?"

"Until tomorrow."

"Tonight with my hubby and me for barbecue then, right? He's looking forward to meeting you."

"You sure he wants me interfering with your date?"

"We've been married more'n thirty years, Cameron. That's right. We started early. Having a young white boy eat with us won't get in our way. You're just afraid to be in the minority; is that it?"

"Hardly."

For the first time since he'd been married, Rayford Steele lied to his wife about where he was going, just so he could see another woman. "Running some errands," he said. "Sports store, then the hardware store. Need anything?"

"Don't think so, hon. But why don't you wait until Raymie gets home and let him go with you? You're going to be gone the rest of this week, and —"

"Nah, just let me get this done, and I'll spend some time with him tonight."

Rayford would have to remember to buy something at both the stores he had mentioned on the way home to cover that he drove straight past them and into Des Plaines.

He picked up Hattie outside her apartment. "What's up?" he said. "You needed to see me?"

"Yup," she said, grinning mischievously. "That's all. I just needed to see you."

He didn't know what to say or do. Had they already been engaged in a full-fledged affair, which seemed not so far off now, he guessed he might have simply asked if he could head back into her apartment with her. But in broad daylight? This was risky enough. He was flattered, but he didn't want to be stupid.

"What do you want to do?" he said, feeling like a thirteen-year-old.

"What do *you* want to do?" she said.

"Don't ask me. This was your idea. I'm running errands. Sports store. Hardware store."

"Ooh, you're good," she said.

"I'm new at this."

"Not for long. Hey, I'm hungry. You?"

"Not really, but I'd love to get you something to eat."

"Let's order Chinese and pick it up. I'll eat it in the car."

That was a relief to Rayford. He wasn't ready to be seen having a meal date with Hattie in the middle of the afternoon. He always figured he could cover if someone he knew saw them dining at night, when they were both in uniform and it should be obvious it was just business. But now both were dressed casually, and it would simply make no sense to anyone.

He called in an order and they drove off to pick it up.

"You sure you don't want some?" Hattie said, trying to feed him rice with chopsticks as they sat in the parking lot next to the place.

He shook his head but had to laugh when she spilled rice in his lap. She broke open a fortune cookie and read, " 'A new friend will make you happy.' "

"That yours or mine?" he said, and she leaned over and rested her head against his shoulder.

Charles Washington proved to be a rangy, bony man with thinning hair and a wise look. He greeted Lucinda first, slipping his long arm around her ample waist and pulling her close.

"Charles!" she said.

"Lu-cinda!" he said, drawing out the first syllable as if savoring it. "Still the best-lookin' gal in Chicago."

"Stop it and be polite," she said, and Buck was amused at how she beamed. "Meet the friend I told you about."

"Pleasure," Charles said, offering a big calloused hand. "Trust me, you've never had ribs like these."

"I've had some good ones."

"They'll be bad memories in about half an hour, young man. Call me racist, but your people don't even start to know how to barbecue. Know how you can tell? You see white people in our establishments. You don't see us in theirs, not that we don't feel welcome. We do. We just go where the food is best, and that's right here."

Charles and Lucinda sat close and giggled like schoolkids until the food came. Then it was time to get down to serious eating. "I'll show you how to do it best," Charles said, "but let me pray first, all right?"

"Sure." *Right here in public?* Buck had never felt so conspicuous.

Charles took his wife's hand and reached for Buck's. "Lord," he began, "we're grateful for everything but most of all for these provisions. Thank You and thanks for our friend. In Jesus' name, amen."

Buck said amen too, almost before he realized it, and after he tasted the ribs, he felt like praying himself.

"I won't put you on the spot this evening, Cameron," Lucinda said, "but one of these times we're going to have to get into why the press — yes, us, the *Weekly* — seems so afraid of God."

"Afraid of God?"

"C'mon, we run articles about Him as if He's some sort of strange phenomenon that has to be examined from every angle. Polls show that more than half the population believes in God. But you could never tell that from our pages or those of our competition."

"Can't argue that."

"We'll solve it another time," she said, smiling. "You look like you need to sleep off some calories."

Sixteen

"I'm not that hungry," Rayford told Irene.

"It's nothing heavy. I just thought we could sit down together before you're off to England."

Rayford shrugged, and as he and Raymie sat at the table, Irene stepped into the garage to toss some trash. She noticed the light on inside Rayford's car. As she reached in to turn it off, she smelled Chinese food and saw an empty soy-sauce packet on the passenger floor mat. She smelled something else too. Perfume? Maybe, but the food smell overpowered it.

In the ashtray lay a receipt from The Happy Lucky in Des Plaines. Well, at least it was for only one meal.

"No wonder you aren't hungry," Irene said, returning to the kitchen.

"Hmm?"

"Your car smells of Chinese food."

"What? Still? Uh, that's from the other day."

"What were you doing in Des Plaines?"

Rayford looked puzzled. "Oh, I was dropping off that flight attendant. Then I was just famished, so . . ."

Why did he seem so nervous? Irene doubted the smell would linger that long. And hadn't Irene been in his car since then? This was new. This was today. And even if he had been alone, what had taken him to Des Plaines?

Irene didn't want to think about it.

The next morning, Irene attended her weekly women's Bible study at Jackie's house. She didn't know why, but attendance was growing there too. Jackie's little home looked even smaller as women crowded in, having to employ the piano bench and even children's chairs. Irene was impressed by a new face, a woman about her age with salt-and-pepper hair, done up right and clearly expensively, and wearing very fashionable clothes. She carried a briefcase and a purse, so Irene assumed she was a businesswoman. Besides her appearance, the woman had a confident air, as if, though in a new and strange setting, she still knew how to conduct herself.

Irene introduced herself and welcomed the woman. She said her name was Amanda White and that she was a local executive who had been to New Hope Village Church once, after her husband had been invited to a men's outing and wanted to check out the services.

During the Bible study, each time Irene caught Amanda's eye, Amanda nodded and smiled. And when Irene contributed to the discussion, she sensed the woman really paying attention.

When the study was over, Mrs. White made a beeline for Irene, thrust out her hand, and said, "Well, aren't you the most precious thing? So vibrant and pleasant."

"Thank you. I hope you enjoyed this."

"Oh, just processing it, you know. My family and I have been churchgoers all our lives, but something's really caught my husband's fancy here. This might all be a little too religious for me, if you know what I mean. It's interesting and all, don't get me wrong, and you ladies seem so into it. To tell you the truth, I didn't know what to expect." She leaned close. "Frankly, I was afraid it was going to be a little hokey. But you're like normal people."

"Oh, believe me, we are," Irene said. "In fact, with my church background, I'm sort of your mirror image. My family — except my son, Raymie — is more comfortable in the typical, less overt church. But my son and I have genuinely encountered God here. We've received Christ."

"*Have* you?"

Irene nodded. "We believe He is the way to God." And suddenly she teared up.

"Oh, you poor thing! What is it?"

"I'm sorry. This is embarrassing."

"Not at all. This is clearly important to you."

"I just pray I'll be able to reach my husband and my daughter before it's too late. That's my greatest fear. I want to know they're going to heaven."

"Well, isn't that something? Isn't that sweet? You know, my own family is saying the same thing to me lately. Got to be saved, they say. Saved by grace."

"You know all you have to do is admit to God that you're a sinner and that you need Christ to forgive your sins and change your life."

"I know. I'm not ready yet, but I do appreciate your concern. I really do."

"May I tell you one more thing, Amanda? I don't mean to be pushy."

"Sure."

"Just let me encourage you not to put off

your decision too long. With all that's going on in the world right now, you just never know what's going to happen, how much time you'll have."

But Irene *had* pushed too far. She could see it in Mrs. White's eyes. She just hoped she hadn't turned the woman completely away.

That afternoon, as Raymie was getting home from school, Rayford was on his way out the door for his London flight.

"My, you smell good," Irene said. "You seem excited about this trip."

"Always love these — you know that."

"But it's not like this is anything new," she said.

"I know."

"Fresh uniform. Wow, you're ready. Almost like you're headed for a date."

He laughed a little too loudly, Irene thought. "Your Des Plaines honey on this flight?" she said lightly.

"Hmm? Who?"

"You know who."

"The young one? Miss Durham? I have no idea."

"You have no idea."

"I haven't checked lately; that's all. So what if she is?"

"Nothing. Just wondering."

"Hey, Raymie! Take care of your mom for me till I get back, eh?"

"Sure, Dad. Have a safe trip and wish me luck."

"Luck?"

"For tonight."

"Tonight?"

The boy's shoulders drooped. "My program, Dad!"

"Oh, yeah! I almost forgot! I'll be thinking of you. You be a good leaf or whatever it is, and —"

"Tree."

"Hmm?"

"I'm the whole tree, Dad. There are four of us."

"Well, see, that's even better. My son the big tree. Break a leg. Or break a branch, or whatever."

"And don't forget your promise, Dad. Sunday?"

"Right. Got it. See you in a few days."

On the way to the airport, Hattie Durham seemed to have lost any trace of inhibition or restraint. As soon as Rayford had put her bag in the backseat and slid behind the wheel, she loosened her seatbelt and leaned against him. She barely moved, pressed against him for the entire drive. He was in heaven. And already debating whether he was going to take this relationship further, once they were on foreign soil. Every few minutes he talked himself out of it, but he knew deep down that the distance from home alone would embolden him.

His number-two man in the cockpit would be Christopher Smith, a pleasant-enough guy he'd flown with before. The closer they got to O'Hare, the more positive he was feeling about the night. Not to mention the weather, which was perfect. His job, once they were in the air and settled into the flight path, should be largely routine until the descent into London.

Dinner at home was rushed as Raymie talked about how embarrassed he was to have to climb inside a cylindrical painted-cardboard tree trunk with his face sticking out. "I have to hold the leaves out and drop them when the north wind comes blowing through. It's such a play for babies. I can't believe they're making us do it."

"But you know your part, and you'll do well. This is probably your last year for stuff like this."

"But, Mom, have you heard my lines?"

"No."

"Just wait."

"Tell me now."

"No chance. It'll be bad enough there."

He was right. When Raymie's big scene came, he was the only tree to forget to drop his leaves. Everybody in the place could hear the stage whispers from the wings: "Drop your leaves! Raymie, drop your leaves!"

Finally he paled and let them go, and the crowed twittered. Then a bird pranced through, asking each tree if she could build a nest in its branches to keep her chicks warm. All, of course, were to sternly turn her down except for the last tree, an evergreen.

When it was Raymie's turn he said, "No! I cannot be bothered with you! I have not yet recovered from the confusion and noise the squirrels made when they tried to gather my acorns for winter!"

This elicited a roar of laughter from the crowd, which warmed Irene but clearly humiliated Raymie. Never had she seen him so eager to be finished with something.

When she met him afterward, she was smiling broadly. He was still blushing.

Irene hugged him and noticed he stiffened a little, looking around. So it was happening already. "I thought you did fine!" she said.

"I was awful. Forgot to drop my leaves. Then I didn't think I sounded like a tree at all. I don't think any of us did."

Irene laughed loudly. "And what do trees sound like?"

"I don't know, but not us."

The more she laughed, the more Raymie lost his scowl. "Well, you've made yourself a memory, anyway, haven't you?"

"That's for sure," he said. "No matter how hard I try to forget this . . ."

By the time they got to the drive–through for milk shakes, Raymie was mimicking his own monotone performance and cackling about how silly it all was. Irene was grateful that he was so good about it. At his age she had been so awkward and shy that a goof like his would have haunted her for days.

The windshield steamed over as they sat and talked. Irene had prayed, including for Rayford's safety and for his soul.

When she finished, Raymie added, "And thanks that he's coming to church with us Sunday."

"That means a lot to you, doesn't it?" Irene said.

" 'Course. Dad just doesn't seem happy anymore. Plus, I want to be sure he's going to heaven when he dies."

"Me too."

They arrived home later than Irene liked on a school night, so she pushed Raymie to get to bed. When she checked on him a few minutes later, he was under the covers. "You're not wearing socks, are you?" she said.

He sighed. "Yeah."

"You know you've got to let your —"

"Feet breathe, yeah, I know. But my feet are so cold. Just let me wear them for a little while, and I'll kick them off later."

"What if you fall asleep? I don't want to have to come in here and pull them off you in the middle of the night."

"Mom, I'm not going to die if my feet don't breathe."

"Just try to remember to take them off, once you've warmed up."

Irene prayed with Raymie again, and as she headed to the lonely master bedroom, she questioned why she was so obsessed over his wearing socks to bed. Feet didn't really breathe, and what was the harm? Had her parents not allowed her to do the same? Where had she gotten that old wives' tale? She could only hope that was the biggest issue she ever had with the boy. Fat chance.

As Irene slid between the cool sheets, she wondered if she too should have socks on. She lay there on her back, silently running through her prayer list. But her mind kept coming back to Rayford. He had been her life for almost as long as she could remember, but things were clearly not the same.

Could he be having an affair with this Durham girl? And if he was, what should Irene do?

She still didn't want to think about it, but she couldn't help it. She would not be walked on, not be treated that way. But if there was something she could be doing differently or better, she hoped God would tell her what it was. In the meantime, Irene would just keep praying for Rayford. She didn't want to lose him, particularly to another woman. But above all, she didn't want to see him lost to the Kingdom of God.

Rayford Steele was a conflicted man. During the O'Hare-to-Heathrow preflight preparation he began to feel less than the professional he had always been. He was not perfect; he knew that. But he was one high-level accomplished pilot, supremely confident in his ability to safely transport hundreds of people thousands of miles in a craft worth millions of dollars. He was well paid and respected, and he believed he deserved both.

The problem was, Rayford had never been this distracted before a flight. He'd always had the ability to compartmentalize the various areas of his life. Irene knew better than to try to call him between the time he left for the airport and when he called her upon arrival at his destination. Only a couple of times during their long marriage had she violated that. Both times she had caught him in the car on the way to the airport, and she was just telling him she missed him or loved him or would be thinking of him. And both times he had realized he sounded distracted and had apologized, but he was — in essence — getting his game face on.

Preflight routine was indeed routine, but it was nothing to sleepwalk through, and he had to start thinking of the myriad checklists and protocols so necessary to safety and efficient flight operation. He was not just the pilot; he was the captain, responsible for everything, and he would have to answer for anything that went wrong.

Rayford loved the responsibility and his ability to focus on it. He was known as a nice, friendly guy, a captain that people enjoyed flying with. His first officer tonight would be Christopher Smith, an earthy, down-home kind of guy he enjoyed chatting with. Chris had a couple of young sons he liked to talk about, and he also seemed to get a kick out of reverting to his youthful colloquial language. Rayford and Chris Smith had flown a good bit together and had even been through a dangerous incident together, but Rayford had to admit that they had never bonded to the point where Rayford even knew where that accent had come from. Not quite Southern. But country. Could have been southern Indiana or even Oklahoma.

Rayford knew Chris had the skills to become a captain but perhaps not the demeanor or character. If any first officer of Rayford's ever violated protocol, like trying to sneak a nap during a flight or exhibiting a bit of selfishness, it would be Chris. Not to the point that he required more than a reminder rather than an official reprimand, but enough that Rayford had to wonder about his future. And Chris was an ambitious guy. Rayford couldn't figure it. He would've thought a guy who had his sights set on the top job would do everything in his power to show everybody he was dead serious and committed to it.

Hattie had informed Rayford that one of his favorite attendants would be aboard. Antonio Salazar was a veteran and a passenger favorite. A family man, he was funny and entertaining and helpful, seemingly a ball of indefatigable energy with a great smile. He was just one of those types who appeared happiest when busy and helping people. Tony had actually turned down a promotion to senior flight attendant, citing his pleasure with his current role as well as family responsibilities that made him want more control over his own schedule.

Rayford's problem this evening, however, was the new senior flight attendant herself, the leggy young woman who had ridden from Des Plaines to O'Hare with him. Their flirtation dance had accelerated, and something had to give. Either Rayford would have to nip it in the bud and tell Hattie it simply wasn't wise and wasn't going to work — the old "I really can't do this to my loyal wife and kids" tack — or he was going to have to quit pretending he didn't notice her every look, touch, and remark.

The conflict, then, was not really over whether he was going to pursue this out-of-bounds relationship. Rather it was tension between knowing full well that this was his intention — especially since they would have a couple of days in London with time and distance from his conscience (which he had apparently left at home) — and his need to keep his professional mind on his business.

While boarding and greeting the crew and getting himself situated, Rayford knew he should be in full preflight mode, eyes and mind on the task. But he was formulating his approach to Hattie. She seemed on high alert, excitedly talking about her new role as senior attendant, yet giving him other obvious signals that she knew they were headed toward the inevitable point of no return.

Even while lugging his boxy flight attaché case, shedding his coat, greeting Antonio and the others, and finding Chris already in the cockpit, Rayford had to admit his mind was elsewhere. Salazar had been busy in the galley when Rayford moved through, and the smaller man flashed a smile and shook the captain's hand warmly.

"Hey, Tony," Rayford said. "Good to see you."

"Likewise. Diet Coke with a lime or are you ready for some coffee?"

"Oh, thanks," Rayford said, "but I think Miss Durham's already on it."

"We're excited about her, sir. She's going to be a good senior. And she credits you for being a great mentor."

"Really?" Rayford said, trying to appear

pleasantly surprised.

Hattie was accomplished at hiding her feelings for Rayford from the rest of the crew. She always referred to him as the captain or Captain Steele or the pilot, never using his first name. And she didn't ogle him on board as she did in the car or from across the table at a restaurant. How she was able to lightly touch him as they passed each other or when she delivered something to him in the cockpit without anyone else being the wiser, Rayford would never know.

Even now, when he finally settled in behind the controls and she brought him a Diet Coke, she shielded Christopher Smith's view with her body as she leaned to hand Rayford the drink. Meanwhile, with her left hand she dragged a finger across his shoulder to the base of his neck. There was nothing but professionalism in their tones of voice and thus seemingly no suspicion aroused on anyone else's part.

When she left the cockpit, Smith chortled, "Whoo, boy, that is one gorgeous young thing, ain't she?"

"Miss Durham?" Rayford said. "She *is* attractive."

"Attractive?" Smith said, adding a crude remark about his own fantasies concerning her.

"Pretty young for you, wouldn't you say, Chris?"

"May it never be so, Cap'n. Tell me you'd turn down a chance with her."

Rayford pursed his lips and shook his head, as if admonishing a student. "Let's have a little class, man. She's not much more than a child. And you, a family man."

"Well, I'm not dead, and I'm sure not blind."

"Back to business there, cowboy."

Seventeen

Irene Steele was not the type of person that bolted straight up in bed, regardless of what she felt or heard. Rayford might sit up or even creep out to see what had awakened them, but Irene tended to freeze if something startled her awake.

And that's what happened this night. She'd had trouble falling asleep, as usual when Rayford was away. But soon she was soundly out, hands clasped under her cheek as she lay on her side.

What woke her was a shout so loud that it was as if someone were in the room. Clear as day came the piercing precision of every syllable, and her eyes popped open, her heart resounding against her ribs.

"IRENE STEELE!"

Liem, a graduate school student, had worked in the Jakarta, Indonesia, Sunrise

Crematorium throughout his university tenure. In fewer than three years he had risen to the point that he was responsible for the actual burning of corpses.

The hardest part of the job was the paperwork. Obviously one had to be sure he was cremating the right body and following whatever religious instructions had been outlined.

The modern ovens, which each held one standard-size cremation coffin and remains, burned at more than 1,650 degrees Fahrenheit and consumed approximately 175 pounds every thirty minutes.

Liem left everything on the coffins except the nameplates, as ornaments and fittings were combustible plastic. Once he was certain the paperwork matched the corpse, he would slide the coffin out of storage and onto an oversized steel gurney, which he would then roll to the oven door. The coffin was then transferred to the top level of the chamber, the door secured, and the burners turned to maximum.

During the process, the heavier bones and calcium deposits would fall through openings to the lower chamber. When what was left had cooled, Liem would use a magnet to separate surgical pins, nails, screws, or other artificial elements. He would then grind the final residue into a fine powder and deposit it in a decorative urn selected by the family.

Liem was cremating the body of a missionary pilot whose religion was designated *Christian*. Without incident, he made certain of the paperwork, slid the coffin into the chamber, adjusted the settings, and left for his late-morning lunch break.

Upon his return just after noon, Liem noted that the burning was finished and the cooling had begun. But when the remains should have been cool enough to begin the magnetic procedure, Liem was stunned to find nothing in the lower chamber. His brow knit with confusion, he rushed to his supervisor.

"Show me the paperwork," the man said. "Did the coffin feel full?"

"Absolutely. I know the difference."

"Then what happened in the process that kept the bones and calcium from dropping?"

"No idea, sir."

They checked the upper chamber and found only the ashes and dust from the coffin and plastic.

"Liem, you were mistaken. That coffin had to have been empty."

"How could that be? That has never happened before. And no . . . no, sir. I clearly recall that coffin being difficult to get rolling from the gurney. It was not empty."

"Liem, see for yourself. No residue of human remains. What will we tell the family?"

Liem was terrified, though he could not imagine he bore responsibility for this. "I will open every coffin before burning it from now on. But what could have caused this?"

"You said you took a break. Do you suspect body snatchers?"

"I cannot imagine. That is the stuff of horror movies. How would anyone get in here to steal bodies? And I put the coffin in the oven myself. Someone would have had to remove it, take the body, and replace the coffin into the fire."

"How many more do you have today?"

"Four."

"Check them now."

Liem found all the paperwork and began comparing it with the form affixed to each coffin. The first body, a local whose family had checked *None* for religion, was there. The second, a young female exchange student from Canada, had *Unknown* listed under religion.

Another Christian was supposedly in the third coffin, but as soon as Liem slid it onto the gurney, where he would have room to open it, he could tell it was empty. "We've got no body here either, sir."

"How do you know?"

When the lid opened, the supervisor gasped. Only the clothes remained. "This suit was buttoned back up after the body was stolen. What kind of a sick — ?"

Liem's cell phone rang, and he took a call from his sister.

"Turn on the news," she said.

"We don't have a television down here."

"Find one and turn it on."

"Maybe after my shift."

"Trust me, Liem — do it now!"

Liem hung up and told his boss that something big was on the news.

"Unless it has something to do with missing bodies, we don't have time for that, Liem. We're in big trouble."

The door burst open at the end of the corridor. "You guys hear what's going on? Get up here!"

Liem and his boss ran up the stairs and joined a scrum of fellow workers crowded around a TV. News footage showed a funeral parlor with coffins empty, save for the clothes and artificial body parts of the deceased. Panic broke out and people rioted. A fresh story, fed from a network TV station in California, showed an anchorman disappear from his clothes on camera as the nine o'clock news began. His coanchor frantically pulled the clothes from the man's chair, screaming.

Liem, unable to get his mind around any of this, staggered out into the noonday sun and was struck to see the traffic hopelessly gridlocked. From his first moment in Jakarta years ago, he had heard the cacophony of car horns as he heard them now. And while the traffic had always been insane, it somehow kept moving. Even when cars brushed against each other in the roundabouts, people had kept their heads and managed to pick their way through.

But now no one was moving. Liem walked into the street and joined others who peered speechlessly into driverless cars — cars with engines running, radios on, even airconditioning humming. But in each no one sat behind the wheel. Shoes and socks lay on the floor. Pants on the seat. Shirts on the back of the seat. Eyeglasses, hearing aids, jewelry — all still there.

From one of the radios Liem heard a horror-stricken reporter say that this sudden disappearance had struck all over the globe at the same time and that experts were already predicting the toll would rise to more than a billion. Other major cities where this phenomenon had occurred in broad daylight, including some during the afternoon rush hour, saw traffic disasters just like this one.

Liem slapped himself to be certain he was not dreaming. This was a living nightmare.

In cities where the disappearances had happened in the middle of the night, those left behind were awakened by frantic phone calls from loved ones in other time zones. Soon the modes of communication were hopelessly jammed as the biggest news story in history swept the globe.

For an instant, Irene Steele had lain terrified, but before she could move even an inch she heard a loud trumpet blast and felt transported out of her bed, passing through the ceiling, the attic, the roof, and into the dark night sky. Strangely, though she had left her jewelry and nightgown, she did not feel naked, nor was she cold. Not for a second did she believe this was a dream or anything other than real. She was more in the moment than she had ever been in her life.

And there was Raymie, right next to her, as they soared.

"Is this it, Mom? Is this it? Somebody shouted my name!"

She could see clearly, even in the dark, and as they rose Irene saw millions rising with them from horizon to horizon. Oh, praise God! She would soon see Jesus!

But for now she was fixated on Raymie. She had known it was her son; she had recognized his face and his voice, though it had changed, and he was a full-grown man, over six feet tall with a clear face and chiseled features. She too had changed. Her face felt smoother, her skin taut. And while she still bore nicks and scars from various minor injuries over the years — even Jesus' scars would still be visible, she knew — her body and tone reminded her of several years before, when she had been in her early thirties.

When she and Raymie reached the clouds, they slowed and were suspended there. Irene could not keep from grinning. She had always been afraid of heights, but here she was, higher than she'd ever been outside a plane, and she feared nothing. She wondered aloud where Jackie was, and suddenly, there she was, with Dooley and their grown-up child. They embraced and stared and shook their heads.

"It was you, you know," Irene said. "You really led me to Christ."

"Me too," Dooley said. "I wonder if Pastor Billings —"

And there he was with them, embracing everyone, rejoicing. "I always wondered what this would feel like," he said, looking half his age.

"Thank you for your faithful preaching and teaching," Irene said.

It was then that she realized that there was no barrier between thought and action. "Raymie, it seems everything we think about happens instantly. I mentioned Jackie and here she is. Dooley mentioned the pastor, and here he is. It's as if time has stood still and all of this is happening simultaneously."

"I want to see Grandma and Grandpa," Raymie said, and they appeared, youthful, lucid, no trace of the Alzheimer's that had claimed them both.

"Irene," Rayford's father said, "you led us to Jesus. We are eternally grateful."

"Yes," her mother-in-law said, "and we must pray for Rayford, who is not here, is he?"

Irene shook her head, and the four of them huddled to pray. "I don't know what comes next, Lord," Irene said, "but I know Rayford must endure difficult days. Give him strength to resist the evil one, and bring him to Yourself, God."

All around them Irene could hear cheers

and squeals of delight as more reunions took place. People of all races and creeds celebrated. Irene knew they had to be speaking in their own languages, yet she understood every word.

A Chinese woman announced for all to hear, pointing at another woman, "My daughter was in a wheelchair twenty years! Look at her now!"

From somewhere else, a father introduced a handsome, smiling young man. "This boy was born with Down Syndrome."

"I can't wait to sing to Jesus," the boy said.

Irene saw two women embracing and weeping. "Your child?" Irene said.

One met Irene's eyes and nodded. "I had her aborted sixteen years ago. She forgives me."

"I have both arms!" a man shouted, waving.

"I'm whole!" came from somewhere else.

Had they been here for an hour or only a second? Irene couldn't tell. All she knew was that anticipation crashed over her like a waterfall. She turned to Raymie, and they said in unison, "I want to see Jesus."

And the entire throng from all over the world ascended yet again.

Eighteen

Everything in Irene's past paled to insignificance as she soared into the heavens, the earth shrinking from sight. She had to wonder how the billions of people in the air would ever be able to share the attention of the One they had believed in, the One who had beckoned them home.

But then it hit her. If Jesus' shout had been heard in the same instant by true believers all over the world as their own names, it proved yet again that He was omnipotent and omnipresent, unbound by space or time. He could do anything and everything all at once.

As Irene's new, glorified body was transported through Earth's atmosphere above the clouds, she let her head fall back and spread her arms wide, closing her eyes tight. When the light of glory flooded her being, she had to peek.

High above her was Jesus, His gleaming incandescence brighter than a million suns. With arms outstretched He welcomed His beloved, and while Irene remained vaguely aware that she was just one of so many on this same journey, His beautiful piercing eyes seemed to bore into hers alone. She wanted to cry out, to thank Him a thousand times a thousand for forgiving her, for saving her soul, for calling her to Himself. His face shone with love and compassion and welcome, as if her arrival was His highest joy.

Irene immediately felt unworthy, and all she had wanted to express seemed to leak from her mind. She could not speak. She tried to bow, to lower herself, to hide from Jesus' perfection, which seemed to permeate her own darkness like a beacon.

But He reached for her, lifted her to Himself.

"Irene," He said as He enveloped her. "My child, My own. I praise you for believing in Me, for trusting in Me, for calling upon My name to be saved. This is what you were saved for, to be with Me. And yet it is only the beginning of a journey that has no end. Come with Me to My Father's house, for as I promised, 'If anyone loves Me, he will keep My word; and My Father will love him, and We will come to him and make Our home with him.' "

Irene was aware only of blinking, and in the next instant she had been transported into outer space and then into what Pastor Billings had called the third heaven, into the presence of a vast and beautiful crystal city so overwhelming that she could scarcely take it in. This made Soldier Field and Wrigley Field look like toys. From certain vantage points, even when those stadiums were full, she had been able to see almost everyone at once. With a mere turn of the head on Earth, her eyes could take in forty, fifty, sixty thousand people. But this. This was something else.

Clearly there were hundreds of millions of others, more than a billion, maybe two. Yet without rising above their heads, Irene was aware of them all. And not just aware. It was as if, without so much as moving an eye — let alone her head — or even standing on tiptoe, she saw and recognized every one. She knew them. Their histories, their stories, were known to her. She could pause and concentrate on one or another or a thousand at a time.

There was a reason for this, she knew. Irene had never realized how limited her mind had been until now when all things became known. Every story, every person, every insight and intuition, had a purpose. And the purpose was Jesus. Everything here was for and about and because of Him. Irene's eternal life was for the purpose of worshiping Him. As people's stories were revealed to her heart and mind, Irene's entire focus was on the work Christ had done in their lives. Forgiving them. Loving them. Saving them.

No amusement-park imitation of a real experience came close to this. There were no holograms, no 3-D, no pretending. Friends and loved ones left behind would assume her dead, but Irene knew with all of her being that she had never been more alive.

Had Raymie had the same experience?

He appeared next to her. "Jesus welcomed me personally," he said. "And this is the house of God."

Irene was agape. It seemed that if she were able to back up a million miles into space she would not be able to see the beginning and end of this masterpiece built four-square. Her pastor had recently reminded the congregation that if God had created the entire world in seven days by merely speaking it into existence, imagine what He could do with two thousand years to fulfill

Jesus' promise of going to prepare a place for them. The Scripture told that it was just under fourteen hundred square miles, the length, breadth, and height the same. If superimposed on the earth it would extend from Canada to the Gulf of Mexico and from Colorado to the Atlantic Ocean. With the raptured saints and the resurrected dead, perhaps two billion people would be there, with enough room for each to inhabit a cubed space of seventy-five acres. Talk about high ceilings!

It all lay before her in incomprehensible grandeur, radiant and delicate and yet somehow, she knew, indestructible. Gold and silver and brass and platinum complemented diamonds, rubies, emeralds, and pearls, and these were so perfectly arranged that the appearance did not offend as gaudy or extravagant. Naturally, everything looked perfect, every gate — consisting of one giant gem each and attended by angels — every wall, every pillar. And yes, its roads were as glassy as spun gold.

Irene noticed not a shadow anywhere. None. Yet there was no sun. The light of God illumined this place from within and cast no shadow in any direction. Irene had always wondered and, frankly, worried about what heaven would look and feel like.

Would it feel alien to her? Would it appear as such a great monument to God that she would be merely a spectator, a museum patron?

This, however, immediately felt like home. It was as if she had been an alien on Earth, just waiting for the day when she could return here. In spite of its immensity and splendor, a strange intimacy radiated from it, and she felt it had indeed been prepared for her.

Irene did not know how she knew that the next voice was of God Himself; she simply did.

"This is the city I have prepared for those who had the faith to believe My Word and follow My will. Behold the city of the living God, the heavenly Jerusalem where are now gathered the general assembly of the church of the firstborn and the just, whose spirits have been made perfect in the great resurrection. To this city came all the spirits of those who died in Christ and have now been resurrected. The resurrected and the living saints shall dwell here until the earth is made new, when this city shall descend to abide there forever."

This, Pastor Billings had taught, was the new Jerusalem that would descend onto the new earth after the seven-year tribulation and Jesus' glorious appearing. So Irene would live here until Jesus' second coming upon the earth and then would remain in this relocated city for eternity. She wondered how long the next seven years would seem from this perspective.

And God said, "Behold, the tabernacle of God is with men, and I will dwell with them, and they shall be My people. I will be with you and be your God. And I will wipe away every tear from your eyes; there shall be no more death, nor sorrow, nor crying. There shall be no more pain, for the former things have passed away."

Irene had read those words and heard them read, but what an unspeakable thrill to hear them from the very mouth of God. Their truth resounded and engulfed her. No more tears, death, sorrow, or pain. The former things had passed.

In the next instant, along with everyone else, she was inside the ground floor of the cubic city where a crystalline sea led to a gleaming throne. There sat Jesus, majestic, triumphant, and again, somehow making Irene feel as if she were the only other person in the room. Her eyes riveted to the eternal embodiment of unconditional love and sacrifice, she could assume only that everyone in the vast multitude somehow had the same supernaturally unobstructed view and that Jesus was interacting with them personally as He was with her.

Irene felt no farther from Jesus as she saw Him from what on Earth would have been hundreds of feet away than when He had pressed her against His chest. How was this possible? She would have to stop asking herself such questions. She was not aware of flying or walking or even moving, and yet she had traversed thousands of miles from her home in just moments. As she merely thought about things or conjured questions, her new body darted here and there, and everything was answered and understood.

The entire first floor of the colossal house of God had been fashioned into a great hall, a vast beautiful gathering place where the Spirit of God dwelt and the Son of God presided. Irene was not aware of turning her head or even her eyes, yet she was aware of everything around her. Inexpressible splendor filled her senses, and while she knew she was in a place that had foundations, whose builder and maker was God, she was unaware of a floor or ceiling, and the walls seemed transparent, though the open gates were made of precious stones and attended by angels.

She again tried to imagine this scene on

Earth, as if she had gone to a great venue to see someone perform or speak. Monitors would have been set up to allow everyone to see what was really happening onstage. But here she sat, unaware of the weight of her body, in the middle of this enormous throng, yet she saw Jesus as clearly as if she were sitting at His feet. As He appeared to take in the crowd with His eyes, still it seemed His attention was solely and fully on her, and she could hear His thoughts.

"I am so glad you are here, Irene. I chose you before the foundation of the world. I came to Earth for you, lived and died for you, forgave your sins, and claimed you as My own. Welcome to the house of God."

Around His throne four creatures hovered, with eyes all around their heads. The first was like a lion, the second was like a calf, the third had a face like a man's, and the fourth was like an eagle. Each of the four had six wings and seemed to never alight. They called out, "Holy, holy, holy, Lord God Almighty, who was and is and is to come!"

As the creatures gave glory and honor and thanks to Jesus, twenty-four men in a semicircle before Him fell and worshiped Him and cast crowns before the throne, saying, "You are worthy, O Lord, to receive glory and honor and power; for You created all things, and by Your will they exist and were created."

Thousands upon thousands of angels appeared and surrounded the throne, joining the men and the living creatures in praising Jesus and saying with loud voices, "Worthy is the Lamb who was slain to receive power and riches and wisdom, and strength and honor and glory and blessing!"

Suddenly Jesus said, "Behold, I make all things new. It is done! I am the Alpha and the Omega, the Beginning and the End. I give the fountain of the water of life freely to all who thirst."

Irene had no emotion from her past to compare with what she had felt from the time she heard her name and the sound of the trumpet of God and began to rise. It was as if every happy, fulfilling, thrilling moment of her life combined in one instant, never to abate, would only begin to hint at the feeling that permeated her entire being. She felt she would never again need sleep, would never be hungry or thirsty. All she wanted was to be in the presence of her Savior and to worship Him with her whole self.

But were the stories of delicious foods in heaven merely apocryphal? Because Irene didn't need food, did that mean she would not want it? With that mere thought came a cornucopia of delights that dwarfed anything she had ever hungered for — sizzling meats, fruit, vegetables, crystal glasses full of nectar.

Irene wondered if she had time to partake, not wanting to miss a thing while concentrating on her own satisfaction. She found herself able to consume more food in a split second than she had ever eaten in one sitting. Yet there was not an iota of discomfort. Every bite and sip brought bursts of flavor unlike anything Irene had ever imagined, and the taste stayed with her as the foodstuffs disappeared.

She wondered where Raymie was now, and instantly he was at her side, telling her of friends he had discovered whom he had not even known were believers.

"How wonderful," she said as he darted away, and immediately she had the same experience, recognizing people, some surely miles away, whom she had known on Earth but not really known. Had they had any more clue that she was a believer than she had that they were?

Nicolae Carpathia slid from under his blankets and sat on the edge of his bed with his head in his hands. Bucharest was normally quiet at dawn, but now he heard the dissonance of sirens and car horns and weather-warning alarms. He moved to the window and pulled back the drapes to reveal the mix of pastels emerging from the eastern horizon. Such a beautiful day for so much racket.

But there was as much noise in Nicolae's mind as in his ears. It tormented him, this mix of terrible screams and maniacal laughter, driving him to his knees before the window. He hung his head and lifted his arms. "Speak to me, spirit," he pleaded. "Tell me!"

"Our enemies have been rescued," came the haunted, rasping, echoing voice. "Saved, snatched from our grasp! But all is not lost. Those who remain are ours. And we are in the vast majority!"

"I do not understand," Nicolae whined.

"Are you prepared to lead those who remain?"

"I am willing, but I do not know —"

"Your time has come. You must merely obey."

"I will do your bidding, master. But what has happened? Master? Spirit? Tell me more."

"Obey!"

"I am yours, but —"

"Obey!"

"I shall, but I —"

"Obey!"

"I am at your service." Nicolae struggled to his feet, his face wet with tears. Phones were ringing all over the house. He reached for the intercom. "Gabriella!" he barked. "Who is answering the phones?"

Another maid's voice came back, shaken. "I'm trying. Do you know what has happened?"

"No. Tell me."

"Turn on your TV."

"I will, but tell me first."

"I'm sorry, sir, but I must get these phones, and Gabriella is missing."

"Missing?"

The woman had clicked off, so Nicolae grabbed the remote and flipped through a hundred channels, all reporting the same news. The greatest catastrophe in history had claimed hundreds of millions around the globe — billions when the dead were added. People had disappeared in an instant, leaving everything material behind.

Nicolae felt his lip curling into a snarl. Had he been duped? Was this, then, what he was to inherit, to rule? A world decimated by chaos and tragedy, reeling from the vanishing of more lives than had been claimed by all the wars and plagues and natural disasters of history combined?

All the kingdoms of the world were to be his, and this was the shape they were in?

Nicolae was again driven to the floor, this time from a blow to the back of his neck, just above his spine. As he teetered on all fours, trying to regain his equilibrium, the spirit again communicated to his soul. "Do you not see how we can use this to our advantage? Our soldiers do not need uniforms! Our enemies have retreated, separated themselves from the battleground. The earth and all that is in it is ours! We have won! We have driven our enemies from us and we are left with the spoils.

"Remain alert. Remain on the offensive. Fight to maintain every soul. We must not lose even one more to the other side. This tragic day can be laid at the feet of the Enemy. Those who believe this was an act of God will hate Him for it. The terrified, the suffering, the needy, the war-weary will look for a man of peace, of compassion, of understanding, of hope. You can be that man if you can comprehend the unlimited possibilities and seize the moment. Are you that man? Can you accomplish that task?"

"I am that man."

"Rise. And obey."

When Nicolae emerged from the shower and dressed in one of his finest suits — anticipating the crush of the press — phones were still ringing all over the estate, and Gabriella's assistant had called in even those who were supposed to be off today.

"TV, newspapers, magazines," she called out, covering the phone as he strode past. "What can I tell them?"

"I am unavailable until after lunch."

"Do I tell them about our own losses?"

"I am sorry?"

"Gabriella's uniform is on the floor where she stood. One of our drivers was checking an engine. His clothes are draped over the car under the open hood."

"Anyone else?"

"Not sure yet. Some of those I'm calling are not answering."

Enemies on my own staff. "Tell the press that I do not anticipate being up to speaking until after lunch as I am in seclusion, grieving the losses of several on my own staff. And get someone to show you how to program those phones so that they ring directly to Ms. Ivins and Mr. Fortunato in New York."

Leon had been dozing before the television in anticipation of going to bed when his room phone jangled.

Viv Ivins was on the other end. "Do you see what has happened?" she said.

Leon fought for clarity from the loginess of his nap. The TV news showed alarming images from all over the world.

"Millions have disappeared right out of their clothes."

"What is it?" Leon managed. "Am I dreaming?"

"No, you are not dreaming. And you know precisely what this is. It is the day of reckoning. The ultimate war has begun."

Nineteen

Irene Steele had long wondered what heaven would be like. She had heard there would be different priorities, that things on Earth that had seemed so important would become inconsequential. But what of her heartache over Rayford and Chloe? Somehow the pain was muted in the presence of God. She felt an optimism deep within, and her prayer life had already been radically altered.

Anytime Irene was moved to communicate with God through Christ, she merely thought what she wanted to say, and God was in her and she in Him, the conversation direct and instantaneous. And His message? It was always filled with encouragement and security. There was no earthly word for this heavenly feeling of welcome, of belonging, and — strangest of all — praise that went both ways.

In her humanity on Earth she praised had

Him and longed to do so in His presence for eternity. But she would not have been able to even comprehend God praising her. On Earth Irene had had the most difficult time accepting and feeling God's love for her, even though she knew it was true. It was what had drawn her to Him, and she could identify with the biblical truth that "we love Him because He first loved us."

That Jesus, the only perfect man who ever lived, would have gone to the cross and suffered and died for her had she been the only sinner in history, had often caused her to break emotionally. And yet Irene had to admit that she had never, ever understood God's love. She had always regretted that, because she sensed that God wanted her to not only accept His gift — which she had — but to also understand that she was the object of His great love, the apple of His eye, the reason He did what He did.

Now, here, in His presence, she got it. She understood. In herself she found no more worthiness, yet she could not deny the look in Jesus' eyes and the thrill it seemed was His to see her. She only hoped her countenance showed the same, as being in the eternal presence of her Savior had been her loftiest hope and dream ever since she had received Him. How could He seem as overjoyed to see her — one of so many — as she was to be in His presence?

Irene had assumed all the attention would naturally and rightfully be on Jesus here, so it stunned her to feel His love and acceptance in a whole new way. Everyone here — she knew that each was feeling this as personally as she — was the object of Jesus' love.

On Earth she would not have been in a place even a tenth this massive without keeping an eye on Raymie every second. Now, though he may have been miles from her with the ability to move at the speed of thought, she was entirely aware of his presence and knew he was safe and, in essence, still with her. With his having been transformed into an instant adult — seemingly in mind as well as body — he exuded a wisdom far beyond his years. Irene knew he was experiencing every detail the way she was, and she couldn't wait to talk with him, though she resisted the urge to request his presence. When they needed to be together, both would come to that conclusion simultaneously, and it would happen.

For now, as the colossal hall hummed with excitement, Irene settled in for what was to come. She had an eternity to enjoy this, and her prayer became that her husband and her daughter would somehow see the truth and make their decisions to follow Christ before it was too late. The way she understood it, only one in four people alive at the time of the Rapture would survive the Tribulation. With odds like that against them, she prayed they would early turn to Christ. She wished them no danger or pain or death. She would gladly wait to reunite with them following Jesus' glorious appearing and the setting up of the millennial kingdom if it meant they didn't have to endure tragedy in the meantime.

The question looming in Irene's mind was whether it was possible to maintain this delicious, overwhelming feeling she could barely describe. She felt full of God, full of light, full of His righteousness and perfection. How she had felt when she made her husband or kids happy or when everything seemed to go right just began to hint at this sense of well-being. In her old life, Irene would have been able to maintain such an emotional high for only so long. Now it seemed it would never fade, and something told her that she had the capacity to more than endure it but to also luxuriate in it.

From what seemed miles behind the throne came a tiny beam of light that grew slowly as it drew nearer. Soon Irene could make out that this was another band of angels, thousands of them. And they were singing. Rich basses and clear tenors combined for the most magnificent sound she had ever heard.

How she had always loved music! And how bad she had always been at it. Though she was not tone-deaf — she always knew when the right notes were being played and sung, and she could detect the clunkers — Irene had never been able to carry a tune. For years that had been her little secret. She enjoyed singing nonetheless, but she had learned to keep her voice down, because there was no hiding her monotone, and it had surprised even Rayford and the kids.

She had joked to Jackie that one thing she looked forward to in heaven was being able to sing. As the angel choir drew nearer and their magnificent voices filled the place, the redeemed saints began to join in singing praises to God.

Suddenly Jackie and Dooley appeared next to Irene, and Jackie said, "This is your moment. Let's hear it. Let it go!"

Irene did not even have to listen to learn the simple song. It was as if the words and the melody had been written on her heart. The great multitude, led by the angel choir, blended beautiful voices, drawing Irene to her feet and causing her to raise her chin. And with a dramatic, crystal-clear soprano she had never heard — and certainly never produced — she raised her hands high and joined the triumphant, majestic multitude, singing, "Alleluia! Salvation and glory and honor and power belong to the Lord our God! For true and righteous are His judgments, because He has judged the great harlot who corrupted the earth with her fornication; and He has avenged on her the blood of His servants shed by her.

"Alleluia! Her smoke rises up forever and ever!"

And the twenty-four elders and the four living creatures fell and worshiped God. "Amen! Alleluia!"

Then a voice came from the throne, saying, "Praise our God, all you His servants and those who fear Him, both small and great!"

In unison, the voices of the vast host, sounding like rushing water and mighty thunder, proclaimed, "Alleluia! For the Lord God Omnipotent reigns! For the Father judges no one, but has committed all judgment to the Son, that all should honor the Son just as they honor the Father."

The music stopped as quickly as it had begun, and a holy hush fell over the place.

Irene was feeling the crackle of anticipation but not knowing what they were waiting for.

With the four creatures hovering quietly behind Him; the countless angels, heads bowed, crowded around for what seemed like miles; and the twenty-four elders on their faces before Him, Jesus stood. Despite royal robes, the magnificent throne, the galactic beauty of the house of God, and the encompassing host of worshipers, there was not even a hint of pride in Jesus' bearing. He merely regarded the crowd.

And again, Irene felt as if His look was for her alone. How He could single out each of the hundreds and hundreds of millions, she would never know. She wanted to cheer, to clap, to shout, to sing, to fall prostrate, yet that thrum of expectancy, that heightened edge, had caused not only all sound but also any movement among the masses to cease.

When the great gathering place and all those souls were finally dead silent and motionless, the booming voice of God shook the place: "This is My beloved Son, in whom I am well pleased. Henceforth He shall be known to all as KING OF KINGS AND LORD OF LORDS. I have highly exalted Him and given Him the name which is above every name, that at the name of Jesus every knee should bow, of those in heaven, and of those on earth, and of those under the earth, and that every tongue should confess that Jesus Christ is Lord, to the glory of God the Father."

As Jesus again sat on the throne, Irene instinctively reached toward Him and saw that everyone else was doing the same. Then the chant started, picked up by all: "King of kings and Lord of lords. King of kings and Lord of lords. King of kings and Lord of lords . . ."

Again silence washed over the multitudes, and one of the twenty-four elders slowly rose and stood before the throne. Irene saw him as if standing next to him, a plain, earnest-looking man, quivering with emotion. She knew without being told that he was the apostle Peter.

He said, in a voice so soft that Irene knew only God could make it resonate so clearly in the ears of so many, "Blessed be the God and Father of our Lord Jesus Christ, who according to His abundant mercy has begotten us again to a living hope through the resurrection of Jesus Christ from the dead, to an inheritance incorruptible and undefiled and that does not fade away, bestowed here now for you, who were kept by the power of God through faith for salvation to be revealed in the last time.

"In this you greatly rejoice, for you were grieved by various trials, that the genuineness of your faith, being much more precious than gold that perishes, though tested by fire, may be found to praise, honor, and glory in the presence of Jesus Christ, whom having not seen you loved. Now you see Him, and you rejoice with joy inexpressible and full of glory, receiving the end of your faith — the salvation of your souls.

"Everyone here shall receive praise for receiving the gift of salvation through God's Son, Jesus the Christ. Those who have served Christ will be honored, for as the Son Himself has proclaimed, 'If anyone serves Me, let him follow Me; and where I am, there My servant will be also. If anyone serves Me, him My Father will honor.'

"And those who have suffered for the sake of Christ and the gospel will be glorified. So, beloved, do not think it strange concerning the fiery trial which tried you, as though some strange thing happened to you; but rejoice to the extent that you partook of Christ's sufferings, so that now that His glory has been revealed, you may also be glad with exceeding joy. If you were reproached for the name of Christ, blessed are you, for the Spirit of glory and of God rests upon you and through you He is glorified.

"The time has come for judgment to begin here at the house of God. Therefore let those who suffered according to the will of God and yet committed their souls to Him in doing good, as to a faithful Creator, be commended by Him whom they served." Peter returned to his place and prostrated himself before the throne.

Next the voice of God began to praise all believers for their faith. Again, though Irene had been taught that this would take place and had felt this attention and honor since the moment of her arrival, it struck her as bizarre even as it warmed her beyond measure.

She knew that if God gave every redeemed saint even ten seconds of praise, it would take thousands of Earth years. So when Irene was addressed by Him personally, she knew that everyone else was getting their commendation at the same time.

"Irene," He spoke audibly to her heart, "I have loved you with an everlasting love. You believed in My Son and followed Him, despite opposition within your own family. Though you have belonged to Me only a short time, you have been faithful in studying My Word, in teaching it to children, in leading your in-laws and your own son to Christ. From the time of your salvation, your concern has been not for yourself, but for others. I love you and welcome you home. Well done, good and faithful servant."

The words of God from His own mouth humbled Irene so much that she could no longer stand. Enraptured as she was, all she could think of was her shortcomings, the times she had failed God and how puny her service had been in the short time she'd had to offer, especially compared to so many of those around her. Just this brief moment with her God gave Irene a whole new view of her temporal life and what a waste it now seemed in light of eternity. She had heard the quote "Only one life 'twill soon be past; only what's done for Christ will last," but how true and real it was to her now. What had all the rest of that busyness been about? It amounted to less than nothing in the cosmic scheme.

Irene had been praised for receiving Christ and honored for a bit of service: teaching Sunday school and leading three others to Him. But there was another category of blessing for which she knew she was not qualified. Yet it buoyed her to see others glorified for having suffered for the sake of Christ and the gospel.

Countless thousands were brought before

Jesus and honored for years and years of service in various capacities, and this was when Irene realized the truth of the adage that "the last will be first and the first last" in heaven. Irene looked forward to seeing and hearing about the exploits of all the heroes of the Bible and leaders of the church throughout history, but clearly they were at the other end of the godly schedule. For as God praised the saints, He began with the behind-the-scenes people, the lesser knowns, those unrecognized outside their own small orbits.

There was the woman from Indiana who had raised four sons in spite of an alcoholic husband who abused her. She had continued to pray for him, protect her sons, and work to provide for them all. While she had refused to be walked on and injured by this man, she treated him as a lost soul and not as an enemy, and God honored her for that example to her sons. Under her tutelage and Bible teaching, all four became excellent students, graduated from seminaries, and went into full-time Christian work. The adult Sunday school class she taught grew to more than seven hundred members.

Another honoree was a prodigious pianist who had taken the gift God had given him and devoted himself to ministry rather than exalt himself by pursuing what was guaranteed to be a lucrative career in the great concert halls. He taught piano in remote areas of the world and used his giftedness to spread the Word of God, eschewing personal glory and wealth.

On and on they paraded by the throne, receiving honor from the Lamb who had been slain for the sins of the world. As Jesus embraced them and spoke to them, Irene could hear and see it all as if she were in the front row. And it was as if time stood still. She felt no passage of minutes or hours, experienced no fatigue or restlessness or impatience. If this went on for the rest of eternity, it would have been fine with her. She was exposed to heroes of the faith she had never even heard of, and they proved to be quiet, unassuming giants.

Through sheer force of his own will and personality, Abdullah Smith had wrestled his decimated life back to some semblance of normalcy. For many, many months he laid low at the Amman air base, not making it obvious that he still lived there, though he had been divorced for so long. His ex-wife, Yasmine, still lived in their modest home with their son and daughter, and Abdullah had cleaned himself up enough that she allowed brief visits every couple of weeks or so.

He had quit drinking, quit chasing women, quit being slothful, and returned to his old disciplined ways with the Royal Jordanian Air Force. Abdullah was always the first one up and on the job in a crisp, shining uniform. He regained his sense of class and purpose and style, but, sad to say, his old personality seemed lost forever.

He had always been a man of few words while bearing the ability to be quick-witted and pleasant. Now his professionalism and leadership in the cockpit had returned, but he was largely a sullen, silent man. *Wounded* was how he would have put it. With the loss of his wife and children, he was devastated.

And it was obvious that this was not going to change. He and Yasmine still traded letters occasionally, but it was nearly impossible for him to remain civil in his, always moving from desperate lovelorn pleas to get back together to rants and raves about her infidelity to Islam and her treachery in "stealing" his own children. Yet it was Abdullah who was not devout in his faith, and it had been he who initiated the divorce. That made everything worse; he had no one to blame but himself. Yes, she had turned her back on her religion, but he had intended to make her pay. He was the one, however, who was now suffering.

Abdullah had, as usual, been up since the crack of dawn on the fateful day that changed the world. He had already eaten and begun his round of preflight training chores when the warning sirens sounded and military personnel were rallied from all over the base. He'd seen enough similar drills, so he never even asked what was going on. He just assumed it was a routine test and that he would be expected to muster next to his fighter plane until the thing was called off.

Instead, he and several colleagues were marshaled to take off and defend the skies of Jordan. Against who or what, no one could or would say. But as Abdullah's fighter screamed into the air over Amman, his view of the carnage on the ground horrified him. What could have caused this on such a beautiful, sunny, cloudless day?

He stared at hopeless rush-hour traffic jams — nothing new except for the number of smoking and burning accidents and the fact that nothing was moving. Helicopters were the only craft able to get on and off the main roads, carting the most seriously injured to overtaxed hospitals.

"What in the world has happened?" Abdullah cried into his radio.

But his dispatcher was so harried that he merely responded, "Find the news on the radio. Everyone's carrying it."

Abdullah had always been one who knew the difference between his dreams and reality. He had never had to pinch himself to determine whether he was awake. For the first time ever, he was not so sure. To hear the frantic reports of the disappearances of people in Jordan, the rest of the Middle East, Europe, Asia, even his beloved America, was almost too much to take in. People had disappeared, disintegrated, dematerialized — whatever one could call it — right out of their clothes, regardless of where they were or what they were doing.

Pots boiled over and started fires that were burning homes and apartment buildings. Driverless cars careened into trucks, buses, other cars, bridges, and abutments, resulting in the mess Abdullah saw below. Doctors had disappeared during operations, instruments falling into body cavities, colleagues collapsing in horror.

A baby had disappeared while being born. A nurse's uniform had floated to the floor. An entire soccer team, save for one hysterical teammate, left their uniforms, shoes, and socks on the field as the ball trickled out-of-bounds. Stories like this poured in from all around the world.

Something niggled at the back of Abdullah's brain, but it didn't hit him full force until panicky commentators — usually so all knowing and aloof — began speculating on the various theories. Radiation. Spontaneous combustion that somehow eluded clothing and jewelry. An entirely new form of weaponry. Or the old religious saws: the end of the world. The Rapture.

Not many seriously considered that one, but it had to be raised because nobody had a better idea. And as it gathered steam, supporters and detractors called in with what they had heard and learned over the years from the few kooks who believed such things.

Abdullah shuddered. Yasmine had warned him of this. She had spelled it out plainly in one of the letters that had so enraged him. And he was certain it was one he had not destroyed.

He had wanted to shred and burn it, had meant to. He had balled it up and thrown it across the room because it also contained the step-by-step instructions for becoming a follower of Christ. But if memory served, this was one of the letters he had smoothed back out and put in his metal lockbox. Now he was desperate to check it again, because if she had been right and this was what he feared, she and the children were gone.

Twenty

Had Irene Steele been forced from her reverie — impossible, of course, in the very presence of God — and asked her most stark impression of heaven so far, she would have had to admit that most jarring was her new concept of time. On Earth she had been in an hourly, daily, weekly, monthly, yearly cycle sometimes carved into semesters or trimesters or even gestation periods. She was aware of interminable dark winter months, the elusive spring, and flashbulb summers she couldn't make linger.

But here . . . here it was so different. She simply could not put a clock on how long it had been since she had been awakened from a deep sleep and delivered to the portals of heaven. So much had happened that she could have been here an hour or a week or — who knew? — longer.

Yet it seemed like an instant. She had

been told that time would have no meaning in the light of eternity, and she had to chuckle to recall what she once thought that meant. Perhaps she would set up whatever kind of housekeeping one set up in glory, visit Jesus, talk to God, meet friends and biblical saints, see the sights, and then settle in, realizing she had a long, long time ahead of her.

She had not, however, expected time to simply have no bearing. Irene had zero sense of the passage of time, and only in those fleeting moments when she wondered what was going on on Earth did she think about what might have happened between the shout, the trumpet sound, and right now.

She could only imagine the chaos below. What Rayford and Chloe were thinking. Whether they were reunited. Were communication and travel impossible? How long would it take them to remember what she and Raymie had talked of, warned them about? In one sense, she thought, this should be easy for them. They had not believed, but now what could they think? Would it be obvious to anyone who had had exposure to believers that, as crazy as it had all sounded, clearly what their friends, loved ones, and acquaintances had predicted had come true?

Everything about this place, needless to say, constituted sensory overload, and Irene realized that her mind had to be as new as her glorified body. Otherwise, how could she manage to take it all in? Things like this happening on Earth would have either driven her mad or made her pass out from their sheer implausibility. This ability to move about at the speed of thought, to understand what was going on without being told, to communicate with people and, best of all, with God instantaneously, almost without a back and forth. She wondered and knew at the same time.

The "leaders" of this massive meeting did not step to a microphone and announce the program or introduce the participants. They spoke to the hearts and ears and minds of everyone all at once, and you simply knew. God had honored His Son, of course, and His voice was unmistakable, but it wasn't as if anyone assembled in the house of God wondered who sat on the throne.

Irene sat enthralled, unaware of the weight of her body on a chair, with no feeling of fatigue or ache or pain or that charming memory: time. Impatience was not an issue. Boredom she could never imagine again. Heartache and loss were strange, muted, overwhelmed in the presence of her Savior. She was still concerned about her family, but something — actually Someone — had embedded into her new mind and body a deep sense of contentment and peace that told her she had no part in that which was to come as it related to Rayford and Chloe. Still she prayed for them and somehow believed without question that God knew best and that His will would be done.

Seemingly from nowhere, a translucent podium appeared some thirty feet to the left of the throne, emitting from its center a piercing flame so white and bright that all Irene could compare it to was the flash of burning magnesium from a high school experiment. That had required that students wear welding masks to protect their eyes, but she was able to gaze at this great light without danger and sense its powerful, incomparable heat. Something told her that in her mortal body she would not have been able to stand within twenty feet of it.

The apostle Paul left his place before the throne and humbly addressed the masses: "We were God's fellow workers; we were God's field, we were God's building. According to the grace of God which was given to me, as a wise master builder I laid the foundation, and another builds on it. But each was to take heed how he built on it. For no other foundation could anyone lay than that which was laid, which is Jesus Christ. Now if anyone built on this foundation with gold, silver, precious stones, wood, hay, or straw, now one's work will become clear; now it shall be declared, because it will be revealed by fire; and the fire will test each one's work, of what sort it is. If your work built on the sure foundation endures, you will receive a reward. If your work is burned, you will suffer loss; but you yourself will be saved, yet so as through fire."

So this was what Pastor Billings had been teaching about recently. While salvation was free and granted by grace through faith, still the works of the righteous would be tested. God looked at sinful people through His perfect Son and saw only His perfection, so their salvation was secure, regardless of how their individual works were judged. But their rewards, their various crowns for service to Christ, would be determined by whether the fire exposed precious gems and metals or resulted in ash from the wood, hay, or stubble of bad works or even good deeds done with bad motives.

Irene knew she had precious little that could even be tested and only wished she had had more time, more knowledge, less selfishness, so that she could present many good deeds for the test. She was grateful that the destiny of her eternal soul did not rest on the work she had or hadn't done, but in her gratitude for that gift, she wished she could somehow have done more to make obvious her devotion and thanks to God.

Would she be embarrassed? She couldn't imagine that, not here, not in the presence of God. Certainly she would bear shame and regret for wasted time, and she would have to rest and glory in the fact that her soul was saved no matter what. But surely the God who loved her would not expose her to ridicule in front of all the believers from time immemorial.

Irene could only hope that she would be dealt with with some dispatch so that regardless of how she fared she would be able to enjoy seeing crowns bestowed upon the heroes of the faith she had known and read about.

As soon as Abdullah had completed his first run and reported what he could, he took advantage of a break and landed back at the base. He hurried to his quarters, unlocked his metal box, and tore through the letters from Yasmine, finally finding the wrinkled, faded one that spoke of this very eventuality.

Abdullah, I believe — and I am certain you agree — that God hates divorce. It was not my intention that my new faith would result in the end of our marriage. This was your choice, but I concede that staying with you and allowing you influence over our children would have also been untenable as long as you feel the way you do about me now.

I know this letter will anger you, and neither is that my intention. We have talked and talked about the differences between Islam and Christianity, but please indulge me and allow me to get my thoughts down in order. Hopefully God will help me make them clear.

I do not expect that you will suddenly see the truth because of my words, but I pray that God will open your heart and will one day reveal Himself to you. As I have said over and over, the difference between what you call "our religions" is that mine is not religion. I have come to believe that religion is man's effort to please God. I had always been bound by rules, acts of service, good deeds. I was trying as hard as I could to win the favor of Allah so that in the end I would find heaven on Earth.

But I could never be good enough,

Abdullah, and as wonderful as you were for many years, you couldn't either. That became clear with your unreasonable reaction to my coming to faith in the one true God and Father of Jesus Christ. To you it was anathema, despite the fact that, like me, you had drifted even from the tenets of Islam.

I believe that to you, my converting was a public humiliation. I regret that, but I could no more hide my true feelings and beliefs than I could ask you to give up flying.

Just once more, let me clarify: Christians believe the Bible teaches that everyone is born in sin and that the penalty for sin is death. But Jesus paid the price by living a sinless life and dying as a sacrifice for all who believe. Abdullah, you must admit that you have never met a perfect person, and we each know the other is not perfect. We are sinners in need of salvation. We can't save ourselves, can't change ourselves. I am most encouraged by your discipline and your efforts. You are now more like the man I married, but don't you see? You will never be good enough to qualify for heaven, because you would have to be entirely perfect.

Someday, when you are ready — and I hope it will not be too late — just pray and tell God that you know that you are a sinner, that you are sorry and want to repent and be forgiven. Ask Him to take over your life. The day is coming, prophesied in Scripture, when Jesus will return in the clouds and snatch away all true believers in an instant. No one will see this happen except for those to whom it happens. Those left behind will simply realize that it is all true. Christians from all over the world will disappear. I hope it does not take a tragedy like that — though it will be anything but tragic for those of us who go — to get you to swallow your pride, examine yourself, and humble yourself before God. Of course, if this does happen before you come to true faith, you will know what has occurred. And you will be without excuse. I just pray that you do not lose your life in the resulting chaos before you can become a believer, not in a religion but in a person. Jesus the Christ.

With fond memories and deep affection, praying for you,

Yasmine

Was it possible? Could she and the children be gone? If they were, she had been right. Abdullah could not control his shuddering body. He had to know. He had to get there.

He dashed outside and found a lone helicopter sitting on the tarmac. It's pilot, Khalid, stood next to it. *"Ya Sidi,"* Abdullah said, "Might you have time to run me to my home? I must check on my family."

"Of course, *Ya Bek*. I have just refueled."

On the way, Abdullah asked Khalid what he had heard from his own family.

"They are safe, praise Allah. But of course they are terrified, as we all are. No one can imagine what has happened."

Twenty minutes later the chopper kicked up a cloud of sand as Khalid put down in the narrow, steeply inclined space between Abdullah's former home and the house behind it. Abdullah was immediately struck by the absence of children. His was a neighborhood full of families mostly larger than his, and by this time of the morning it was usually teeming with activity, children of all ages running around. Now all he saw were wailing adults and a few teenagers, wandering, horror etched on their faces.

"Would you like me to go in with you, *Ya Bek?*"

"No, thank you, friend. I'll be right back."

As soon as Abdullah entered the back door, he was overcome by the odor of burned food. He rushed to the tiny kitchen to find a pan over an open flame, the residue of falafel and hummus blackened and smoking. Abdullah grabbed a towel and slung the red-hot pan into the sink, quickly turning off the gas. Only then did he realize he was standing on something.

Yasmine's *thiyab* was underfoot, and as Abdullah stepped back, he realized her undergarments and slippers were there too. In all their years together he had never known her to leave her clothes on the floor, even in the bedroom. Clearly she had been standing here. Yasmine had long made a practice of rising before the family and waking them with the smell of breakfast cooking.

He moved to the tiny bedroom the children shared. There, on their mats, lay their nightclothes. Abdullah's mind tried to play tricks on him, to tell him this was a mistake, that his family was elsewhere, that there was some explanation for the appearance that they had disappeared right out of their clothes.

But he knew the truth. In a stupor, his hands shaking, Abdullah grabbed the children's clothes, picked up Yasmine's outer

269

garments, and walked stiff legged back to the copter.

As he climbed in, Khalid said, "What, *Ya Bek?* Are they all right?"

Abdullah could not speak. He shook his head.

"Gone?"

Abdullah nodded, lips quivering.

"You want to go back to the base?"

He nodded again, and yielding to emotion so overpowering that he was incapable of keeping himself from doing something he had never before done in front of another man, Abdullah buried his face in the clothes of his beloved family and wept.

Again Irene was fascinated that she merely knew what was going on without anyone saying so. Somehow God revealed to her — and, of course, to everyone else at the same time — that it was time for the next phase of the *bema* or the judgment seat of Christ. Works were to be tested by fire to see what remained and what ignited like kindling, and then the judged would receive from Jesus at least praise for trusting Him for salvation but ideally one or more of four separate crowns.

The Crown of Life would be awarded to those who had remained faithful through trials, some even to the point of martyrdom. Irene was reminded of the admonition in the book of James: "My brethren, count it all joy when you fall into various trials, knowing that the testing of your faith produces patience. . . . Blessed is the man who endures temptation; for when he has been approved, he will receive the crown of life which the Lord has promised to those who love Him."

Pastor Billings had recently taught on the statement of Jesus Himself from John's Revelation: "Do not fear any of those things which you are about to suffer. Indeed, the devil is about to throw some of you into prison, that you may be tested, and you will have tribulation ten days. Be faithful until death, and I will give you the crown of life. . . . Behold, I am coming quickly! Hold fast what you have, that no one may take your crown. He who overcomes, I will make him a pillar in the temple of My God, and he shall go out no more. I will write on him the name of My God and the name of the city of My God, the New Jerusalem, which comes down out of heaven from My God. And I will write on him My new name."

The Crown of Righteousness was reserved for those who had eagerly awaited the Lord's return. Irene had long admired this in the apostle Paul, who, when standing in the courts of Rome, had been more concerned about the court of heaven.

> For I am already being poured out as a drink offering, and the time of my departure is at hand. I have fought the good fight, I have finished the race, I have kept the faith. Finally, there is laid up for me the crown of righteousness, which the Lord, the righteous Judge, will give to me on that Day, and not to me only but also to all who have loved His appearing.

The Crown of Glory was promised to those who had shepherded God's flock with pure motives. Irene enjoyed hearing Pastor Billings talk about the heavy weight of stewardship and accountability he felt to serve willingly rather than out of some compulsion. He often cited 1 Peter in relation to his calling:

> Shepherd the flock of God which is among you, serving as overseers, not by compulsion but willingly, not for dishonest gain but eagerly; nor as being lords over those entrusted to you, but being examples to the flock; and when the Chief Shepherd appears, you will re-

ceive the crown of glory that does not fade away.

The Crown of Rejoicing would go to the soul winner. Paul had written to the Thessalonians:

For what is our hope, or joy, or crown of rejoicing? Is it not even you in the presence of our Lord Jesus Christ at His coming? For you are our glory and joy.

To the Philippians he had written:

Therefore, my beloved and longed-for brethren, my joy and crown, so stand fast in the Lord, beloved.

In John 4, Jesus taught that those who shared His passion for the lost and were active in evangelism were gathering fruit for eternal life. "Behold, I say to you, lift up your eyes and look at the fields, for they are already white for harvest! And he who reaps receives wages, and gathers fruit for eternal life, that both he who sows and he who reaps may rejoice together. For in this the saying is true: 'One sows and another reaps.'"

Khalid carefully set the chopper down on

the tarmac at the Amman air base and asked Abdullah if there was anything he could do for him.

Abdullah shook his head, his jaw set and his lips pressed together. Still tears escaped him. "Thank you, my friend," he managed hoarsely.

The walk to his quarters, fewer than a hundred steps, seemed the longest of his life. He dropped his family's clothes onto his cot and knelt next to them. "Dear God," he sobbed, "does it matter that I am coming to You out of fear and remorse? I believe You exist because of what has happened. I don't know about this matter of being a sinner, but I know I am not perfect, not even close. Please, if I am to believe in Jesus, make it plain to me. I know I do not measure up to You, a God so mighty and powerful that He can make people disappear. It seems to me I have no choice, and so I need to know whether my motive is pure enough."

Suddenly Abdullah realized that he was not facing east, not praying toward Mecca, not addressing Allah but rather the God of his wife, the God who had clearly made hundreds of millions vanish from around the globe. And yet the Jordanian man somehow knew, was touched deep within his heart and soul, that this God was hearing him. With everything else that had to be on His mind, with the unnumbered prayers that must be rising to Him right now, He was listening; He was communicating.

Abdullah felt loved. Now here was a God worthy of fear, worthy of praise, worthy of devotion. No longer was he undecided about his status as a sinner. He slid from the pile of his family's clothes on his cot until he was prostrate on the floor. Somehow the weight of his imperfection bore down on him in the presence of the one true God.

Abdullah began to weep anew. "I am unworthy, God. I see myself for who I am. Selfish. Prideful. Lustful. Angry. Unloving. Mean-spirited. Can You forgive me?"

It was as if God was speaking directly to his heart. Abdullah was reminded of everything Yasmine had said and written. Everyone was born in sin. There was "none righteous, no, not one." And even though some people seemed better and nicer and less selfish than others, all were hopelessly lost in their sin. They fell short of God's perfection and needed Christ's sacrificial death on the cross as payment for their sins. And how was it that one appropriated that for his own life? He was merely to believe and receive it?

"I believe and receive!" Abdullah cried out. "Forgive me and save me from my sins. Make me one of Your own children!"

As he lay there sobbing, Abdullah was overwhelmed by a sense of peace. The loss of his family was biting and bitter and deep, and he knew on some level that he could lay such a tragedy on the very One to whom he was now pledging himself. But Abdullah also understood that this act of God had a purpose. It had been prophesied. Yasmine had told him that God might someday intrude so dramatically into human affairs that no one would be able to doubt His existence.

Abdullah stood shakily and sat on the cot, running his fingers over the clothes of his loved ones. Tears dropped from his chin to his lap. He had no idea where to go or what to do next, but he felt like a different man. What would his new God want of him? He was desperate to find someone who understood, but would they not all be gone?

In the meantime, he would serve God the only way he knew how. Abdullah would be the best servant, the best military man, the best pilot, the most giving person he could be. He would find a Bible; Yasmine had one at home. He would study it, look for books that might help explain it. And he would pray that perhaps God would bring into his life others who were only now realizing that they had missed the truth. Surely there would be others on this vast planet who found themselves in the same spiritual place as he.

Twenty-One

Everything in God's house stopped. Irene had not even considered that billions of people, all in one place, were capable of producing no sound. But the stillness pervaded, and she could imagine no greater feeling of anticipation. Anytime anything here changed, something important was about to happen. She scanned the great hall, watching to see if Jesus would stand, listening for God to speak, looking to see if one of the twenty-four elders would step forward.

But no, just several seconds of silence. And then, suddenly, a crashing burst of music from the thousands upon thousands of angels behind the throne and attending the gates. In a sustained, harmonic eruption, on perfect cue they sang just one word:

"HALLELUJAH!"

Slowly, throughout the house of God, people began applauding, cheering, and murmuring. This was how the angels rejoiced when someone on Earth received Christ. Such outbursts began to come more and more frequently as the fire and Bema judgments continued. Sometimes three or four hallelujahs would be sung at once, then, after a moment, ten or twelve more.

The longer Irene was there, the more celebrations of conversions surged from the angels, and the saints applauded and cheered. Would this ever get old? Irene could not imagine.

Every so often, newcomers would join the throng, clearly those who had just died, some having been believers for only hours. Irene prayed that some of the rejoicing was for Rayford and Chloe and that they would reunite with her seven Earth years later at the establishment of the millennial kingdom.

Irene's new heart was warmed by insight. As she sat thrilling to the fire test and the awarding of crowns to believers from every tongue and tribe and nation, she realized that she had lost her fear of shame. Irene was no longer worried about being humiliated in front of others because of her sin. What God seemed to be implanting in her mind and, she knew, in the minds of everyone else too, was that this was not a sin judgment.

Her sins, as well as the sins of all the other saints, had been dealt with long ago on the cross. They had already been removed as far as the east is from the west, so there were no sins to be tested in the fire. What, then, would be considered dross and burn away to leave only the precious metals and stones? Irene knew, as if Pastor Billings or even God had been sitting next to her, advising her.

Her work for the Kingdom would go into the fire along with everything else she had done — apart from her sin — and the wasted time, the frivolous things, the activities not devoted to eternity, would be burned away. The time she spent nurturing and serving her family would surely survive. Her church attendance and Bible reading, personal devotions, acts of service, recreation to refresh herself for more of the same, exercise to keep herself fit for service — all those would survive the fire and be burnished to a beautiful glow.

But what of the times she had not been educating or inspiring herself? What of the time she simply wasted on trivial matters, on things of interest but not of value? Irene was reminded of time frittered away on things that had little meaning beyond diversion. There were movies and TV shows that quickly proved other than educational or even uplifting, which she could have turned off in order to make better use of her time. Books that proved titillating but pointless. Shopping sprees merely to make herself feel better, short of anything she really needed.

Irene did not get the impression that she had been expected to fill every waking moment with acts of service. But clearly it was true that only what was done for Christ would last. Much of her life had been filled with stuff . . . not wrong, not sin, just waste.

One of the most delightful parts of the Bema Judgment, to Irene, was how Jesus handled the people who had been nearly anonymous on Earth. People who worked with their hands were lauded if they had performed their tasks as unto the Lord, rather than unto men. They may have been engaged in work as routine as auto mechanics or carpentry or shipping. But if they had dedicated themselves to Christ and worked to honor Him — especially when coworkers slacked or management was dishonest or others cut corners — Jesus had high praise for them. They were rewarded on par with those who had dedicated themselves to full-time Christian work in which their income was garnered from ministry. In fact, some of the latter found that more of their works were burned to waste than survived, due to poor motives or laziness.

Musicians — singers, composers, and instrumentalists — were surprised to hear the heavenly choir break into their songs. But Irene's favorite musical moment was when the famed blind gospel hymn writer Fanny Crosby, who had penned some nine thousand songs before her death in 1915, came leaping with joy at her ability to see.

Her works were tested in the fire, and all that was left were precious metals and gemstones. From the silver and gold Jesus fashioned a beautiful, simple crown, embedded with the gems that had been forged in the fire, and presented to her the Crown of Life for living through her trial of blindness and glorifying Him nonetheless. He also gave her the Crown of Righteousness for clearly loving the hope of His appearing, as well as the Crown of Rejoicing for the fact that her work brought so many souls into the Kingdom.

Jesus said, "Well done, good and faithful servant. Would you sing for me?"

Mrs. Crosby knelt and covered her mouth with both hands, but the heavenly host cheered and she began, backed by an eternal chorus nonpareil.

From "Pass Me Not, O Gentle Savior" she sang lyrics she adapted on the spot:

Finally at Thy throne of mercy
I find sweet relief,
Kneeling here in deep contrition;
No more unbelief.

Jesus stood and stepped from the throne, standing beside Mrs. Crosby as she continued to sing from another of her most famous hymns:

When my life work is ended, and I cross the swelling tide,

When the bright and glorious morning I
    shall see;
I shall know my Redeemer when I reach
    the other side,
And His smile will be the first to wel-
    come me.
Oh, the dear ones in glory, how they
    beckon me to come,
And our parting at the river I recall;
To the sweet vales of Eden they will sing
    my welcome home;
But I long to meet my Savior first of
    all.
Through the gates to the city in a robe
    of spotless white,
He will lead me where no tears will ever
    fall;

In the glad song of ages I shall mingle
   with delight;
But I long to meet my Savior first of all.

And with that, the entire heavenly host, including Irene and all the redeemed saints, stood to sing:

I shall know Him, I shall know Him,
And redeemed by His side I shall stand,
I shall know Him, I shall know Him,
By the print of the nails in His hand.

Rayford Steele's mind was on a woman he had never touched. With his fully loaded 747 on autopilot above the Atlantic en route to a landing at Heathrow, Rayford had pushed from his mind thoughts of his family. Over spring break he would spend time with Irene and Raymie. Chloe would be home from Stanford too. But for now, with First Officer Chris Smith breaking the rules by dozing, Rayford imagined Hattie's smile and looked forward to their next meeting. He hadn't seen her in more than an hour.

Rayford used to look forward to getting home to Irene. She was attractive and vivacious enough, even at forty. But lately he had been repelled by her obsession with religion. It was all she could talk about. Rayford tried to tell himself it was her devotion to a divine suitor that caused his mind to wander. But he knew the real reason was his own libido.

Besides, Hattie Durham was drop-dead gorgeous. No one could argue that.

Maybe today. Maybe this morning, if her coded tap on the cockpit door didn't rouse Chris, he would reach and cover the hand on his shoulder — in a friendly way he knew she would recognize as a step, the first from his side, toward a relationship.

In a couple of hours Rayford would be the first to see hints of the sun, a teasing palette of pastels that would signal the reluctant dawn over the continent. Until then, the stars this far above the clouds shone brightly through the window. His groggy or sleeping passengers had window shades down, pillows and blankets in place. For now the plane was a dark, humming sleep chamber for all but a few wanderers — the attendants and one or two responders to nature's call.

The question of the darkest hour before dawn, then, was whether Rayford Steele should risk a new, exciting relationship with Hattie Durham. He suppressed a smile. Was he kidding himself? Would someone with his reputation ever do anything but dream about a beautiful woman fifteen years his junior? He wasn't so sure anymore. If only Irene hadn't gone off on this new kick.

Would it fade, her preoccupation with the end of the world, with the love of Jesus, with the salvation of souls? Irene had become a full-fledged religious fanatic, and that somehow freed Rayford to daydream without guilt about Hattie. Maybe he would say something, suggest something, hint at something as he and Hattie strode through Heathrow toward the cab line. Maybe earlier. Dare he assert himself even now, hours before touchdown?

Twenty-Two

Rayford Steele Jr. sat in the house of God with a friend, Jeremy Phillips, he had known from his sixth-grade class in Mt. Prospect, Illinois.

"Calling you Raymie seems strange now," Jeremy said, his shock of dark hair reminding Raymie of the boy he had known.

"I know. And you look so much like your dad. Is he here?"

"Of course!" Jeremy said. "Dad?"

Instantly Jeremy's parents were at his side, smiling. "Raymie!" Mr. Phillips said, and his wife embraced Raymie.

"You look younger!" Raymie said.

"You look older," Mr. Phillips said.

"The strangest thing is that I *feel* older."

"Me too," Jeremy said. "It's as if I understand stuff now I never even thought about before."

"So did you even know Raymie was a believer?" Mrs. Phillips said.

Jeremy shook his head. "We've been talking about that. I guess neither of us was too bold in our faith. I mean, I knew Raymie was a good kid, never got into trouble, didn't swear — that kind of thing. But I never put two and two together."

Raymie was laughing.

"What's funny?" Jeremy said.

"Just that I never knew you were a Christian either, but you weren't always such a good kid."

"Yeah, I got in my share of trouble. And I didn't always use the best language, did I?"

"That was my fault," his father said. "I didn't become a Christian until Jane here did, so there was a lot of garbage in my life that it took the Lord a few years to clean out. How about your folks, Raymie? They here?"

"Mom is. Pray for my dad, will you?"

"We'll put him on our list," Jane Phillips said. "There are a lot of people on it, but I have a hunch they will figure this out pretty quickly. They can't say we didn't warn them. In fact, I fear we turned a few people off, always talking about this very day."

"Has it only been a day?" Jeremy said. "It seems like we've been here a month already."

"I have a feeling," his dad said, "that it hasn't been more than a few minutes."

The angel host burst forth with more hal-lelujahs.

"Maybe one of those was for your dad, Raymie," Mr. Phillips said.

"I can only hope. Put my sister on your list too, please."

Irene felt she had almost gotten used to her glorified body. To not worry about aches and pains and strain and fatigue was too good to be true. But she decided it was un-likely she would never take her new mind for granted. As any mortal, she had often won-dered what it must be like to have the mind of God. To be able to know all and re-member all and know the future. That last didn't happen to come with her new equip-ment, but the idea of knowing and under-standing everything all at once — now there was a novelty.

Irene couldn't see Raymie, but she knew instinctively that he was within a quarter mile of her, and she even knew he was talking about her and Rayford and Chloe. *The Phillipses,* she thought. *How won-derful. Who knew?* Irene could transport herself directly into their presence, but that could wait. They had to be enjoying these festivities as much as she was.

What a parade of saints had already

passed by the throne, their works tested by the fire, their crowns produced from the treasured residue. Irene thrilled to every story of a behind-the-scenes saint, unknown outside their tiny church or town, who had represented Christ every day for decades. From every city and village on every inhabited continent they came, people of all colors and tongues. From a woman in the bowels of India who had spent her own meager income on materials to teach the Bible in her squalid neighborhood, despite opposition from her government and people of other religions — to the man who had sold his lucrative businesses in Australia to move into the outback and spend his life reaching Aborigines for Christ.

Irene couldn't get enough of this. She had expected, of course, to see preachers and pastors and evangelists getting their rewards, but she had not considered that most of these would be men and women from places she had never heard of. Many had lived on pennies, wearing at most two sets of clothes, opposed by the enemies of God, often persecuted by the state, and yet persevering in spite of it all.

An invalid woman was praised by Jesus for making her sickbed an altar of prayer for more than fifty years, daily petitioning God for countless ministries and missionaries. Now she jumped and ran and skipped before the throne, whole, young, vibrant, and the recipient of the crowns of Righteousness, Life, and Rejoicing.

Next to a window in first class on a 747 bound for London, Buck Williams sat hunched over his laptop, executing the slow blink of the sleep deprived. He had intended to do so much, to get himself newly organized, but he felt unconsciousness invading. And it was such a warm, inviting wave that he knew he would be unable to resist it for long.

The elderly couple in front of him — he could see only the woman's head now — and the overweight, heavily lubricated businessman next to him were already sound asleep. Buck would be next, but he wanted to keep the computer screen from swimming before his eyes for another minute or so.

No luck. He roused with a start to realize he had keyed gibberish onto his calendar. And then he was out again.

Irene estimated that she had witnessed the judgment of more than two thousand saints so far. Only about 19,999,998,000 to go. Still getting used to her new abilities, she debated whether to bother God with her question, but as soon as she allowed the thought, He spoke to her heart.

"Just ask."

"Well," she said, "You see, I know time is different here, and —"

"In fact, nonexistent," He said.

"Yes, right. But just out of curiosity, how long have we been here?"

"In earth time?" A heavenly chuckle. "Approximately four minutes."

"See, now, Amy, this is our problem. Here it is, nine o' clock on a weeknight, and here we sit."

"We've been through this," Amy said as Chloe closed her books. "You're going for best student in history, and that doesn't allow for much of a social life."

"But how about you? Do something! Go somewhere!"

"Yeah, I should call one of my dozen boyfriends, all of whom own Porsches, of course, and see which wants to take me on a pizza run."

"Pizza!" Chloe said. "That sounds fantastic. Who has a car?"

"You done studying?"

"I'm out of gas," Chloe said. "I could read

some more, but I need fuel. Pizza would be just the thing."

"Let's order delivery."

"Nah. I need to get out of here awhile. Don't you?"

Amy nodded. "But we still need wheels. You want to borrow someone's car?"

"Whose?"

"Well, Phoebe's, but you don't like her."

"It isn't that I don't like her, Amy. I hardly know her. She just reminds me too much of my mother; that's all."

"She is a little old for her age, isn't she? But on the other hand, she does have a car. And what are you saying about your mom? She's so sweet."

"I know, but she and Phoebe only want to talk about God. God this and God that and 'you should really come with me to Campus Crusade sometime.' "

"I know," Amy said. "And don't you think it's a little disingenuous that they never use the full name of that club?"

"Campus Crusade for Christ?" Chloe said. "Sometimes they do."

"Yeah, but too often they don't. It's like getting invited to a party and finding out it's one of those multilevel marketing things."

"Ah, I guess they mean well. So, call Phoebe."

"You know her better, Chloe."

"I do not! She just thinks I'm a better candidate for Campus Crusade than you are. How does that make you feel?"

"Hopeless . . . or maybe she thinks I'm already in."

They both laughed. Chloe said, "You know she's going to want to go. She'll offer to drive."

"Don't tell her where we're going. Just tell her it's an errand. C'mon. Call her."

Chloe grabbed the phone and called the floor below them.

Phoebe's roommate answered. "Just missed her, Chlo'. She was running out to get us something to eat."

"That's what we wanted. How long ago did she leave?"

"I don't know. Five minutes maybe? Call her cell."

Chloe tried but got Phoebe's voice mail. She moved to the window and saw Phoebe's car still in the lot. "Maybe she's got her phone off, Amy. Let's see if we can catch her."

The girls pulled on jackets and headed for the elevator. "This'll take too long," Amy said. "The stairs!"

They raced down the steps and burst out the door, and in the dim light from the lampposts in the parking lot they saw shoes, socks, jeans, a sweater, and undergarments between them and the car. Also in the grass, next to the concrete walkway, lay a purse and a cell phone.

"What is this?" Amy said, kneeling and reaching for the phone.

"Wait!" Chloe said. "Don't touch it! Maybe she was attacked. I'm calling the police."

"I'll call her roommate."

Chloe got a busy signal, even from 911. She dialed campus security. Same thing.

Soon Phoebe's roommate appeared in pajamas and slippers. "This *is* her stuff," she said, ashen faced. "Call somebody."

Chloe told her she had tried, and the girl, shaking, whispered, "I don't want to scare you any more, but on my way down here, I heard screaming on every floor."

"Stay here, Amy," Chloe said, dashing back inside. She found students everywhere, shaking, crying, running, trying to call for help. In her building alone, more than ten students had disappeared right out of their clothes, most in front of their friends or roommates.

Chloe, a knot forming deep within, dialed her father's cell phone, wondering what time it would be where he was. She got the message that the system was overloaded and that she should try later.

A girl grabbed Chloe from behind, hanging on as if she were drowning. "What's going on?" she wailed.

"I don't know!" Chloe said.

"Have you heard? Lots of students' kids are gone. Some say all of them. And a couple of professors." The girl ran off.

Chloe tried her home number. "Mom? Dad? Are you there? Have you seen what's going on? Call me as soon as you can. We've lost at least ten students and two profs, and all the married students' kids disappeared. Is Raymie all right? Call me!"

Chloe ran to her room and began packing, hardly thinking about where she was going. Kids had TVs and radios blaring the news that this was a worldwide phenomenon. She had to get home. Why, she didn't know. She just had to. She threw anything and everything she needed into one suitcase and dragged it downstairs.

Amy was still standing guard over Phoebe's clothes.

"You might as well take that stuff up to her room," Chloe said, and she told Amy what she had heard. "I'm going to keep trying to reach my family, but if you hear from them, tell them I'm trying to find a way back there. I'll try to call them tomorrow if I can get a flight. Can you do that?"

"Sure. And, Chloe . . . be careful."

.

Twenty-Three

On Earth Irene would have called it telepathy; she had never had the gift and doubted anyone else ever really did either. She had heard stories and pseudomagicians make claims and demonstrate what seemed like impressive feats of clairvoyance, but she was a skeptic. No one had ever proved to her that the gift was real, except perhaps in rare cases of demonic activity. In fact, she had enjoyed reading books by debunkers or those who explained the secrets behind the tricks.

But here in God's house, she was able to communicate with Raymie without opening her mouth or even being in his presence. It was as if they were together, regardless of how far apart they were. Irene knew she could merely desire his company and he would be there. But she wanted to be sure he was free and wouldn't feel as if he were abandoning Jeremy or his parents.

In an instant, Raymie was at her side. "I suppose you've noticed that things are different here," he said, smiling.

Irene still found it disconcerting that he had recently looked and acted and thought and spoken like a boy twenty years younger. She laughed. "Yes. I've noticed."

"I mean, there is no offense. If I leave Jeremy and Mr. and Mrs. Phillips, it's not as if I have snubbed them. We're all still here, we can still talk, and I can be back with them immediately. I could bounce back and forth between here and there every nanosecond, and you would all feel as if I were with you alone."

"Interesting," she said, "but please don't. It's just that I'm finding this judgment so fascinating that I wanted you next to me as I watched. Needless to say, I'm anxious about my own appearance before that flame."

"Me too," Raymie said. "I was so young, and I'm satisfied that I was earnest and devout enough. But even you were young in your faith, and we really didn't know what to do, did we?"

"I do now. From a whole new perspective. I'd like to have another chance at living the Christian life."

Raymie cocked his head at her. "No, you wouldn't. You have no more interest in leaving this place than I or anyone else here does."

"That's for sure," she said, interrupted by hallelujahs from the angels. She joined in the cheering and applause, then said, "I only wish I'd known then what I know now."

"I especially wouldn't want to be on Earth now," Raymie said, "with what has to be happening. I mean, I would be a better witness. I'd be more overt about my faith, more enthusiastic, more bold, more insistent. I wouldn't be afraid or embarrassed. I might even be able to endure all the hardships. But I can't imagine ever again being out of the physical presence of Jesus."

Irene stared at the line that seemed to stretch for miles as saint after unknown saint was called to face the flame of judgment for their works on Earth. "I just want everyone I knew and loved to be here."

Over what seemed like the next week — but what Irene knew was more likely just a matter of minutes — she and Raymie watched and listened as the white-hot finger of fire rose and fell with the tempering of the gold and silver and precious stones of some works and the gush of flame at eternally valueless wastes of earthly time. Irene felt electrified to realize how many believers there had been in the world during her time on

Earth. Names of every length and form represented millions of unknown Christians who had served Christ in unseen places and in unknown ways. Here the last were first and the first would be last. Irene looked forward to witnessing the judgment of the works of the heroes of the faith, contemporary and from the past, but she found the rewarding of these otherwise unknowns just as fascinating.

It had been during the middle of the morning rush hour in Bucharest — and for many the workday had just begun — when the Rapture occurred. Minutes later television news helicopters began landing on the lawn at the estate of the new Romanian president, Nicolae Carpathia. He immediately took Gabriella's assistant maid off phone duty, had her dressed in a business suit, and coached her on what to say:

"President Carpathia will address the nation in a few minutes. He is currently in seclusion, mourning the loss of some key members of his staff."

In truth, of course, Nicolae was on the phone to New York, being debriefed by Leon Fortunato, who agreed that he should not face the cameras until the international media arrived. "You are no longer the man of the Romanians," Leon said. "You are the man of the hour for the world. Do you know yet what you will say?"

"Of course. Words of peace and comfort."

"Excellent. Scripted?"

"Of course not. The spirit will give me utterance."

"Amen."

"Leon, some of the press are peeking in the windows even now as we speak. I must appear to be about earnest, important business."

"Well, you are."

"Tell me, what do you make of the fact that some on my staff here have vanished? How could I not know of their true allegiances?"

"Perhaps they were loyal to you as well, Nicolae. Unless they were God, they would not have detected where your loyalties lay or who you are."

"Could they be that naïve? Would not our adversary have informed them, the way our spirit guide informs us?"

"Apparently not."

It was not unusual for Bruce Barnes — visitation pastor of New Hope Village Church in Mt. Prospect, Illinois — to read in bed as his wife slept. Too often his reading and turning pages kept her awake, and after wrestling with three kids, five and under, all day, she frequently asked how long he would be reading.

That night he was enjoying his favorite sports-weekly magazine, and, as usual, his wife gently murmured, asking how long the light would be on. Not long, he told her, hoping she would soon fall asleep and not hear the pages turning or be bothered by the light.

She sighed a few times as the pages crinkled, but soon he heard her breathing slowly and steadily and knew she was out. He resituated himself with his back to her and kept reading, planning to finish the entire magazine.

Soon Bruce felt the bed move and sensed that his wife had gotten up. He assumed she was going to the bathroom and hoped she wouldn't rouse so much that she would complain about his still having the light on when she got back. It didn't strike him until later that he had not heard her walk to the bathroom or heard any water running. She was a tiny little thing, so the lack of her weight on the bed was pretty much all he noticed.

Engrossed in his reading, Bruce suddenly became aware that his wife had not returned. He called over his shoulder, "Hon, you okay?"

No response. Maybe she was checking on the kids. Or maybe it had been his imagination that she had left the bed. He read for a few more minutes, then reached behind him to be sure she wasn't still there. She was gone. He turned over and noticed that she had also pulled the covers back up to the pillow.

Great. She was angry with him for still being up and having the light on, so she had likely retired to the couch. Bruce felt terrible. He went to apologize and coax her back to bed, resigned to quit reading and turn out the light.

But his wife was not on the couch. Not in the kitchen. Not in the bathroom. Not in the kids' rooms. He didn't want to call out for her and wake the children. The lights were off all over the house, so he turned on the one in the hall to check their rooms again. Perhaps she was in a corner, rocking one of the younger ones.

From the dim shaft of light in the hall, Bruce thought the baby's crib looked empty. He turned on the room light, stuck his head out the door, and called down the hall for his wife. When he got no response, he turned back to the crib, saw the empty footie pajamas, and knew.

Bruce ran to each of the other two rooms, yanking back the covers and finding the kids' pajamas. Hurrying back to the master bedroom, he pulled back the covers on his wife's side to find her nightgown and her rings.

Bruce grabbed the phone and called Pastor Billings. He got the answering machine. He called other staff members. Same problem. He dug through the church directory, looking for older people who might not like answering machines. No answers.

As alone as he had ever been, Bruce jumped in his car and drove to the church. There he found one of the older New Hope secretaries sitting in her car, sobbing. They both knew what had happened. They had been left behind, and they knew why.

Chloe was horrified at what she saw as she dragged her suitcase through the campus and out onto the streets of Palo Alto. Bedlam everywhere. People cried and screamed, some ran, some collapsed into the fetal position. Others held each other. Many cried out to God. Some yelled for help, but there was nothing she could do for them. She just wanted to get home.

But there were no cabs, no buses, no

trucks moving. A few small cars and motor-cycles picked their way around the mayhem, but no one was stopping for hitchhikers. Chloe resolutely soldiered on with a vague notion that she was heading toward the San Jose airport. If she could just find a ride to the 101 . . .

Raymie Steele sat next to his mother, mesmerized by the myriad stories that flashed across his mind's eye as thousands upon thousands of people faced the fire judgment of their works and then the Bema Seat for their rewards. As a couple and a woman — all appearing about the same age now, of course — approached the altar, the crowd, Raymie and Irene included, rose with applause.

Without announcement or fanfare, God somehow impressed on the hearts and minds and souls of the spectator saints the entire story of each supplicant. Raymie received the entire fascinating story of this couple and their daughter all in one piece and ruminated upon it as their works were burned to precious metals and gems and they were awarded crowns by Jesus.

John and Betty Stam of America had been missionaries to China. In 1934, John and Betty and their three-month-old daughter,

Helen, were taken as hostages by the advancing Communists. When their attackers demanded a $20,000 ransom, John wrote in a note to mission authorities: "The Lord bless and guide you. As for us, may God be glorified, whether by life or by death."

During the night John was tied to a post out in the cold while Betty tended the baby. Before dawn she hid the sleeping Helen in a sleeping bag, praying she would be found by someone who would take care of her. In the morning John and Betty were stripped and led through town like common criminals, their hands bound behind them.

Along the way a man stepped from the crowd and pleaded for their lives. The guards ordered him to be silent, and when he would not desist, they dragged him away to be killed. John begged the guards to spare the man's life, but they ordered him to kneel. John was still speaking when one of the guards decapitated him with one ferocious swing of his sword.

Betty, kneeling beside her fallen husband, was murdered by the sword.

A local pastor was told that a baby had been left in the house where John and Betty had been chained. He hurried to find Helen in the little sleeping bag, hungry but alive. He bravely spirited her away, and a week later she was delivered to another missionary in a nearby city. Eventually she was returned to the States, where she lived until her death.

Raymie felt as if he had known the Stams and their daughter, even though all of them died long before he was born. He found it thrilling to see John and Betty receive their martyrs' crowns and be reunited with the pastor who had saved their daughter and with those who had raised her.

Stories like this were repeated hundreds, thousands, tens of thousands of times as Raymie sat there with his mother. He tried to compare it to the best entertainment he had ever enjoyed on Earth, but nothing matched this. He had loved a great ball game on TV, a last-minute victory. He had enjoyed mystery stories and heroic tales that kept him turning the pages until long after his bedtime. He had been to movies that amazed and delighted him and made him remember them for days.

But this made those seem like nothing. As each person approached the flame and the throne, his or her history was implanted in Raymie's mind. In full color with every sound and emotion he followed their feats as they served God, fighting persecution and the sword, trusting the Lord to deliver them, many dying for their faith, now enjoying their rewards.

From every century and every corner of the world they came, the throng rising to applaud them as everyone enjoyed the dramas of their heroic highlights. In every case, as their stories unfolded, the crowd exulted and the principals bowed at the feet of Jesus, deflecting all praise and honor to Him. The stories of humble pastors of tiny churches, persevering for decades in spite of seemingly no results, were just as uplifting as the dramatic tales.

Raymie had been fascinated by his mother's report that she had asked God how long they had been here — in terms they would understand from an earthly standpoint — and found it had been just minutes. He wondered if God would feel he was being trivial if he asked for his own update.

And as soon as the thought crossed his mind, God spoke to his heart. "You are anything but a nuisance, Son. Still only moments have passed since you arrived."

Raymie hoped this would never end and then realized that it would not.

Twenty-Four

Nicolae Carpathia waited until his people told him that the largest international-media outlets had arrived; then he took his time having his valet dress him in his most elegant, sedate, black suit with black tie and white shirt. Lingering in his dressing closet a few more beats, he finally left the mansion in a slow, seemingly sad gait with his head down, approaching the microphones on his vast back lawn.

Carpathia stepped to the makeshift podium as still cameras clicked and reporters jostled for position. Pressing his lips together in what appeared to be an attempt to control his emotions, he stoically raised his head and cleared his throat.

"Forgive me, but like so many around the world, I am grieving this hour as well. It appears no one has been left untouched by this tragedy. I know that even now, virtually moments after the cataclysm has struck, people all over the globe are already expounding theories. At the risk of adding to the confusion, for now let me say that the idea that makes the most sense to me is briefly as follows:

"The world has been stockpiling nuclear weapons for many years. Since the United States dropped atomic bombs on Japan in 1945 and the Soviet Union first detonated its own devices on September 23, 1949, the world has been at risk of nuclear holocaust. I would not be surprised if scientists discover some atmospheric phenomenon interacting with all these stockpiled weapons that may have caused the vanishing of so many people instantaneously.

"I am not a scientist, but I am well-read in these subjects, and it could very well be that some confluence of electromagnetism in the atmosphere, combined with as-yet-unknown or unexplained atomic ionization from the nuclear power and weaponry throughout the world, could have been ignited or triggered — perhaps by a natural cause like lightning or even by an intelligent life-form that discovered the possibility before we did — and caused this instant action.

"Why the disappearances seem so

random, striking some societies and cultures more than others, I am not prepared to speculate upon. It is possible that certain people's levels of electricity made them more likely to be affected. That would account for all the children and babies and even fetal material that vanished. Perhaps their electromagnetism was not developed to the point that it could resist whatever happened.

"I have already heard postulated that this may have been some cosmic act of God. Let me be careful to say that I do not and will not criticize any sincere person's belief system. Such tolerance is the basis for true harmony and brotherhood, peace and respect among peoples. I do not accept the so-called Rapture theory already being bandied about, because I know many, many more people who should be gone if the righteous were taken to heaven. If there is a God, I respectfully submit that this is not the capricious way in which He would operate. By the same token, you will not hear me express any disrespect for those who disagree.

"There may come a time when I will be presented the opportunity and privilege of addressing in a more appropriate setting my views of millenarianism, eschatology, the

Last Judgment, and the second coming of Christ, but until that time I feel it would be best if I did not attempt to speak on those subjects informally.

"Let me just close by adding my condolences to all who have suffered loss this day and to respectfully decline questions at this time. Thank you."

As Carpathia strode back toward the house, the press called out, "Mr. President!" "Dr. Carpathia!" "Just one question, sir."

But he neither turned nor slowed. This had been his show, not theirs.

Raymie had never heard of Cyrus Ingerson Scofield, but he was certainly intrigued by the man's story. Scofield had been a successful lawyer and politician in the nineteenth century but had resigned from the United States Attorney's office under charges of political corruption.

By the time he was thirty-six, in 1879, Scofield had suffered spiraling losses in his personal life, having ended his political career in humiliation, lost a son, turned to drink, and undergone a divorce. He was also involved in many controversial court cases.

Raymie thought Scofield appeared repentant, kneeling before the flame as his works were tested in the fire. Despite his history, his judgment resulted in precious gems and gold and silver that shone. Jesus fashioned these into a Crown of Life for Scofield's persevering in ministry despite opposition to his theological views. Jesus also presented him a Crown of Glory, citing his feeding of several flocks as pastor of various churches. He also received a Crown of Righteousness as one who stood out as loving the very idea of Christ's appearing. And finally he was given the Crown of Rejoicing for his work having resulted in so many coming to faith in Christ.

"But, Lord," Scofield said, "I am unworthy. I wasted nearly half my life."

Jesus embraced him and said, "You of all men should know that the sins and omissions of the old life are not counted against you at this judgment. Your sins were covered and forgotten, and all that remains is what you did for Me after you were regenerated. Well done, good and faithful servant."

Raymie enjoyed the Scofield life story passing his mind's eye. A change had certainly been needed in the man's life. And now the masses were treated in their minds' eyes to the time in 1879 when Scofield had asked God to forgive his sins and for Jesus to take over his life.

From that moment the brilliant but flawed Scofield began to study and live for his newfound Savior. He stopped drinking, was discipled by a prominent pastor and Bible teacher, served many organizations, and was eventually called to be a pastor.

He led people to Christ, began cottage prayer meetings, married a Christian, saw his Dallas, Texas, church send out missionaries, and also saw the work grow and spawn new churches. He designed the Scofield Correspondence Course, which was later licensed to Moody Bible Institute and taken by more than 100,000 students. And he created a reference Bible to aid those just beginning to read the Bible, which became an authoritative guide to millions for more than a century.

Raymie had heard Pastor Billings mention his Scofield Bible, but he had never quite understood what he meant and was fairly certain he had never seen one. Now, as Raymie watched Jesus give Cyrus Scofield his crowns, he thought this was a man he'd like to talk with, and it was nice to know he had an eternity to do it.

Chloe caught a clumsy ride on the back of a motorbike, during which she and the young, terrified Asian rider struggled to keep her suitcase aloft. "You want to try the new Palo Alto airstrip?" he said.

"I can't imagine anything's going out of there," she said. "I was hoping to make it to San Jose."

"Definitely closed," he said. "Heard it on the news."

"Palo Alto then," she said, which proved providential.

A harried, middle-aged woman behind the counter, her mascara having run from recent tears, told Chloe she was in luck, "in a manner of speaking." She said she was going to try and see how many rules she could break, learning that Chloe was immediate family of a Pan-Con captain. "Somehow I'll get you onto Pan-Con by the last leg of your trip, if I find even one plane on its way to Chicago."

The woman spent several minutes tapping away at her keyboard, talking to herself and maintaining a running commentary as she went. "Um-hmm. Interesting. Okay. Fine, let's try this. Nope. Here. Oh, my. Well, worth a try."

"What?" Chloe said, checking her watch. It had been an hour since she and Amy had discovered Phoebe's clothes on the ground.

"It's something — a long shot, not much."

"I'll try anything."

"I figured that. Because San Jose is shut down, we're getting some rerouting. More than we're used to and more than we can handle. There's a little military strip between here and San Jose, and it looks like there's going to be an Air California jet stopping there to refuel. I can get you on that. Some back roads are clear, so we can bus you to the strip."

"Air California? They don't leave the state, do they?"

"You do know your air travel, young lady. AC is an in-state airline, yes, but this one is on its way to Salt Lake City, only major airport open for hundreds of miles. There's an old piece of Pan-Con equipment there that's going to Oklahoma."

"Thought you said the only major —"

"I'm not talking Oklahoma City or even Tulsa here, doll. Enid. Middle of nowhere. Military town."

"That's not on Pan-Con's routes."

"No, but Dallas is, and Enid's getting lots of DFW's slopover."

"Okay, where do I go from Enid?"

"There's an Ozark flight to Springfield, Illinois. I suppose you know that Ozark spelled backwards is Krazo."

Chloe was not in the mood. "Yep, I've heard 'em all. What are the chances I can get to O'Hare from Springfield?"

The woman shrugged. "That's as far as I can guarantee. Maybe you can get a bus from there. Looks like Pan-Con is running some ancient turboprops out of there, but who knows how long Chicago will be open. JFK is already closed, and O'Hare is taking every jumbo jet within five hundred miles. Can't imagine they won't run out of room soon. You want this or not? Got to get you on that bus right now if you're in."

"I'm in."

"Isn't this something, Mom?" Raymie said. "You're getting these mind pictures, right?"

"I am."

"These next two guys are from the first and second centuries!"

"I don't recognize their names," Irene said.

"I have a feeling we'll both be experts on them soon. Papias and Polycarp. Weird. And they were friends of John, the one who wrote the Gospel."

"And the epistles and Revelation."

"Just wait till it's his turn, Mom." But Raymie would find these two men every bit as captivating.

Twenty-Five

Hattie Durham enjoyed the delectable secret that she was not quite as ditzy as she seemed to be. How people reacted to her — particularly men — she had recognized so many years before that she couldn't remember not using it to her advantage. Women seemed to baby talk to her, as if because she was a beautiful blonde she couldn't have a brain. And men seemed to talk to her with their eyes, as if their gibberish was meaningless, which it often was.

It was, however, not true that Hattie was other than calculating. She had largely charmed her way to senior-flight-attendant status just after her twenty-seventh birthday — no small feat — but these jobs were not just handed out. She had had to study, to be a quick learner, to gain favor with passengers, fellow crew members, and superiors. They didn't give such a title to a body, a face, a hairdo, and makeup in uniform.

And now she was enjoying her new role, especially on a 747 streaking toward London. Hattie didn't want any mistakes, no complaints. There would be issues, sure, but that's why she and her crew were here. They would deal with everything and everyone quickly and efficiently. Tony Salazar, who had been with the airline since Hattie was in grade school, was already proving most helpful. He was one who could easily have had her promotion, had he merely wanted it. Clearly there was no animosity there. He apparently wanted her to look good and seemed to be doing everything in his power to effect that.

They were several hours into the flight already. Two meals had been served, the movie had ended, and except for just a few wanderers and the rare night owls still hunched over their laptops under their individual reading lamps, the plane had become dark and quiet.

"You want to make points with this staff," Tony whispered, "urge them to finish breakfast prep now and let them take a load off until sunup."

"Great idea," Hattie said.

When they were finished, she swept through the cabins a few times herself, then finally sat, feeling the nervous energy drain from her and wishing she could close her eyes. The last thing she would do, however, was actually sleep on the job. Here and there other attendants were sitting, chatting, and watching and listening for any call buttons.

Hattie glanced idly up the aisle, where a woman was either getting some exercise or on her way to the lavatory. Funny. In the dim light she seemed to be there one second and gone the next.

Something else was on Hattie's mind. Rayford Steele. She had never seen herself as a home wrecker, though Captain Steele was hardly the first married man who seemed eager to throw away his family for her. She had merely teased previous conquests, knowing full well they were not responsible people and were merely lusting rather than loving her.

But Rayford. He was something different. It had not been lost on her that he had been more than careful. He had a beautiful family. He never bad-mouthed his wife. It was clear he was not happy at home; otherwise, what was he doing with his looks, his body language, his conversation? Yet it was his very discipline that attracted her . . . not to mention his striking appearance.

Okay, he was forty-two. Had forty-two

ever looked so good on a man? He kept himself in shape and looked great in and out of uniform. They were headed for something, and Hattie didn't want to scare him off and mess it up. She knew enough to let Rayford make the next move, and from what she could tell, he was well on his way. She had made clear her own intentions — or at least willingness — but this was a different relationship — for certain a different potential — than she had ever had.

Hattie's goal was nothing short of claiming Rayford as her own. An affair was not enough; for one thing, given their situation, it would ruin her career. No, she wanted him. He would have to be willing to divorce his wife and pursue her to the altar.

If her instincts were right, London would be a city where memories were made.

Irene Steele took great pleasure in her new ability to — what else could she call it? — multitask. She was able to watch and listen to the exhilarating judgments — which were, in reality, another way to bring honor and glory to Jesus — exult at the rejoicing of the angels every time someone received Christ, "view" as it were the stories of each supplicant in her mind's eye, and simultaneously feel overwhelmed with joy at being able to take this all in in the presence of her son, now a full-grown man. Irene felt as if she would never be able to lose her eternal smile, nor did she wish to.

She quickly understood why Papias and Polycarp, those of the strange names, seemed to be dealt with together. They had been contemporaries, friends, and their most stark bond was that they had both been acquaintances of the disciple whom Jesus loved: John.

Papias proved to be a Greek Christian leader who had written a five-volume commentary on the sayings of Jesus. Jesus praised him for his efforts in offering one of the earliest records about the writing of the Gospels. While his work was lost to history after several centuries, it had been used in the early church to help give credence to the veracity of Scripture.

"Though some questioned your intellect and scholarship," Jesus said, presenting him the crowns of Glory, Righteousness, and Rejoicing, "you proved authentic and devoted. You fed your flock, you anticipated My return with gladness, and you became My glory and joy by winning souls."

Papias's friend Polycarp had been a disciple of the apostle John and eventually became the bishop of the early church in

Smyrna. Irene soon learned that he was one of the most celebrated characters in ancient Christendom, reminding her again how embryonic and provincial her faith was. The idea of having eternity to learn all this warmed her.

As a pupil of John, Polycarp had talked with many who had been with Jesus Himself. He became a bold pastor, preacher, and witness for Christ in spite of dangerous opposition from Rome, and indeed he was eventually martyred for his faith while serving as the bishop at Smyrna.

Jesus used the precious residue from the flame judgment of his works to make for him all the crowns he had given Papias, adding the Crown of Life, reserved for martyrs or those who had suffered undue trials.

Hattie Durham had enjoyed only a brief respite before feeling that she should get back on her feet and continue to monitor the needs and comfort of her passengers. She was aware that other attendants glanced curiously at her, probably wondering if they too were expected to get back to work. But really, there was little to do.

She missed Rayford, but she had decided the next move was his. And he certainly wasn't going to do anything during a flight.

Hattie moseyed to the back of the plane, idly checking to see how many lavs were occupied. Only one, and that soon became free too. Then she quietly began her stroll up the long aisle. Nearly everyone was asleep, so Hattie was careful to keep her steps light. When she was a passenger she could always tell when someone was coming, and nothing was more irritating than a lumbering staff member, interrupting someone's rest.

Some passengers had their seats reclined, and they lay back, snoring softly or with their mouths open. Most had heeded the advice to fasten their seat belts outside blankets and sweaters so Hattie and her team would not have to rouse them to be sure they were buckled in. Others had slid down in their seats and slept in various curled-up positions of repose.

Strange though. Maybe it was the darkness. It seemed at least one seat in each row was empty. Several seemed to have two or more. Yet Hattie had seen only one woman in the aisle several minutes before. And she had not seen that woman return.

With every lav now vacant, Hattie's eyes had to be playing tricks on her. Surely she was simply missing these people in the shadows, under blankets and pillows. But as her eyes widened — partly in alarm, she knew — it was as if her night vision improved. About a third of the seats she studied looked empty.

This was a full flight. Hattie scowled in concentration. Focus. There had to be an explanation. It had to be her. She was missing something. Or was she still sitting, taking a break, dozing, dreaming this? That had happened before. Once, thoroughly sleep deprived, she had drowsed in a jump seat, only to dream that the craft had landed, but everyone was asleep and she couldn't wake them to disembark.

Hattie took a deep breath. She was awake. She knew it. And this would all make sense in a moment when it would somehow come together in her mind. But she couldn't help leaning past a sleeping man in an aisle seat and feeling the two seats beyond him. Both were empty. All she felt were blankets and what seemed like clothes. On the second seat she felt earrings. What was going on?

Six straight aisle seats on both sides had heads silhouetted in the dim light, but the next three, on both sides, were empty. The first one she checked revealed a man who had slid down beyond her view. But the others were vacant, blankets and clothes and jewelry lying there.

Hattie couldn't breathe. Where were these people? She hurried up the aisle, no longer caring about the weight of her footfall.

A woman turned to see her coming and whispered, "Is anything wrong?"

Hattie mustered her cheerful voice. "No, ma'am. Everything's fine." But she couldn't slow herself. Several more seats were empty before she reached the bank of lavs, and all of them still showed "Vacant" on the doors. She knocked and opened each, hoping they were full of people answering nature's call who had somehow suffered from mass forgetfulness, leaving the doors unlocked. But no. All were empty.

Hattie rushed forward, only to trip on a pile of . . . what? She bent to examine it and picked it up to clear the aisle. It was a woman's complete outfit, including hosiery, undergarments, and accessories. Hattie felt a sob rising in her throat. She must not cry out. This was where the woman she had seen had seemed to disappear.

Right out of her clothes?

And then it hit Hattie. At least a couple dozen children had boarded this flight. She now saw none. She pushed toward the galley to dump the pile of clothes.

There she met another flight attendant,

who said, "Miss Durham, what's up?"

"I don't know."

Call buttons began to ding. Reading lamps came on. People called out, "Hey! What? Ma'am? Sir?"

Hattie toyed with illuminating the cabin lights, but if that revealed her worst fears that a hundred or more passengers had disappeared out of their clothes, she could incite a riot.

"Have you seen Tony?" an attendant said. "He was back there, and now I don't see him. Something's going on and we need him. We need everybody. Hattie, where are all these people?"

Hattie held a finger to her mouth and trotted toward the stairs at the front of the plane. She was going to see if this craziness extended to first class, and then she was heading for the cockpit.

Irene had heard of an organization called Wycliffe Bible Translators, but she knew little about it and nothing about whomever it had been named for. That was soon remedied as John Wycliffe, a fourteenth-century saint, reached the fire judgment and his story was impressed upon the minds of everyone in the house of God.

Wycliffe had been a scholar who apparently had almost as much to do with the reformation of the church as had the more famous Martin Luther of the following century. Like Luther, Wycliffe came to believe that the essence of the gospel was that Christ's own righteousness is imputed to those who believe, and on that ground alone they are accepted by God.

Wycliffe faced persecution and opposition from religious leaders of his day, but he persevered and eventually led the way in translating the Scriptures into the language of the people, a revolutionary concept at that time. He also expounded upon his theological ideas and sent out preachers to do the same.

Irene had always taken for granted that she was able to read the Bible in English, but until Wycliffe's translation, Jerome's Latin Vulgate had been the only Scripture available. Also, anyone other than clergy had been prohibited from reading the Bible. Wycliffe's work was so controversial that years later the church actually prohibited the translation of the Bible.

But Wycliffe believed it was crucial that Christians be able to read God's Word in their own language. He believed the Scriptures were inspired of God and should be accepted without reserve.

Because the printing press had not yet been invented, every word had to be handwritten. More than six hundred years later, over one hundred and fifty handwritten copies still existed.

Wycliffe also trained and sent out "Bible-Men," students who had been ordained but without a bishop's license. He instructed them to not settle in any particular area, to avoid worldly pursuits, and to study and preach the Bible. They wore long reddish gowns and carried staffs, but they were barefoot. They carried at least a portion of Wycliffe's translation and preached wherever they could find an audience.

Wycliffe had been widely thought the best preacher of his day. He centered his sermons around the meaning of the Bible passage and then the application of the text to the lives of the hearers.

Jesus presented him the crowns of Glory and Rejoicing.

Twenty-Six

Not sure he'd follow through with anything overt, Captain Rayford Steele felt an irresistible urge to see Hattie Durham right then. He unstrapped himself and squeezed his first officer's shoulder on the way out of the cockpit. "We're still on auto, Christopher," he said as the younger man roused and straightened his headphones. "I'm gonna make the sunup stroll."

Christopher squinted and licked his lips. "Doesn't look like sunup to me, Cap."

"Probably another hour or two. I'll see if anybody's stirring anyway."

"Roger. If they are, tell 'em Chris says, 'Hey.' "

Raymie Steele found it interesting that God seemed to have a theme going that was giving him a crash course in church history. The next supplicant was a contemporary of

Wycliffe who was also instrumental in translating the Scriptures. As a young man, John Hus had worked in churches in Prague and become known as a humble servant and a devoted student. He was eventually ordained to the priesthood and assigned as the preacher in the new Bethlehem Chapel in Prague.

Hus was impacted by the writings of Wycliffe and helped translate and circulate much of Wycliffe's work. At first Hus did not face opposition for his views but was actually a favorite of his archbishop. Eventually, however, the archbishop was ordered to speak out against what were considered the heresies of Wycliffe and to forbid any further criticism of the clergy.

Later the church ordered that all Wycliffe writings be surrendered for correction. Hus obeyed and publicly declared that he condemned whatever errors existed, but he was eventually called to account by the archbishop for what were termed his "Wycliffite tendencies" and was reported to Rome.

Wycliffe's writings were withdrawn from circulation and burned, and when Hus protested, he was excommunicated, along with his sympathizers. When he continued supporting the work of Wycliffe, he was summoned to appear before the pope. Hus further protested practices of the church and the pope, resulting in a papal edict that he be imprisoned and that the Bethlehem Chapel be destroyed. The order was not obeyed by the king of Prague, and at the end of 1412, Hus wrote a treatise about the errors of the church and later posted it on the walls of the Bethlehem Chapel.

From these works of protest the church extracted propositions it considered heretical, and the Council of Constance was assembled. Hus was urged by the king to appear there and defend his doctrine. At Constance he was condemned and burned at the stake.

Jesus presented Hus the crowns of Glory and Life.

Hattie Durham was in shape. She worked out nearly every day. Why, then, was her heart pounding and her lungs overtaxed from the short flight of stairs to first class? She knew.

As she moved through the cabin she found a good-looking, blond man sleeping, his laptop open, his reading lamp on. She reached across a heavyset, snoring man who smelled of too many drinks and switched off the light. As she backed away she noticed that the dapper old man on the aisle just ahead of those two was gone. His clothes were on the seat. To Hattie's great relief, the man's wife still dozed.

Relief? That was a laugh. Hattie was starring in the horror film of a lifetime.

A young woman on the other side of the aisle frantically patted the empty seats beside her, calling out, "Bill! Where are the kids?" She spotted Hattie. "Ma'am?"

Hattie held up a hand. "I'll be right with you." And she sprinted toward the cockpit.

Next on God's list of those honored for the ministry of His Word was a twentieth-century saint who had made the Scriptures even more understandable to the masses by crafting them to be understood by his children. His laborious private effort was eventually recognized by Christian leaders, and the explosion of his paraphrase, *The Living Bible*, resulted in worldwide publishing ministries.

He too suffered for his work, virtually losing his voice for the second half of his life. Ken Taylor was presented with crowns rewarding his enduring trials, feeding the flock, and winning souls.

His appearance before the flame and the throne began what seemed to Irene an endless parade of more contemporary Christian heroes, missionaries, pastors, evangelists, personal witnesses, and martyrs. Learning all their stories and — amazingly — now being able to remember every detail of thousands of the same was such a rich experience that Irene only occasionally reverted to her curiosity about how much time this might be taking in Earth minutes. It seemed she had been here a year already, but still she felt no hunger, no fatigue, no flagging of attention. And if what God had told her before remained operative, all this was happening in mere Earth moments.

As Captain Rayford Steele opened the cockpit door, Hattie Durham nearly bowled him over.

"No need to knock," he said. "I'm coming."

The senior flight attendant pulled him into the galley, but there was no passion in her touch. Her fingers felt like talons on his forearm, and her body shuddered in the darkness.

"Hattie —"

She pressed him back against the cooking compartments, her face close to his. Had she not been clearly terrified, he might have enjoyed this and returned her embrace.

Her knees buckled as she tried to speak,

and her voice came in a whiny squeal. "People are missing," she managed to whisper, burying her head in his chest.

He took her shoulders and tried to push her back, but she fought to stay close. "What do you m— ?"

She was sobbing now, her body out of control. "A whole bunch of people, just gone!"

"Hattie, this is a big plane. They've wandered off to the lavs or —"

She pulled his head down so she could speak directly into his ear. Despite her weeping, she was plainly fighting to make herself understood. "I've been everywhere. I'm telling you, dozens of people are missing."

"Hattie, it's still dark. We'll find —"

"I'm not crazy! See for yourself! All over the plane, people have disappeared."

"It's a joke. They're hiding, trying to —"

"Ray! Their shoes, their socks, their clothes — everything was left behind. These people are gone!"

Hattie slipped from his grasp and knelt whimpering in the corner. Rayford wanted to comfort her, to enlist her help, or to get Chris to go with him through the plane. More than anything he wanted to believe the woman was crazy. She knew better than to put him on. It was obvious she really believed people had disappeared.

Irene had heard of Campus Crusade for Christ, but as a fairly new believer, she knew nothing of its history or its founder. Thus she was amazed as Bill Bright's story was revealed and his works were burnished to a huge pile of gold and silver and precious gems.

Dr. Bright had founded and spent more than fifty years leading an organization that became the world's largest Christian ministry. He was so motivated by Christ's command to spread the gospel throughout the world that in 1956 he wrote a booklet titled *The Four Spiritual Laws*, which was eventually printed in two hundred languages and became the most widely disseminated religious booklet in history. Bright also commissioned the *JESUS* film, a documentary on the life of Christ, which was translated into more than nine hundred languages and seen by more than 5.4 billion people in 228 countries and became the most widely viewed film in history.

Bill Bright began his ministry in college by sharing Christ with fellow students at UCLA, which developed into a full-time calling and spawned the eventual worldwide ministry of Campus Crusade for Christ. What began as a campus effort grew to deal with almost every segment of society, including inner cities, governments, prisons, families, the military, executives, musicians, athletes, and others.

Irene and Raymie rose with the rest as Jesus pronounced Bill Bright's well-done and embraced him, crafting for him from the residue of the flame the Crown of Rejoicing, the soul-winner's crown.

The loudest cheers came from the hundreds of millions who were in heaven due to the ministry of Campus Crusade for Christ.

Rayford Steele stepped into first class, where an elderly woman sat stunned in the predawn haze, her husband's sweater and trousers in her hands. "What in the world?" she said. "Harold?"

Rayford wanted to be strong, to have answers, to be an example to his crew, to Hattie. But when he reached the lower level he knew the rest of the flight would be chaotic. He was as scared as anyone on board. As he scanned the seats, he nearly panicked. He backed into a secluded spot behind the bulkhead and slapped himself hard on the cheek.

This was no joke, no trick, no dream.

Something was terribly wrong, and there was no place to run. There would be enough confusion and terror without his losing control. Nothing had prepared him for this, and he would be the one everybody would look to. But for what? What was he supposed to do?

First one, then another cried out when they realized their seatmates were missing but their clothes were still there. They cried, they screamed, they leaped from their seats.

Hattie grabbed Rayford from behind and wrapped her hands so tight around his chest that he could hardly breathe. "Rayford, what is this?"

He pulled her hands apart and turned to face her. "Hattie, listen. I don't know any more than you do. But we've got to calm these people and get on the ground. I'll make some kind of announcement, and you and your people keep everybody in their seats. Okay?"

She nodded, but she didn't look okay at all. As he edged past her to hurry back to the cockpit, he heard her scream. *So much for calming the passengers.* He whirled to see her on her knees in the aisle.

Hattie lifted a blazer, shirt, and tie still intact. Trousers lay at her feet. She frantically turned the blazer to the low light and read the name tag. "Tony!" she wailed. "Tony's gone!"

Rayford snatched the clothes from her and tossed them behind the bulkhead. He lifted Hattie by her elbows and pulled her out of sight. "Hattie, we're hours from touchdown. We can't have a planeload of hysterical people. I'm going to make an announcement, but you have to do your job. Can you?"

She nodded, her eyes vacant.

He forced her to look at him. "Will you?" he said.

She nodded again. "Rayford, are we going to die?"

"No," he said. "That I'm sure of."

But he wasn't sure of anything. How could he know? He'd rather have faced an engine fire or even an uncontrolled dive. A crash into the ocean had to be better than this. How would he keep people calm in such a nightmare?

Twenty-Seven

Irene was well aware that what seemed to be problems in heaven were not problems at all. Only as she tried to consider things from a human, earthly perspective was she able to wonder at the difference in her new view. For instance, the idea of sitting — while not being aware of one's weight on a chair — in God's house (and only the first-floor assembly hall) with some 20 billion others was so ludicrous to the other-than-glorified human mind that all she could do was shake her head.

Imagine someone inviting me to a function like this. Had she had the opportunity to attend a concert of her all-time favorite performer, the idea of a crowd of even tens of thousands would have made her rather just listen to a CD or watch a DVD. Of course she would have gone anywhere to see Jesus, even from a distance. But to be in a crowd so massive that you couldn't see either end of it for days simply would have held no appeal.

Yet somehow this worked. Irene was so happy she could not stop grinning. Emotionally she was full to overflowing. While the crowd was enormous, she didn't have the feeling of being lost among the masses or being hemmed in shoulder to shoulder as if on the midway of a county fair. Everyone was here for the same reason, and that kinship was pervasive. There were no sight-line issues, no audio problems, and the very idea that God could be limited in His ability to make everything plain and clear to everyone all at once had, needless to say, never crossed Irene's mind.

What crossed her mind now, though, was spectacular. Nothing in her previous life compared to having this personal, one-on-one, constant interaction with God while simultaneously being able to hear and see everything — even these life histories at the same time as the judgments and rewards.

It all seemed to be happening at once, and despite the fact that she had witnessed thousands of people meeting Jesus and being tested and blessed, Irene had no trouble remembering every detail of every one. Her earthly mind might have been forced to categorize them, compare them, list them from

342

favorite to so-so. But somehow she found each and every story endlessly fascinating. And endless was what she longed for. If this went on for all of eternity, that would be more than all right with her. This was akin to reading a book so engrossing that you never wanted it to end.

Irene and Raymie enjoyed watching a tall, handsome woman running, leaping, dancing, and spinning toward the altar, all the while praising God and singing. A diving accident as a teenager had left her a quadriplegic, and she had spent the rest of her life in a wheelchair.

As the life story of Joni Eareckson Tada streaked across the theater of Irene's new mind, she was intrigued by the initial devastation of a beautiful young athlete, artist, and horsewoman's being so cruelly incapacitated. Her vibrant, loving family was changed forever by the tragedy. Joni herself — though a believer in Christ — had to battle the seemingly endless winter of depression as she faced a lifetime of dependence upon others for every basic need.

Irene was gripped by the invasion of friends and counselors into Joni's young life, gradually drawing her out of her wish to die and away from her penchant for withdrawing from reality in her mind. There had been no miracle turnaround but a gradual turning to full dependence upon God. Joni's life never got easier, and never did she get to the place where she would have chosen her disabilities over wholeness. But she did come to the point where she gave herself wholly to her Savior and dedicated herself to others.

Despite life in a chair, Joni became a student of God's Word, her life story became a best-selling book and a movie, she sang and recorded — despite needing help with her breathing for the sustained high notes — learned to continue to draw and paint beautifully with a pen or brush held in her teeth, and became an exceptional speaker. She eventually founded Joni and Friends, an organization aimed at accelerating Christian ministry in the disabled community.

Joni's works were tested in the fire, and Jesus bestowed upon her the Crown of Life. And with her embrace and "well done" came a surprise. Jesus restored to her one of the joys of her youth, producing a white stallion for her to ride.

Cameron Williams had roused when the old woman directly in front of him called out to the pilot. The pilot had shushed her, causing her to peek back at Buck. He dragged his fingers through his longish hair and forced a groggy smile. "Trouble, ma'am?"

"It's my Harold," she said.

Buck had helped the old man put his herringbone wool jacket and felt hat in the overhead bin when they boarded. Harold was a short, dapper gentleman in penny loafers, brown slacks, and a tan sweater vest over a shirt and tie. He was balding, and Buck assumed he would want the hat again later when the air-conditioning kicked in.

"Does he need something?"

"He's gone!"

"I'm sorry?"

"He's disappeared!"

"Well, I'm sure he slipped off to the washroom while you were sleeping."

"Would you mind checking for me? And take a blanket."

"Ma'am?"

"I'm afraid he's gone off naked. He's a religious person, and he'll be terribly embarrassed."

Buck suppressed a smile when he noticed the woman's pained expression. He climbed over the sleeping executive on the aisle, who had far exceeded his limit of free drinks, and leaned in to take a blanket from the old woman. Indeed, Harold's clothes were in a neat pile on his seat, his glasses and hearing aid on top. The pant legs still hung over the edge and led to his shoes and socks. *Bizarre,* Buck thought. *Why so fastidious?* He remembered a friend in high school who had a form of epilepsy that occasionally caused him to black out when he seemed perfectly conscious. He might remove his shoes and socks in public or come out of a washroom with his clothes open.

"Does your husband have a history of epilepsy?"

"No."

"Sleepwalking?"

"No."

"I'll be right back."

Raymie Steele had sat through sermons in which Pastor Billings had tried to prepare the congregation for the types of things they would experience in eternity. He had to confess, however, that to his twelve-year-old ears and brain, it had all sounded a little abstract and ethereal. But to be here, to live it, now it all made sense. Of course, he had a new mind, an adult mind, but it was the wonderful assault on his senses that made everything come together.

If Raymie had a regret it was that he had made heroes of athletes, TV and movie actors. Personalities. People famous for being famous. Raymie had had no idea how many heroes of the faith there were and that there had been a treasure trove of reading material he could have enjoyed, had he only known.

Admittedly, most of the people he was now being exposed to had not been famous or had anything written about them while on Earth. Many were homemakers who had invested their lives in their families and loved ones and had contributed time and effort and sometimes money to widows and orphans and others of society's castoffs. Clearly, not one of them had gone unnoticed by God. Each of the downtrodden they had served, Jesus said, actually represented Him. He made clear that every time someone fed or clothed or in any way helped even "the least of these," he or she was doing it as unto Jesus.

Pastor Billings had often said that the biggest mistake a Christian — especially those who loved the idea of the return of Christ — could make was to give up on the world as they knew it. "Just because you may be rescued someday before the Tribulation hits doesn't mean it's time to sell all you own and sit on a mountaintop waiting for a chariot to haul you away. If you truly believe Jesus is coming and that He could be coming soon, you ought to be about His work. And that's more about widows and orphans than it is about setting dates, figuring out who the Antichrist might be, waiting for pie in the sky by and by."

When the works of unknown saints were tried in the fire, the flame seemed to burst forth — not because there was waste that ignited like hay and stubble, but rather because the gold and silver and gems were shimmering, iridescent in the heat. It seemed the greatest rewards and loudest applause and cheering were reserved for "the last" who were among the first to be judged and praised.

It was still a delight to hear and see the stories of the heroes, and Jesus praised them for their service. But Raymie thought that perhaps because these had already been given much of their due while they were alive, here they came last.

One such, whose fame long outlived him on Earth, was a man named Dwight Lyman Moody. How Raymie would have loved to read about him before and how he looked forward to chatting with him. The very idea that he would never run out of time and would be able to interact with everyone here was comprehensible only to his glorified mind.

Moody had been one of history's most dynamic pioneering servants of Christ. Having died before the dawn of the twentieth century and having thus predated the automobile, still he had traveled more than one million miles, spoken to more than 100 million people, and been responsible — on a human level — for having seen perhaps millions coming to saving faith in Jesus Christ. Many considered him the greatest evangelist since the apostle Paul and the forerunner of such preaching giants as Billy Sunday and Billy Graham.

Both Abraham Lincoln and Ulysses S. Grant had attended his revival services. More than 125,000 attended in one day when he preached at the Chicago World's Exhibition in 1893.

Moody became so famous that he began to travel and preach internationally, and some said he was as well-known as the president of the United States. For a time his birthplace, Northfield, Massachusetts, was actually considered the most famous city in the world.

D. L. Moody's works radiated from the heat, and he was awarded the crowns of Glory, for feeding the flock, Righteousness, for "loving His appearing," and Rejoicing, the soul-winner's crown.

★ ★ ★

The first-class lavs were unoccupied, but as Buck headed for the stairs, he found several other passengers in the aisle. "Excuse me," he said, "I'm looking for someone."

"Who isn't?" a woman said.

Buck pushed his way past several people and found lines to the washrooms in business and economy. The pilot brushed past him without a word, and Buck was soon met by a flight attendant.

"Sir, I need you to return to your seat and fasten your belt."

"I'm looking for —"

"Everybody is looking for someone," she said.

Twenty-Eight

When it was Irene's turn to have her works tested by fire, it was as if she reverted to her earthly self and emotions. Scared, nervous, on the edge of embarrassment. But just when she was about to wonder if this had all been for real and demand to know why there would be discomfort in God's house, He spoke directly to her heart.

"Your son will be with you," God said. "And I am with you always, now and forever. Remember, it is only from one to whom much is given that much is required. You have been Mine for only a short time, and while there will be some waste in the fire, you also redeemed much of the time you served Me."

With that and with Raymie at her side, Irene moved through the long line, watching, listening, experiencing with others their testing and rewards, and having their stories projected onto her soul. What would others think of hers? She had always believed she was a nobody, a boring Midwestern girl who had met the love of her life at college and then seen him drift from her when she became a follower of Christ. That was no story. It was simply a history.

As she approached the altar, however, Irene was overcome with praise for Jesus and a renewed feeling of unworthiness to even be in His presence. Though she was aware that Raymie was right there, he was largely irrelevant at this moment. She prostrated herself and heard the whoosh of the fire as every moment of her life from the time Jackie had led her to Christ seemed to spill from her and into the flame.

Her own life flashed before her as it was beamed to everyone else, and she saw it in a new light, almost as if for the first time. Irene was seeing herself through the eyes of God. She had never before seen herself as sweet and precious and an object of desire. But the army brat who cavorted in rapid-fire scenes, the little girl Irene had always thought was conniving and selfish — because she had been told that over and over — had another side to her personality. Lost. She was lost for sure back then but didn't even know it. And how could she have?

Irene saw the young version of herself as a wandering, needy, longing, searching person who only grew and matured into more of the same. She was reminded of conversations she'd had in elementary and junior high school with other girls who wanted only to talk about boys. And yet young Irene was already asking questions about life and truth and the big picture.

Irene had not even remembered those days, let alone wondered what it was she had really been after. But now it was so clear. She was seeking God. Seeking love. Seeking belonging. Purpose. A sense of family. Boyfriends had not brought that. Moving had only exacerbated her problems. It was as if she'd had no choice but to fall for the handsome jock and would-be pilot who had fallen for her.

But what she was really looking for in a man she could find only in God. She had given the marriage and the kids everything she had, but she was still empty, still searching, still facing a void in her life nothing else could fill.

Her eyes downcast yet her body feeling the warmth of the fire, Irene cringed at the wood, hay, and stubble of wasted hours as they burned to ashes. She hadn't known; that was all. Her sin had been dealt with, but how she wished she could have back every day she had spent as a child of God. What she would do with every minute now!

Her time reading, studying, working out, learning, discussing important matters, thinking and caring and praying about people — these were clearly lauded. And all that time was not necessarily Christian or even religious. Wasted were the times she devoted to herself alone and not for rest and recuperation or recharging her batteries. Rather it was the trivia that had filled much of her life that she now bitterly regretted.

And yet what was this? Not much flame had been spent consuming her wasted time. She lifted her face to see a rainbow of colors emitted from the flame. There, before Irene's eyes, came scenes of a woman she barely recognized praying, reading her Bible, studying, volunteering at a food bank, sending clothes to charity, teaching Sunday school, attending church, going to Bible studies, praying to receive Christ, being discipled by Jackie, and finally, leading Raymie to Jesus.

The flame disappeared, and in its place lay the ash from the wasted days and gold and silver and precious stones from her good works. She knew they had contributed nothing to her salvation but were rather spawned by her gratitude for the gift she had received. But now Jesus stood before His throne, arms outstretched, beckoning her once again.

As the masses stood cheering and clapping, Irene felt loved and affirmed and whole.

Jesus gathered her into His arms and said, "Well done, good and faithful servant. Yours are the Crown of Righteousness for loving My appearing and the Crown of Rejoicing for having won your own son's soul for My Kingdom."

Buck was steered back toward the stairs by a flight attendant with "Hattie" on her nameplate. She slipped past him and took the steps two at a time.

Halfway up himself, Buck turned and surveyed the scene. It was the middle of the night, for heaven's sake, and as the cabin lights came on, he shuddered. All over the plane, people were holding up clothes and gasping or shrieking that someone was missing.

Buck felt the same terror he had endured awaiting his death in Israel a little more than a year before. What was he going to tell Harold's wife? "You're not the only one"? "Lots of people left their clothes in their seats"?

As he hurried back to his seat, he searched his memory banks for anything he had ever read, seen, or heard of any technology that could remove people from their clothes and make them disappear from a decidedly secure environment. Whoever did this, were they on the plane? Would they make demands? Would another wave of disappearances be next? Would he become a victim? Where would he find himself?

Raymie's time before the judgment and the throne was brief, befitting his short time as a believer. But he found it nonetheless fascinating and thrilling to be welcomed to eternity by Jesus Himself. And he had to agree with his mother that seeing a replay of his own life from God's point of view would change forever how he saw the person he had once been.

How fun it was to see Jeremy and his parents, Jackie and her husband, and especially Pastor Billings get their rewards. The pastor was especially lauded for his foresight in leaving behind a recording to be discovered by those left, explaining what had happened and telling them how they could still come to Christ.

Fear seemed to pervade the cabin as Buck

climbed over his sleeping seatmate again. He stood and leaned over the back of the chair ahead of him. "Apparently many people are missing," he told the old woman.

She looked as puzzled and fearful as Buck felt.

The first officer came rushing from the cockpit, hatless and flushed. He hurried down one aisle and up the other, gaze darting from seat to seat.

Buck's seatmate roused, drooling, when an attendant asked if anyone in his party was missing. "Missing? No. And there's nobody in this party but me." He curled up again and went back to sleep.

William Franklin Graham had likely been the best-known Christian of the twentieth and early twenty-first centuries. From the moment he became a true believer, Billy Graham had been a devout follower of Christ, earnest in sharing his faith with others.

Graham's tent crusade in Los Angeles in September of 1949 was intended to last three weeks, but the preaching of the dynamic young evangelist was so compelling that it continued for eight weeks and saw several famous and high-profile people come to faith.

From there Billy Graham began to conduct mass evangelistic campaigns throughout the United States and Europe, filling the largest of the great arenas and stadiums of the world. He was soon the confidant of heads of state around the globe, never hesitating to share his personal faith with anyone. In whatever media situation he found himself, whether on a TV talk show or even a variety show, Mr. Graham found a way to share the gospel.

Throughout his life and ministry, Mr. Graham faced opposition, often from within the church, and also suffered myriad physical disabilities, including Parkinson's disease, fluid on the brain, pneumonia, broken hips, and prostate cancer. Through it all he never compromised his message that Jesus was the only avenue to God and that men and women needed to repent of their sins and be saved.

Irene particularly enjoyed seeing episodes in Mr. Graham's life that reflected his passion for Christ. She "watched" as Mr. Graham lay suffering at home with a broken hip and his doctor arrived to give him an injection, directly into the affected bone. He told Mr. Graham, "This is going to be extremely painful. You need to imagine yourself anywhere else you'd rather be than right here, right now — some Shangri-la."

Irene assumed Billy Graham would transport himself to heaven in his mind, but he said, "No, there's nowhere I'd rather be than right here, right now."

"How can you say that?" his doctor said. "I told you, this is really going to hurt."

"Because I believe I am in the center of God's will, and if this is where He wants me, this is where I want to be."

Billy Graham's works left a store of precious metals and stones from which Jesus formed the Crown of Life for all the trials he had suffered, the Crown of Glory for having taught and discipled so many over the decades, the Crown of Righteousness for his frequent emphasis on the appearing of Christ, and of course the Crown of Rejoicing for winning more souls to the Kingdom than anyone else who had ever lived.

As Mr. Graham left the throne there approached a small band of men and women, and as their story began to unfold, Irene glanced at Raymie. Something told her that to him this would prove the most captivating of all.

Twenty-Nine

First Officer Christopher Smith had been gone only a few minutes when Rayford heard his key in the cockpit door and it banged open.

Chris flopped into his chair, ignored the seat belt, and sat with his head in his hands. "What's going on, Ray? We got us more than a hundred people gone with nothing but their clothes left behind."

"That many?"

"Yeah, like it'd be better if it was only fifty? How the heck are we gonna explain landing with even one less passenger than we took off with?"

Rayford shook his head, still working the radio, trying to reach someone — anyone — in Greenland or an island in the middle of nowhere. But they were too remote even to pick up a radio station for news. Finally he connected with a French jet several miles away heading the other direction. He nodded to Christopher to put on his own earphones.

"You got enough fuel to get back to the States?" the pilot asked Rayford.

Christopher nodded and whispered, "We're halfway."

"I could turn around and make Kennedy," Rayford said.

"Forget it. Nothing's landing in New York. Two runways still open in Chicago. That's where we're going."

"We came from Chicago," Rayford said. "Can't I put down at Heathrow?"

"Negative. Closed."

"Paris?"

"Man, you've got to get back where you came from. We left Orly an hour ago, got the word what's happening, and were told to go straight to ORD."

"What *is* happening?"

"If you don't know, why'd you put out the Mayday?"

"I've got a situation here I don't even want to talk about," Rayford said.

"Hey, friend, it's all over the world, you know?"

"Negative, I don't know," Rayford said. "Talk to me."

"You're missing passengers, right?"

"Roger. More than a hundred."

"Whoa! We lost nearly fifty."

"What do you make of it? What are you going to tell your passengers?"

"No clue. You?"

"The truth," Rayford said.

"Can't hurt now. But what's the truth? What do we know?"

"Not a blessed thing."

"Good choice of words, Pan Heavy. You know what some people are saying?"

"Roger," Rayford said. "Better it's people gone to heaven than some world power doing this with fancy rays."

Why twenty people approached the altar and throne together, Raymie had no idea, until their unique story began to unfold on the panoramic screen in the theater of his mind. It was as if he had been carried to another century, living and breathing and experiencing the sights, sounds, temperatures, hopes, and fears of people from another generation.

It soon became apparent to Raymie that these twenty people included five missionary men and their families at the time the men had been martyred. He — and he knew this was true of everyone else in God's house — followed Jim Elliot, Nate Saint,

Pete Fleming, Ed McCully, and Roger Youderian to the jungles of Ecuador in January of 1956 as their small plane landed on a tiny strip of land in the midst of a violent tribe, the Waodani.

They were all aware of the danger. Jim Elliot told his wife, Elisabeth, that if it was what God wanted, he was ready to die for the salvation of the Waodani.

The initial approaches seemed favorable. The missionaries were able to coax one of the first Waodani they met into their plane, and Nate flew him over his tribespeople, who waved and smiled as he waved down at them. When they landed, the man jumped out, clapping and smiling.

But then Nate's plane was discovered on the beach, stripped of its fabric. There was no sign of anyone, neither the men nor the Waodani. When the missionaries were reported missing to the American military, the news spread quickly around the world.

After a search, the bodies of the missionaries were found in the river, speared to death. A *Life* magazine photographer arrived just as the last body was being buried by the overland search party, and the massacre became the most celebrated missionary story of the 1900s.

Now as the five missionaries knelt before

the altar and were then welcomed to the throne, Jesus praised them and their families, who had all continued in Christian work despite their grief and loss. The outcry from around the world had given voice to some who thought the men had died in vain. Yet their deaths created the biggest influx of new missionaries the world had ever seen.

After the missionaries' deaths, members of their families had moved in among the Waodani, and the children played with the children of the men who had killed their fathers.

First one, then another of the six murderers became believers in Christ. "Jesus' blood has washed my heart clean," one told Rachel, Nate's sister. "My heart is healed." The other five killers soon believed.

The five missionaries had not died in vain. Countless thousands who heard their story came to faith and dedicated their lives to mission work. God's house resounded as billions celebrated the awarding of martyrs' crowns to the missionaries.

Thirty

Christopher Smith saw himself as a good 'ol boy, and that was the way he liked to portray himself to colleagues and passengers. He was no Rayford Steele; he knew that. Steele seemed to have his whole life together. Wonderful wife, beautiful family.

Chris knew people saw him in much the same way, even though he frankly didn't think his wife was much to look at, and he didn't look the part either. He was slight and some might have said weak-looking. He didn't have that great bearing that the six-foot-four and darkly handsome Steele had. Chris got his share of action though, and that was the problem. That was his ugly secret. Part of it, anyway.

He'd grown up a nerd, had never been an athlete, not even close to being popular. So he buried himself in academics, had a scientific bent, and decided the shortest route to the kind of income and respect he wanted was in aviation. How could Chris know that with accomplishment and a uniform would come opportunities he had only dreamed of?

He had married another academic type and at least knew enough to never tell her that he assumed her romantic prospects were as limited as his. She had never been described as cute by anyone but her parents, and Christopher couldn't imagine even they had called her that since she was about nine years old. Her name fit. Jane. Plain Jane.

What made Chris feel so bad, though, was that despite her virtual invisibility and a shrill voice that could make him cringe even after sixteen years of marriage, Jane had actually turned out to be a good friend and a good wife. She was efficient and hardworking, and she seemed to care for and about him, even though he had quit trying years ago.

He had simply wanted more than he was capable of achieving, and it didn't help to have other than a trophy wife. Chris knew he had no business even dreaming of one, but once he found that certain flight attendants and even some lonely passengers were impressed by his station and uniform, his wedding vows had flown out the window.

A girl in every port? Sure. Any who really cared for him? Only one, from what he could tell, and he had treated her as shabbily as he had Jane. Chris had given up hoping that one of the attractive ones would really take to him for more than a salve to her own loneliness or the occasional gift he brought from faraway destinations. Those secret liaisons left him miserable and depressed, but not enough to get him to quit. In fact, he had made a huge mistake with the only one he thought really cared. He had married her too. Under a different name. Chris was living a double life.

What should have been complicated he had found easy. His second wife thought he was an international cargo pilot, gone for days and weeks at a time.

Since his sons had become teenagers and developed minds of their own, Chris's trysts — private and short-lived and with no futures — seemed all he was really living for. The bigamy was merely for convenience, and that hadn't amounted to much.

Now as he sat stunned in the cockpit with some sort of *Twilight Zone* cosmic phenomenon having affected not just Steele's and his plane but also apparently all planes and every country of the world, Christopher Smith was overcome with fear and dread.

Overhearing his captain discuss the possible religious aspects of all this didn't do much for him either. All that did was remind him of his sons.

Those boys had once been the joy of his life. Then in junior high school they had become troublemakers, both of them. He was constantly being called in to answer for them or to be informed of their latest mischief. On the one hand he liked that they had their own ideas, but he didn't like what was happening to their grades and their reputations. *His* reputation.

But what had happened with them lately was worse. They had found religion. One of their friends invited them to some sort of church activity, and while they got into trouble there too, they all of a sudden decided they wanted to go to summer camp the year before with that same bunch. That was all right with Chris and Jane, even though it cost them a little money. Maybe the kids would learn something. Maybe they wouldn't. But at least they would be out from underfoot for a couple of weeks.

Well, the worst happened. They came back Holy Rollers. There was no other way to put it. Now they were churchgoers, and not only that, they thought everybody else in the world — Chris and Jane included —

ought to go too. But Chris knew better. Thankfully, so did his wife. They'd both had enough religion as kids, and the best they could hope for was that the boys would grow out of this.

But they didn't. It had been nine months now, and the boys were worse than ever. Carried their Bibles to public school, no less. Became known as church kids. Their grades perked back up. That was all right. But the cost.

Oh, my, Chris thought, *the terrible cost.* Now he was the Pan-Con first officer with a long, boring marriage, a plain wife, two Christian-kook kids, and a guilt-inducing private life that included another wife. Why did it make him feel so bad when he didn't claim any moral authority? He couldn't say. He just knew that what he was doing on the side was something Jane — for whatever her shortcomings and weaknesses — would never do to him and didn't deserve having done to her.

Strange, Christopher barely thought of wife number two in this moment of crisis, but he found himself frantic to know how his real family was. The boys were supposed to be at some church thing tonight, and Jane was to pick them up when it was over. If these vanishings really happened at the same time all over the world, they could very well have been right out in the middle of it at the time.

As a woman knelt before the altar of fire, Jesus stood and began to narrate scenes from her life depicted in Irene's mind. She noticed that Raymie looked just as fascinated as she.

First Irene watched as the woman, clearly from the first century, buried her husband. Then she moved from a comfortable home into a small room at the back of a hovel shared with two other families who seemed to ignore her. Irene watched her visit the Temple in Jerusalem and pray.

The woman ate from gleanings of the fields she passed on her way to sweep out the home of a rich family in an area where she had once lived. Often she stopped to pray. At the end of each week the house owner pressed into her palm a single coin.

Now she was visiting the Temple again, standing in line behind wealthy people making a show of dumping huge amounts of money into the coffers. In the background Irene could see Jesus sitting opposite the treasury.

As the woman's works were tested in the fire and resulted in precious metals and stones, Jesus said, "And many who were rich put in much. Then one poor widow came and threw in two mites — the least valuable Roman coins, two of which make a farthing. I called My disciples to Myself and said, 'Assuredly, I say to you that this poor widow has put in more than all those who have given to the treasury; for they all put in out of their abundance, but she out of her poverty put in all that she had, her whole livelihood.' "

Chris Smith hadn't talked — really talked — to his boys for years. Oh, they'd had shouting matches, threats, reprimands, punishments. There had been a full complement of cold shoulders, slammed doors, epithets, and ultimatums. But in the end, just before the boys had found that old-time religion, Chris had given up. He'd been no prize as a teenager either, and look how he turned out. Yeah, just look.

Did he want them to turn out as he had? A dishonest, cheating weasel? A bigamist? All Chris knew was that no matter what he did or said, he was no example to them and they were going to do what they were going to do, regardless.

But he was curious. Could this, whatever it was, be a religious thing? a God thing?

And if so, what did it mean? Would the boys know? They really seemed into church, and they were smart, but had they learned enough to know about stuff like what had happened now? Chris felt an urgent need to talk with them, to see what they made of it all.

He also began having a crisis of conscience. Little from the real world had ever affected him to any significant extent. To Chris, news was news, something that happened to everybody else. But now he was the number-two man in a jumbo jet with a third of her passengers gone. This wasn't going to be something he could watch on TV and gas about with his poker buddies.

Worse, as the 747 made the huge turnaround and he set the coordinates to get them to ORD by early morning Central time, Rayford asked him to start twisting the dials to see if he could dredge up some news signal from anywhere. They were in one of the worst spots in the world for that, but it wouldn't be long before they would come within range of Greenland and Canada and even the eastern seaboard of the U.S. If it was true that this was some kind of global phenomenon, Chris couldn't imagine what the news would sound like.

New emotions began to roll over him as

he played with the dials. Captain Steele seemed preoccupied and wasn't checking in with him for a progress report, apparently assuming that as soon as Christopher found something, he'd let Rayford know. But as Chris encountered solid static for several minutes, he couldn't keep his mind from going where he really hadn't wanted it to go. What was it about a natural disaster that seemed to focus one's inner eye squarely on one's self?

Except for knowing that his private liaisons — and of course the other marriage — were not things he ever wanted Jane to know about — and especially not the boys — Christopher had rarely had a problem keeping his conscience at bay. There was much in his life he wouldn't be proud to have made public, so he just rarely thought about it.

That wasn't working now. It was as if a black cloud was descending on Chris Smith, and he couldn't get out from under it. What kind of person, what kind of man, was he? For whatever shortcomings his wife had, Jane was a good person, surely more than he deserved. She could even be sweet. And she was a servant.

Guilt. That was what Chris was feeling. In one sense he was grateful that he had always been careful and that she had no clue what he did on the road. That was big of him, wasn't it? To consider her feelings? That's what he had always told himself. He deserved these secret pleasures, but he was considerate enough not to hurt or embarrass his wife. Hadn't that been his motive?

Of course it hadn't, and he had known that all along. He had been covering for himself, but now this crazy worldwide-vanishing business was making him focus, keeping him from hiding behind his usual blather. He was feeling like the scoundrel he was.

Chris shook his head and tried to block these thoughts and feelings by busying himself even more with his task. But it wasn't rocket science. He was spinning dials hoping to lock onto some signal strong enough to bring the news into the cockpit. He could have done that in his sleep, and what a relief that would be.

He had to admit that this was becoming a personal crisis. Chris found himself desperately wanting to talk with his wife, yet he knew that it would take an awful lot longer to come within range of air-to-ground telephoning than it would to finally pick up some scratchy radio-news report.

Christopher was actually shaking and

wondered if it showed. What would he do if something had happened to Jane? And the boys? While they had become a nuisance and an embarrassment, he was suddenly overcome with the reality that they were his flesh, his life, his heart. What was this? Love? Was he loving his family, or was he just afraid for them . . . or for himself?

The longer the plane droned on, the deeper Chris felt himself burrowing into a dark hole of despair.

Thirty-One

Irene and Raymie sat fingering their crowns and — Irene knew — thinking the same thing without speaking. It was so joyous to be in the presence of Jesus, the lover of their souls. But just as Pastor Billings had predicted so many times in so many sermons on so many Sundays over so many months, there was something unique not only about their new, glorified bodies but also about the way their new, glorified minds worked.

As wonderful as it had been to hear "Well done" from the only perfect man to have ever lived and to be welcomed into God's house and to receive crowns of reward, none of that hit them as some cheap imitation as it might have on Earth. Irene had attended countless meetings where people were thanked and lauded and presented with plaques, trophies, cups, framed certificates, and the like for any bit of service they had rendered or accomplishment they might have achieved.

But to be holding in one's own hands a reward for your works in service of Christ would have been beyond comprehension and expression on Earth. This gold-and-silver amalgam was unlike anything Irene had ever seen. And the jewels embedded in it were so exquisite and dazzling that even her new eyes had to adjust to light reflected not from the sun or artificial sources but from God Himself.

As she sat there, somehow able to cherish and admire the headpiece while missing nothing of the hundreds of thousands of judgments and rewards as people filed past the altar and the throne, Irene came to realize what her pastor had been driving at all that time.

As thrilled as she was to be here and to feel the personal attention from the One loved and admired and exalted by all of creation, she had no more interest in her crown than she did in leaving this place. As beautiful and meaningful as it was, representing her life in Christ, she simply did not want it and could not keep it. Raymie was experiencing the same emotion; she could tell. They glanced at each other and shrugged.

This jewelry had one purpose only, and

that was to be returned to the Giver, bestowed, laid at the feet of Jesus. In Raymie's eyes Irene saw that he was getting the same impression she was, that the 20 billion or so other saints in God's house had come to the same conclusion. And above the din of constant praise to the Lamb who had been slain for the sins of the world and the bursts of celebration by the angelic choir every time someone on Earth was welcomed into the Kingdom, there seemed a palpable hum, a buzz of excitement and anticipation. For at some point, Irene realized, everyone there was going to cast their crowns at Jesus' feet.

"Mom," Raymie said, "we don't even have to discuss things here, do we?"

She shook her head.

"I mean, at first it seemed like we were on the same wavelength and I could communicate with you without words, but I wondered whether it was true, whether we were thinking about the same thing at the same time. But I don't wonder anymore. I just know."

"Me too," Irene said.

"How much fun is this? What am I thinking right now?"

Irene felt like smiling, only to realize that her grin couldn't get any bigger anyway. She had been in a constant state of euphoria since she had arrived, and somehow it invigorated her, didn't exhaust her. She wanted it to never end, and she knew it would not. "You're wondering how much we can do all at the same time."

"Right."

"You want to study the crown, witness the judgments, talk with your heroes — old and new — sing with the choir, praise Jesus, talk with me, communicate silently with me, and — above all — you want to tour the rest of this place."

"I do. But I'm a little hesitant to ask. What is that? I should know by now that God knows what I want before I say it, even before I am aware of it myself. Why do I wonder if I'm bothering Him or if something is too much to ask?"

Irene shrugged. "We have new minds and bodies, but we have memories. Maybe in a million or so years we'll be completely free of our humanness."

Raymie laughed. "We already are."

"I know."

Christopher Smith was frantic by the time he finally realized the Pan-Continental 747 was within satellite communication range of the United States. For some reason the usual connections with Greenland and

Canada had produced no results. He couldn't make that compute. Had something happened in the atmosphere to interrupt the signals? Radio and TV signals couldn't be jammed from overloading.

A superstation out of New Jersey reached his headphones, faint and staticky and in and out at first. Finally Christopher was able to catch every word if he pressed the earphones tight, shut his eyes, and concentrated. He would let Rayford know as soon as the signal was listenable without such work. The captain clearly had enough on his mind.

Chris's neck and shoulders tightened and cramped as he concentrated, but suddenly, as if they had passed some invisible barrier, the signal came through strong and clear. He flipped a switch that allowed him to communicate directly to Rayford's headphones. "Patching you through to Jersey Shore All-News Radio, Cap."

"Roger, thanks. Keep us on course."

That was Rayford's way of saying he would listen to the radio while Chris did the work for a while. Fat chance. Chris was as curious as the boss was, and the plane was on autopilot. Chris knew how to appear as if he were concentrating on the controls while leaving the radio frequency open to his own headset.

Once the controls were set Chris stared out the window at the strange colors in the sky. Here they were heading back toward the States at an unusual time of day, working with various towers to stay on course and at the right altitude as thousands of planes sought landing strips all over the world. *How different,* he thought, *to have the rising sun at our backs.*

The impact of the global tragedy was transmitted directly into Chris's ears. Depressed, terrified, despairing — that had been one thing. Now thoughts of suicide began to invade, and he knew if he didn't talk to his loved ones soon, he might go mad. *Loved ones.* When was the last time he had referred to Jane and the boys as his loved ones? His women had been his loved ones, but he knew he had never loved one of them. Not even his other wife. Not even Hattie, the young senior attendant on this very flight. Of course, she had not given him the time of day since a one-night stand they had enjoyed in Spain several months before. He'd had no illusions about that. Half the time even then she had peppered him with questions about Rayford. As if she would have a chance with a dyed-in-the-wool family man like Steele.

★ ★ ★

"Yes," God told Raymie Steele, "you can do anything and everything you wish simultaneously."

"Without missing anything?" Raymie said.

God did not answer that, which was okay with Raymie, as he knew the answer as soon as he had blurted the question. And in the next instant he was in his mansion. When first he had heard this business about a "mansion over the hilltop" in heaven, Raymie hadn't known what to make of it. He knew what a mansion was. It was a home much bigger than the comfortable suburban house his father had provided. He had seen incredible houses on TV shows. Maybe it would be something like those.

On the other hand, Pastor Billings had hammered home the point that Jesus had left the earth two thousand years before "to prepare a place for you," so it would have to be something more spectacular even than the earth itself, which was created in six days.

The first surprise to Raymie was that his name was on the door. He had been expected. And inside his seventy-five-cubic-acre estate was a stunning reproduction of Earth, a gigantic sphere suspended before

382

him like a school globe come to life in full color, so bright and glittering that he was irresistibly drawn to it.

There was no chair, no table, no bed — none of the necessities of earthly life. Raymie simply wouldn't need anything like that. The question was, what did he need with this replica of Earth, big enough for him to walk around on and in it? He learned that as soon as he stepped aboard. It proved merely a trigger to his mind. Regardless of where he stepped, artifacts from various periods of history appeared, and by merely looking at them or touching them, he was instantly conveyed to that time and place and could watch as history repeated itself.

Why not start from the beginning? he thought, and he moved toward the Fertile Crescent and found himself in the Garden of Eden. A gleaming piece of fruit caught his eye, and there he was, watching as Eve conversed with the serpent and took the fateful bite. The snake hissed in glee, Eve's countenance fell, and Adam soon joined her.

It had all been true, the biblical record, and Raymie could immerse himself in every incident and see as it played out. He leaped from there to Mount Ararat and saw Noah's ark bobbing on forty days and nights' worth of water. He would get back to this, for there was a pile of bricks and mortar and thousands of men milling about and working, building . . . what? The tower of Babel.

Raymie had all of eternity to watch and listen and experience everything that had ever happened. He experimented with speeding ahead in time and saw the assassinations of Julius Caesar and then Abraham Lincoln. And how about that time his friends had all sworn he was out at second base, when he just knew they were wrong? He touched the base and watched the play, bursting with laughter when his friends were proved right.

All the time Raymie was experimenting, hopping from here to there and from this age to that, he was also enjoying the judgment of the works of the saints from the ground floor of God's house. What could be better than this? In due time he would return and witness the death of Jesus on the cross and then the triumphant Resurrection.

When the captain had come back on the intercom with the information about returning to the United States, Buck Williams was surprised to hear applause throughout the cabin. Shocked and terrified as everyone was, he assumed most were from the States and wanted at least to return to familiarity.

Buck nudged the businessman on his right. "I'm sorry, friend, but you're going to want to be awake for this."

The man peered at Buck with a disgusted look and slurred, "If we're not crashin', don't bother me."

Irene soon realized that with all she had seen in what supposedly was just minutes on Earth, those "first" on Earth who were to be "last" here had finally begun. It seemed that many of the heroes of the Bible, despite all they had been through and all they had accomplished, were considered first because they had been made known to generations through the Bible.

Irene was fascinated by the stories of many of the disciples, some of whom approached the altar from their positions among the twenty-four elders before the throne. Matthew, the tax collector, of course had none of his conniving and scheming held against him, as all that predated his experience with Jesus and his calling as one of the Twelve. Mark and Luke were lauded for their writing and their various ministries, as well as Stephen, the first martyr; the great women of the New Testament; and hundreds of others Irene had heard and read about.

As the line grew shorter and shorter, Irene saw three more rise from the twenty-four elders, plus one more woman and two more men. She had been keeping track mentally of the Bible greats she had seen here and the ones she knew were yet to come. She was pretty sure she knew who these last six were, and she could hardly wait to find out if she was right.

Christopher Smith felt as alone as he had ever been in his life. As he sat listening to the Jersey radio outlet he learned that communication lines were jammed all over the world, so the disappearances affected people from every continent. Medical, technical, and service people were among the missing. Every civil service and emergency agency was on full red-alert status, trying to keep up with the unending chaos. Chris had seen coverage of natural disasters and terrorist attacks and mass-transit crashes that saw hospital, fire, and police personnel called in from miles around. He could only imagine that multiplied tens of thousands of times.

Even the newscasters' voices were terror filled, as much as they seemed to be trying to cover it. Every conceivable explanation was proffered, but overshadowing all such discussion and even coverage of the carnage were the practical aspects. What people wanted from the news was simple information on how to get where they were going and how to determine whether their loved ones were still around and to contact them if they could.

Chris had to flip off the news and reconnect with a tower when they were instructed to get into a multistate traffic pattern that would allow them to land at O'Hare at a precise moment, now just hours hence. Only two runways were open, and every large plane in the country seemed headed that way.

Thousands were dead in plane crashes and car pileups. Emergency crews were trying to clear expressways and runways, all the while grieving over their own family members and coworkers who had disappeared. One report said that so many cabbies had disappeared from the cab corral at O'Hare that volunteers were being brought in to move the cars that had been left running with the former drivers' clothes still on the seats.

Cars driven by people who spontaneously disappeared had careened out of control, of course. The toughest chore for emergency personnel was to determine who had disappeared, who had been killed, and who was injured, then communicate that to the survivors.

"Cap," Chris said, "I hate to ask, but do you think we could get somebody in the Chicago tower to try to connect me — us — to our home phones?"

Rayford shrugged. "Worth a try." So he asked.

He was laughed off.

Thirty-Two

With only half a dozen saints to go and Raymie glorying in what he had found in his personal living space, Irene watched and listened as a tall dark man slowly approached the altar and fell to his knees.

His works were tested and polished by the fire, then formed into a beautiful Crown of Life, which Jesus gave to him following an embrace and a "well done."

"Just as the virgin was chosen," Jesus said, "so were you, My earthly father. This reflects your perseverance through many trials for My sake."

"But at first I was angry," Joseph said. "Frustrated, confused. I did not respond as one chosen."

"As soon as you knew the truth, you gave of yourself for Me and My mother and treated Me as if I were your own."

"It always felt to me as if You were."

Irene enjoyed peeking in on Joseph's life and eavesdropping on his conversations with Mary, with the angel, and with Jesus at various ages. She couldn't wait to test the features in her mansion and physically enter the world at any place and era she wished.

For the first time in his life, Christopher Smith understood what it meant to be beside oneself. His private agony was so acute that it was as if he had left the very presence of his body and could see himself from afar. There he sat in his usual spot behind the cockpit controls he knew so well. And yet his soul wrestled within.

He made himself sick. Something about this horrible universal incident had forced him to shine a spotlight on his character, and he could not hide from himself. His life was a waste. He was worthless. And he was desperate to connect with his real wife, his boys.

Why? Why now after all these years? What could Jane do? What did the boys have to offer, other than some theological treatise they had learned at church or mumbo-jumbo camp? And even if they could tell him this was indeed somehow connected with God, what would that do for him? It was too late to become one of "those." He had traveled his own road much too long and much too far. God could never forgive what he had done, could not really change who he was.

It wasn't answers Chris sought from his wife and kids. It was some remedy for this enormous loneliness. Why did he feel so isolated? Had he done this to himself? Of course he had. He had made Jane in particular an emotional hostage, and he might as well have abandoned his sons. They had offered little protest, apparently not needing him. And that was okay. That helped assuage any guilt. Maybe his presence and support — being the sorry excuse for a man he knew himself to be — should not be missed.

But now. Now. He needed *them!* How might they respond to such a cry of want? He knew them. They were good people at heart. Even with what he had become, they would rally round him, be there for him despite the fact that he had been so detached from their lives for so long.

Chris didn't know what he would do if he could not somehow reach them soon.

"I am most unworthy," the man said who now knelt before the altar of flame.

"You were a doubter, Thomas," Jesus said. "But I forgave you of that, and once you were convinced, you became most energetic and devout. See how you atoned for your disbelief! Your works have tested favorably. The stones will make a beautiful Crown of Righteousness. You were one who wanted to know where I was going, so you could be here with Me."

"And here I am!" Thomas said.

"And here you are."

Funny how a terrifying disaster changes a man's perspective, Rayford thought. Any thoughts, hopes, or desires for Hattie Durham now struck him as the most ludicrous ideas he had ever had. If she had thrown herself at him right then, he'd have cast her aside. Cold? Yes. Mean? That too. Rayford had, after all, been encouraging her for weeks. But what in the world had he been thinking?

All he wanted now was to reunite with Irene and Chloe and Raymie. But deep in his gut he feared the worst: that Chloe and he would be the only half of his family left.

Rayford had told Hattie that he didn't know what was happening any more than she did. But the terrifying truth was that he knew all too well. Irene had been right. He and Chloe and most of his passengers had been left behind.

★ ★ ★

Thirteen-year-old Lionel Washington was proud of his mother, but for reasons other than that she seemed wise in the areas of forgiveness and acceptance. The truth was, with her job as Chicago bureau chief of *Global Weekly* magazine, she was the star of the family. Not just Lionel's family, but the whole Washington clan. They traced their roots to the freedom riders on the Underground Railroad during the days of slavery, and many of his ancestors had been active in the civil rights movement, fighting for equal opportunities among the races. His mother was one who had proved that a person — regardless of her color or the housing project she had grown up in — could achieve and make something of herself if she really committed herself to it.

Lucinda Washington told Lionel that she had been born and raised in a Cleveland ghetto, but "I loved to study. And that was my way out of the projects." She said she fell in love with reporting and writing. She had graduated from journalism school and worked her way up finally to *Global Weekly.*

She made good money, even more than her husband, Charles, who was a heavy-equipment operator. He was as proud of her as anyone, and secretly Lionel was proud of her too.

But Lionel had another secret, and it caused him no end of anxiety. Lionel knew something no one else in the family even suspected. He was not really a Christian, even though the whole family history revolved around church. Family legend said his mother had taken him to church when he was less than a week old.

Actually, he liked church a lot. Church was what the Washington family was all about, but Lionel knew it went deeper than that. His mother not only loved church; she also truly loved God. And Jesus. And the Holy Spirit.

Lionel admitted to his mother's younger brother, his uncle André, that he had never really become a Christian. André was the criminal of the family. Lionel told him, "Everybody thinks you're a Christian who has bad spells once in a while. They think I might become a preacher or a missionary someday."

"You ought to talk with your mother about this," Uncle André said. "I'd rather see you grow up like her than like me."

"I can't. It'd kill her. She thinks I'm one of the best young Christians she knows. Hey, Uncle André, aren't you afraid it might all be true and we might end up in hell?"

André threw back his head and cackled that crazy laugh of his. "Now *that* I do not believe. I may have once, but I've outgrown that. Some of these stories and legends about what's going to happen at the end of the world — I don't know where the preachers get them. I can't imagine they're in the Bible."

The evening before, the last time Lionel had seen his mother, she had pulled him close and said, "Isn't the Lord wonderful? Don't we have a good God? Hmm? Aren't you glad to serve a God who loves you so much?"

"Um-hmm," Lionel said. "Sure, Mama. 'Course I am."

He felt terrible. Like a hypocrite. Like the liar he was.

There was no clock in the basement of the Washington home, where Lionel slept. The next morning it seemed too bright, too late, when he awoke. He didn't feel like moving. He merely opened his eyes, squinted at the sun rays that had somehow found their way through the tiny windows, and watched the dust dance in the columns of light.

When the phone rang upstairs and Lionel heard no footsteps, he groaned and whipped off the blankets, marching up to answer it. It must have been really early for his mother to not be up yet. And his dad usually made some racket heading out. Lionel noticed that his dad's truck was still parked in front of the garage, where his mother's car was kept. Both still sleeping? Strange.

The call was from *Global Weekly*, asking after his mother. Lionel was stunned to see that it was the middle of the morning. He could be the hero, the one who roused everyone so they wouldn't be even later for work.

Lionel went from the kitchen through the dining room toward the stairs that led to the upstairs bedrooms. He noticed something in his peripheral vision. On his dad's easy chair lay his oversize terry-cloth robe. Lionel stopped and stared. He had never known his father to take his robe off outside the bedroom. Mr. Washington considered it impolite to walk around in public in just his pajamas, even referring to his own family as the public.

Maybe he had been warm and shed his robe while half asleep, not thinking. But that wasn't like him. He had always taken great pride in not being "one of those husbands whose wife always has to trail him, picking up after him."

Lionel's father's slippers sat on the floor in front of the chair. The robe lay neatly, arms draped on the sides of the chair almost as if Dad's elbows still rested there. When Lionel saw the pajama legs extending from the bottom of the robe and hanging just above the slippers, it was obvious that his father had disappeared right out of his pajamas and robe.

It was as if life had switched to slow motion. Lionel was not aware of his body as he carefully advanced, holding his breath and feeling only the pounding of his heart. The harsh sunlight shone on the robe and picked up sparkling glints of something where Dad's lap should have been.

Lionel knelt and stared at his father's tiny contact lenses, his wristwatch, his wedding ring, his dental fillings, and his hearing aid. Lionel's hands shook as he forced himself to exhale before he exploded. He felt his lips quiver and was aware of screams he could not let out. He crept forward on his knees and opened the robe to find his dad's pajamas still buttoned all the way up. Lionel recoiled and sat back, his feet under him. He lowered his face to between his knees and sobbed. If this was what he feared it was, he knew what he would find upstairs.

He ran to the stairs and bounded up two

at a time. The master bedroom was more than he could bear. His parents' bed was still made, his mother's nightclothes draped on one side, where it was obvious she had been kneeling in prayer. How Lionel wished he had been taken to heaven with his family and that he had been found reading his Bible or praying when Jesus came.

Only for an instant had Lionel wondered if he was dreaming. He knew better. This was real; this was the truth. All doubt and question had disappeared. His family had been raptured as his church, his pastor, and his parents had taught.

And he had been left behind.

Thirty-Three

Everybody in God's house knew who the young woman who now approached the altar was, and all, including Jesus Himself, rose to cheer and applaud her. As she knelt facedown before the flame, the praise continued as her works were tried by fire.

Irene found it amusing that she felt a kinship with Mary, simply because she also was a woman. There, she decided, any similarity ended. Well, Irene had had children, as Mary had. And she had been married. But clearly Mary had been a young person of such character that God chose her for the greatest responsibility a woman could sustain. Irene was eager to enter that first-century world and get to know Mary as a child and then the young woman so chosen.

As Irene watched, the young Mary was startled to see the angel Gabriel appear to her. Abject terror marred her face, but Gabriel said, "Rejoice, highly favored one, the Lord is with you; blessed are you among women!"

Mary was speechless, pale, and trembling.

Gabriel said, "Do not be afraid, Mary, for you have found favor with God. And behold, you will conceive in your womb and bring forth a Son, and shall call His name Jesus. He will be great, and will be called the Son of the Highest; and the Lord God will give Him the throne of His father David. And He will reign over the house of Jacob forever, and of His kingdom there will be no end."

Mary said, "How can this be, since I do not know a man?"

Gabriel said, "The Holy Spirit will come upon you, and the power of the Highest will overshadow you; therefore, also, that Holy One who is to be born will be called the Son of God. For with God nothing will be impossible."

Mary said, "Behold the maidservant of the Lord! Let it be to me according to your word."

Now, as Mary rose from the altar and approached the throne, Jesus presented her the crowns of Life and Righteousness, embracing her and saying, "Well done, good and faithful servant."

Mary said, "My son has become my Father. My soul magnifies You, O Lord, and my spirit rejoices in God my Savior. For He regarded the lowly state of His maidservant, and all generations have since called me blessed. He who is mighty has done great things for me, and holy is His name. His mercy fell on those who feared Him from generation to generation. He showed strength with His arm; He scattered the proud in the imagination of their hearts. He put down the mighty from their thrones, and exalted the lowly."

By the time the plane began its descent into Chicago, Buck Williams noticed that the senior flight attendant looked dangerously shaky. He beckoned her and reached for her wrist, looking again at her name tag. "Hattie, we're all going to go home and cry today. But hang in there. Get your passengers off the plane, and you can at least feel good about that."

His words didn't help. She began to sob. "You know we lost several old people but not all of them. And we lost several middle-aged people but not all of them. And we lost several people your age and my age but not all of them. We even lost some teenagers."

Buck stared at her. What was she driving at?

"Sir, we lost every child and baby on this plane."

"How many were there?"

"More than a dozen. But all of them! Not one was left."

The man next to Buck finally roused and squinted at the early morning sun burning through the window. "What in blazes are you two talking about?"

"We're about to land in Chicago," Hattie said. "I've got to run."

"Chicago?"

"You don't want to know," Buck said.

The man nearly sat in Buck's lap to get a look out the window, his boozy breath enveloping Buck. "What, are we at war? Riots? What?"

Smoke. Fire. Cars off the road and smashed into each other and guardrails. Planes in pieces on the ground. Emergency vehicles, lights flashing, picking their way around the debris.

As O'Hare came into view, it was clear no one was going anywhere soon. There were planes as far as the eye could see, some crashed and burning, the others gridlocked in line. People trudged through the grass and between vehicles toward the terminal.

The expressways that led to the airport looked like they had during the great Chicago blizzards, only without the snow.

Cranes and wreckers were trying to clear a path through the front of the terminal so cars could get in and out, but that would take hours, if not days. A snake of humanity wended its way slowly out of the terminal buildings, between the motionless cars, and onto the ramps. People walking, walking, walking, looking for a cab or a limo.

Raymie Steele was pretty sure he knew who the next man to be judged was, and his suspicion was immediately proved right as a rugged young man fell weeping before the altar. His works shone brightly in the flame, and there was certainly no wood, hay, or stubble. He had not been a perfect man, and he had failed the Lord more than once, but he had been forgiven his sins and had served God faithfully to the day of his death.

When beckoned to the throne for his crowns and his "well done," Peter hesitated and asked Jesus' forgiveness "for denying You thrice on Your way to the cross."

"My friend, you were forgiven the first time you repented, and it was never remembered again — except by you when you confessed it again and again. I commend you for your faithfulness in leading My early church, for your passionate preaching on what has become known as the Day of Pentecost, and for being the first to communicate My truth to the Jews in Jerusalem. And I praise you for your willingness to preach to the Gentiles, opening the door of faith and salvation to millions.

"You never again denied Me following My resurrection and return to heaven. And when you were martyred for My cause, you chose to be hung upside down, considering yourself unworthy to die in the manner in which I did. I welcome you to the eternal joy of My Father and present to you the crowns of Life, Glory, Righteousness, and Rejoicing."

Jesus placed one of the crowns on Peter's head, and Peter turned to face the masses with the other three in his hands. Raymie thought he looked embarrassed to be holding them.

Raymie and his mother leaped to their feet with the rest of the endless throng, cheering and clapping as Peter turned and praised Jesus. And as they watched, Peter removed the crown from his head and, putting it with his other three, knelt and placed them at the feet of his Savior.

Thus began a parade of saints doing the

same, one after the other in crowds so huge one couldn't tell where they began and ended. And when the crowns piled so high that they nearly blotted out the view of Jesus, they melted away and became part of the glassy sea and the gold-paved streets.

Thirty-Four

Christopher Smith had his cell phone plastered to his ear as he helped the rest of the crew get everyone off the plane, directing them to slide down plastic chutes. A few buses arrived for the infirm, but almost all the passengers walked.

Chris was unable to reach Jane or the boys, so he called everywhere he could think of. Finally he reached his local police department and a desk sergeant so harried that Chris was surprised the man would talk to him at all.

"Your wife was involved in a TA, yes."

"A TA?"

"Traffic accident — sorry."

"And is she all right? Where is she?"

"I am not at liberty to discuss this by phone, sir."

"What are you talking about? I need to know if she's all right and, if not, what hospital she's in. And my sons. Had she picked them up? Were they in the car yet? We both know you know. Now tell me."

"You are to call a Mr. Ira Smith. You know him?"

" 'Course I know him. He's my uncle. Why do I need to call him?"

"He can tell you what you need to know."

Chris was dialing his uncle as he and Rayford and Hattie disembarked. The driver of the last bus insisted that the crew ride with him.

Rayford refused. "I can't see passing my own passengers as they walk to the terminal. How would that look?"

Christopher said, "Suit yourself, Cap. You mind if I take him up on his offer?"

Rayford glared at him. "You're serious?"

"I don't get paid enough for this."

"Like this was the airline's fault. Chris, you don't mean it."

"The heck I don't. By the time you get up there you'll wish you'd ridden too."

"I should write you up for this."

"Millions of people disappear into thin air and I should worry about getting written up for riding instead of walking? Later, Steele."

Only two men remained. When Jesus stood and said, "John," the masses erupted.

The disciple Jesus loved knelt at the altar, and his works also showed no waste — no hay, wood, or stubble. He was awarded all but the martyr's crown, as he was the only one of the faithful disciples who had not been put to death for his faith.

Jesus and John embraced like the old friends they were, and Jesus said, "I commend you for never denying My name before men, for writing your Gospel and the three letters that bear your name. Also for faithfully recording My revelation, chronicling the vision I bestowed upon you. You were a witness for many years as shepherd of many flocks, primarily the church at Ephesus, where you also tutored and mentored so many of those who carried on the work after the deaths of the apostles.

"Thank you for taking care of My earthly mother. Well done, good and faithful servant. Because you have been loyal and trustworthy and dependable in so many things, I will therefore make you ruler over many cities. Welcome into the joy of the Lord forever."

"Chris, you need to get home," Uncle Ira said. "I'll be waiting for you there."

"No, you don't! Tell me right now what's happened to my family!"

"I really need to do this in person. I'm not going to try to get into everything over the phone."

"Yes, you are! Now I mean it, Ira! I'll be hours getting out of here and into the suburbs. Don't make me wait that long. They're dead, aren't they? They were all killed."

"Not exactly."

"What does that mean? If they're there, let me talk to them!"

"If you have to know and won't take no for an answer, I'm sorry to tell you that, yes, Jane is gone."

"What happened?"

"She was on her way to pick up the boys, and a tractor trailer hit her head-on. The driver was one of those who disappeared right out of his clothes."

"No! But the boys weren't with her?"

"No, but, Chris, they're gone too."

"Oh no! No! How did *they* die?"

"Their wallets were found at the church in the parking lot, along with the clothes and personal effects of several dozen other kids and staff from the church. I guess they were out there waiting for their rides when this happened."

Chris was mentally reaching for anything that would keep him from going over the edge. "Then they'll find them. The boys will be back. The boys aren't dead."

"Nobody knows where these people are, Chris," Ira said. "There wasn't one person left at the church. The truth is nobody knows if we'll see these people again."

"Don't say that!"

"You wanted the truth. Now, I'm sorry, but there's both barrels. You come straight home as soon as you can now, hear? Your aunt is putting together a meal for you."

"Tell her not to bother."

"She's already bothered. We can only imagine how awful this is for you. Get here so we can take care of you."

"Yeah," Chris said, letting his phone flap shut. Take care of him? Unless they could bring back Jane and the boys, there would be no taking care of Christopher Smith. That everybody at the church had disappeared told him everything he needed to know. God *was* behind this. His boys had somehow qualified, and he and Jane hadn't. In some absurd way, that made sense.

He deserved this.

But he couldn't imagine life without them. He wouldn't even consider it. Christopher Smith was not about to go home to an empty house, to be the object of concern and pity by his elderly relatives. As soon as he could find a private place and the means, he was going to make sure he didn't spend more than ten more minutes on this godforsaken planet.

"Paul."

There was a reason the apostle who had never personally met Jesus had been saved for last. He was the most well-known person in the New Testament besides Jesus Himself. And he had so profoundly articulated the faith in deep theological treatises that millions through the ages had come to understand and believe the gospel.

What a story, Raymie thought. A scholar who had been so opposed to the Christian message that he had actually killed Christians had become the writer of so much of the New Testament.

Paul seemed eager to meet Jesus, even as he knelt before the flame that left a precious residue of only gems and gold and silver. And when he approached the throne, he dropped to his knees, begging forgiveness for having originally been a persecutor of the church.

"Your sins," Jesus said, lifting him and embracing him, "have been removed as far as the east is from the west. You came to believe in Me so completely that you offered every fiber of your being in service to Me.

Yours was the ultimate expression of a life-time of worship. I award you all four crowns of reward, good and faithful servant. Thank you for being the first to take My gospel to Europe, which became the gateway to the rest of the world."

Facing Jesus, with his back to the crowd, Paul was still able to be heard. "I thank You for Your sacrifice, which provided eternal life to all who believed in Your name, for Your finished work on the cross, for Your resurrection. And thank You for sending Your Holy Spirit to be our Comforter, who guided and strengthened us through all our trials and sufferings. I will praise Your name forever."

And with that, Paul too laid his crowns at the feet of Jesus.

Rayford Steele feared he had a better idea than most of what had happened. If he was right, if it was true, it explained why he was not getting an answer when he dialed home. Most shocking, as he stood in the terminal, was watching a TV monitor above him broadcast images of the chaos. From around the globe came wailing mothers, stoic families, reports of death and destruction. Dozens of stories included eyewitnesses who had seen loved ones and friends disappear before their eyes.

A woman in labor, about to go into the delivery room, was suddenly barren. Doctors delivered the placenta. Her husband had caught the disappearance of the fetus on tape. There was a scream, the dropping of the camera, terrified voices, running nurses, and the doctor. CNN reran the footage in superslow motion, showing the woman going from very pregnant to nearly flat stomached, as if she had instantaneously delivered.

Local television stations from around the world reported bizarre occurrences, especially in the time zones where the event had happened during the day or early evening. CNN showed via satellite the footage of a groom disappearing while slipping the ring onto his bride's finger. A funeral home in Australia reported that nearly every mourner had disappeared from one memorial service, including the corpse, while at another service at the same time, only a few disappeared and the corpse remained.

Unable to reach more than the answering machine at home, Rayford finally caught a helicopter to the landing pad at Northwest Community Hospital in Arlington Heights. He was about five miles from home, and he bet he could hitch a ride easier than finding a cab. As he trudged along, his trench coat over his arm and his bag in his hand, he had an empty, despairing feeling.

A woman of about forty stopped for Rayford on Algonquin Road. As he got in and thanked her, he said, "Have you lost people?"

" 'Fraid so," she said, her voice quavery. "About a dozen nieces and nephews."

As she drove, sniffling, into Mt. Prospect, Rayford felt fatigue he had never endured before. "Can I offer you anything?" he said as she pulled into his driveway.

She shook her head. "You could pray for me, if you think of it."

"I'm not much for praying," he said.

"You will be, sir. I never was before either, but I am now."

Rayford stood in the driveway and waved at the woman until she was out of sight. The yard and the walk were spotless as usual, and the huge home, his trophy house, was sepulchral. He unlocked the front door. From the closed drapes in the picture window to the bitter smell of burned coffee when he opened the door, everything pointed to what he dreaded.

Buck Williams checked the phone log in his laptop and dialed.

A teenage boy answered, "Washingtons."

"Cameron Williams of *Global Weekly* calling for Lucinda."

"My mom's not here. I'm the only one left. Mama, Daddy, everybody else is gone. Disappeared."

"Oh, man! I'm sorry, son."

"That's all right. I know where they are, and I can't even say I'm surprised."

"You know where they are?"

"If you know my mama, you know where she is too. She's in heaven."

Lucinda and Charles Washington, filled to overflowing with what they had already witnessed in the short time they'd been in glory, knew what was coming next. Seven Earth years after the signing of a covenant between the Antichrist and Israel, Jesus would return for His glorious appearing and establish a thousand-year reign of peace.

But just before that would come the marriage of the Lamb with His bride, the church.

Lucinda looked into the eyes of her husband and thought his thoughts. Time clearly meant nothing here. That wedding might seem eons away, yet it could happen within the next few moments. She couldn't wait. Best of all was that when the time came and Jesus rode His white stallion in triumph to the Battle of Armageddon, the saints in heaven would descend with Him and constitute His avenging army. She and her husband would be part of that. Imagine.

Like everyone else in the great assembly hall on the first floor of the house of God, Lucinda Washington was finding heaven way more than she had ever dreamed.

Author's Note

The second coming of Jesus Christ is the most frequently mentioned subject in the Bible, other than the doctrine of salvation, what the Bible is all about. The Second Coming is clearly taught in both the Old and the New Testaments. It was promised 321 times in Scripture, predicted by Jesus Christ Himself, by all the writers of the New Testament and by many of the Old Testament prophets. It is the capstone of all Christianity, without which God's merciful plan for mankind's future cannot be understood.

The Second Coming is easily the most fascinating event predicted anywhere and is the only message that gives hope to the chaotic world in which we live. Jerry Jenkins and I have often been asked why the Left Behind books comprise the most popular fiction series ever. My answer, aside from Jerry's incredible fiction-writing gift, is that it is based on the Bible's forecast of the last days, starting with the Second Coming, which many find fascinating. Surveys tell us that more than 65 percent of the population of America believes Jesus Christ is coming back to this world, just as He promised. It is the last best hope of mankind, if, of course, you are ready for His return by having personally invited Christ into your life. This is the primary reason we wrote the Left Behind series. Fortunately, from the letters, e-mails, and personal contacts we receive, we know that thousands say they have come to faith through reading these books.

Admittedly, there is disagreement even among Christians as to events of our Lord's second coming. The reasons are primarily twofold: First, Satan clearly does not want anyone to understand prophecy, for there is no more spiritually motivating subject than the return of Christ. Jesus called Satan "a liar" and "a deceiver," so we can expect him to "[sow] discord in a family" and confuse those who are seeking the truth (Proverbs 6:19). Second, Jesus predicted there would be "false messiahs and false prophets" who would come on the scene in the last days (Matthew 24:24; Mark 13:22). If these are really the last days, as many Bible scholars believe, I am not surprised to find false prophets and those deliberately teaching error. For that reason it is important for the serious student of the Scripture to learn . . .

The Two Keys to Understanding the Second Coming

1. *You must take the Bible literally, including prophecy.* That does not mean we are "wooden literalists," as some detractors accuse. Every language has metaphors and other figures of speech usually revealed by context. We follow the time-honored principle used by many Bible scholars: "When the plain sense of Scripture makes common sense, seek no other sense, but take every word at its primary literal meaning, unless the facts of the immediate context clearly indicate otherwise." This, of course, allows for no allegorizing or spiritualizing of prophecy, which is what leads to so many divergent and confusing interpretations of end-time events. Most amillennialists, postmillennialists, and preterists fall into this category. Whereas they may take other Scriptures literally, they tend to spiritualize or allegorize prophecy, which, in our opinion, makes it all but impossible to rightly divide the Word of truth (2 Timothy 2:15). As the Old Testament prophecies of Jesus' first coming were literally fulfilled, there is every reason to believe that the New Testa-

ment prophecies of His second coming will also be literally fulfilled.

2. *You must keep in mind that there are two stages to the Second Coming.* By studying all 321 Second Coming passages in context, we find that they fall into one of two categories: They relate either to the rapture of the church — when Christ calls all believers to meet Him in the clouds (1 Thessalonians 4:16–17) just before taking them to heaven as He promised (John 14:1–3) — or they describe the Glorious Appearing (Matthew 24:29–31; Revelation 19:11–21) just before He returns to earth and establishes His one-thousand-year kingdom. In our series we show the Rapture coming just before the Tribulation period, which we cover in books one through twelve, and then the Glorious Appearing, which we cover in book twelve and the final sequel.

In four of my nonfiction prophecy books — *Are We Living in The End Times?*, *The Popular Encyclopedia of Bible Prophecy*, *The Rapture* (not to be confused with this novel), and *Charting the End Times* — I list the fifteen differences between these events. In fact, after you compare them, you will realize that they cannot possibly be describing the same event. For example, the Rapture could take place at any moment without warning; the Glorious Appearing cannot take place for at least seven more years after many prophetically forecast events. The Rapture finds Christ calling believers to meet Him in the air so He can take us to His Father's house as He promised. The Glorious Appearing finds believers coming with Christ to the earth when He sets up His kingdom. This may be why the apostle Paul referred to the Rapture, our Lord's coming, as "the blessed hope," and gave us the name "Glorious Appearing" for the public coming of Christ to earth. Personally, I think Paul was distinguishing these two phases or stages of Christ's second coming.

The miniature chart on page 422 shows these two phases of Christ's coming separated by the seven-year tribulation period. If you have read most or all of the books in the Left Behind series, you will find it easy to locate where each book appears on this chart. I hope you find this exercise helpful in understanding the entire plan of God for your future and that of the rest of the world.

For further information on end-times prophecy, check my Web site, www.timlahaye. com, as well as our publisher's site, www.tyndale.com. And take a look at the entire Tim LaHaye Prophecy Library.

— *Dr. Tim LaHaye*

THE TRIBULATION IN CONTEXT

**Antichrist—
The Abomination
of Desolation**
MATTHEW 24:15
2 THESSALONIANS 2:4

Rapture
1 THESSALONIANS 4:16,17

**Glorious
Appearing**
MATTHEW 24:27-31

| church age | 7-year tribulation | millennium | eternity |

About the Authors

Jerry B. Jenkins (www.jerryjenkins.com) is the writer of the Left Behind series. He owns the Jerry B. Jenkins Christian Writers Guild (www.ChristianWritersGuild.com), an organization dedicated to mentoring aspiring authors, as well as Jenkins Entertainment, a filmmaking company (www.Jenkins-Entertainment.com). Former vice president of publishing for the Moody Bible Institute of Chicago, he also served many years as editor of *Moody* magazine and is now Moody's writer-at-large.

His writing has appeared in publications as varied as *Time* magazine, *Reader's Digest, Parade, Guideposts*, in-flight magazines, and dozens of other periodicals. Jenkins's biographies include books with Billy Graham, Hank Aaron, Bill Gaither, Luis Palau, Walter Payton, Orel Hershiser, and Nolan Ryan, among many others. His books appear regularly on the *New York Times*, *USA Today*, *Wall Street Journal*, and *Publishers Weekly* best-seller lists.

He holds two honorary doctorates, one from Bethel College (Indiana) and one from Trinity International University. Jerry and his wife, Dianna, live in Colorado and have three grown sons and three grandchildren.

Dr. Tim LaHaye (www.timlahaye.com), who conceived the idea of fictionalizing an account of the Rapture and the Tribulation, is a noted author, minister, and nationally recognized speaker on Bible prophecy. He is the founder of both Tim LaHaye Ministries and the Pre-Trib Research Center.

He also recently cofounded the Tim LaHaye School of Prophecy at Liberty University. Dr. LaHaye speaks at many of the major Bible prophecy conferences in the U.S. and Canada, where his prophecy books are very popular.

Dr. LaHaye earned a doctor of ministry degree from Western Theological Seminary and an honorary doctor of literature degree from Liberty University. For twenty-five years he pastored one of the nation's outstanding churches in San Diego, which grew to three locations. During that time he founded two accredited Christian high schools, a Christian school system of ten schools, and Christian Heritage College.

There are almost 13 million copies of Dr. LaHaye's fifty nonfiction books that have been published in over thirty-seven foreign languages. He has written books on a wide variety of subjects, such as family life, temperaments, and Bible prophecy. His current fiction works, the Left Behind series, written with Jerry B. Jenkins, continue to appear on the best-seller lists of the Christian Booksellers Association, *Publishers Weekly, Wall Street Journal, USA Today,* and the *New York Times.* LaHaye's second fiction series of prophetic novels consists of *Babylon Rising* and *The Secret on Ararat,* both of which hit the *New York Times* best-seller list and will soon be followed by *Europa Challenge.* This series of four action thrillers, unlike *Left Behind,* does not start with the Rapture but could take place today and goes up to the Rapture.

He is the father of four grown children and grandfather of nine. Snow skiing, waterskiing, motorcycling, golfing, vacationing with family, and jogging are among his leisure activities.

The employees of Thorndike Press hope you have enjoyed this Large Print book. All our Thorndike and Wheeler Large Print titles are designed for easy reading, and all our books are made to last. Other Thorndike Press Large Print books are available at your library, through selected bookstores, or directly from us.

For information about titles, please call:

(800) 223-1244

or visit our Web site at:

www.gale.com/thorndike
www.gale.com/wheeler

To share your comments, please write:

Publisher
Thorndike Press
295 Kennedy Memorial Drive
Waterville, ME   04901